THE MODERNIST TREND IN
SPANISH-AMERICAN POETRY

THE MODERNIST TREND IN SPANISH-AMERICAN POETRY

*A Collection of Representative Poems
of the Modernist Movement and the Reaction
Translated into English Verse
with a Commentary*

BY

G. DUNDAS CRAIG

GORDIAN PRESS
NEW YORK
1971

Originally Published 1934
Reprinted 1971

Published by GORDIAN PRESS, INC.
By Arrangement With
UNIVERSITY OF CALIFORNIA PRESS

Library of Congress Catalog Card Number — 78-131249
SBN 87752-129-8

To my good friend
MERRITT Y. HUGHES

CONTENTS

	PAGE
PREFACE	xi

Part I

INTRODUCTION	1

Part II
TRANSLATIONS

José Asunción Silva
- Nocturno III . . . 32
- Egalité . . . 36

Rubén Darío
- Yo soy aquel . . . 38
- El cisne . . . 44
- Blasón . . . 46
- Sinfonía en gris mayor . . . 48
- Friso . . . 50
- Canción de otoño en primavera . . . 54
- Mía . . . 60
- Para una cubana . . . 60
- Margarita . . . 62
- Los tres reyes magos . . . 62
- La dulzura del ángelus . . . 64
- Salutación del optimista . . . 64
- A Roosevelt . . . 68
- Salutación al águila . . . 72

Amado Nervo
- Cobardía . . . 76
- El día que me quieras . . . 76
- «Tel qu'en songe» . . . 78
- Si tú me dices:—¡Ven! . . . 80
- No todos... . . . 80
- Delicta carnis . . . 82
- La montaña . . . 84
- En paz . . . 86

Ricardo Jaimes Freyre
- Aeternum vale . . . 88
- Pórtico . . . 90
- El alba . . . 90
- Las voces tristes . . . 94

CONTENTS

	PAGE
LEOPOLDO LUGONES	
El solterón	96
A los ganados y las mieses	106
Desdén	108
Lied de la boca florida	110
GUILLERMO VALENCIA	
Leyendo a Silva	112
Los camellos	122
JULIO HERRERA Y REISSIG	
Alba triste	126
La sombra dolorosa	126
La cena	128
La gota amarga	128
JOSÉ SANTOS CHOCANO	
Blasón	130
Las punas	130
Los Andes	132
Cuacthemoc	132
Tres notas de nuestra alma indígena:	
a. ¡Quién sabe!	134
b. Así será	136
c. Ahí, no más	140
ENRIQUE GONZÁLEZ MARTÍNEZ	
Tuércele el cuello al cisne	146
Y pienso que la vida...	146
Mañana los poetas	148
La piedad que pasa	148
Esta tarde he salido al campo	150
PEDRO PRADO	
Los pájaros errantes	154
Las manos	156
Lázaro	158
CARLOS PEZOA VÉLIZ	
Nada	168
Tarde en el hospital	170
VÍCTOR DOMINGO SILVA	
Balada del violín	172
ENRIQUE BANCHS	
Balbuceo	174
La estatua	176
Espíritu gentil...	180

CONTENTS

	PAGE
Juan Guzmán Cruchaga	
Cuatro caminos	182
Lejana	182
Gabriela Mistral (Lucila Godoy Alcayaga)	
La maestra rural	194
Íntima	196
Balada	200
El ruego	202
Arturo Torres-Ríoseco	
Campanita nocturna	206
Cuando me muera	206
Versos de profecía	208
Ausencia	214
Alfonsina Storni	
Carta lírica a otra mujer	220
Pablo Neruda	
Maestranzas de noche	226
Poemas de amor	226
Vicente Huidobro	
Adiós	236
Horizonte	238
Hijo	238
Mañana primavera	240
La senda era tan larga	240
Campanario	242
Jorge Luis Borges	
Calle desconocida	244
La guitarra	246

Part III
COMMENTARY

José Asunción Silva	251
Rubén Darío	255
Darío's hexameters	274
Amado Nervo	276
Ricardo Jaimes Freyre and the theory of modernist versification	281
Ricardo Jaimes Freyre	286
Leopoldo Lugones	290
Guillermo Valencia	297
Julio Herrera y Reissig	301
José Santos Chocano	306
Enrique González Martínez	310

CONTENTS

	PAGE
Pedro Prado	313
Carlos Pezoa Véliz	316
Víctor Domingo Silva	316
Enrique Banchs	317
Juan Guzmán Cruchaga	319
Gabriela Mistral	320
Arturo Torres-Ríoseco	326
Alfonsina Storni	328
Pablo Neruda	330
Vicente Huidobro	334
Jorge Luis Borges	338
Bibliography	341

PREFACE

THE POEMS in this book have been selected for their representative value both in matter and in style. The field of Spanish-American poetry is wide, and the number of poets is enormous. Even the number of good poets is remarkable, as is evident from a perusal of the various national anthologies. Julio Noé's Argentine anthology, for example, of works written between 1900 and 1925, contains no fewer than eighty-seven writers, and the Chilean volume compiled by Armando Donoso contains forty-nine. Where there are so many writers whose work rises above the mediocre, it is evident that from such a collection as this much excellent material has necessarily been excluded; therefore, if one poet or another does not appear, it is not to be assumed that his work is unworthy of notice. Nevertheless, an attempt has been made to include examples of all the different schools, from Parnassianism to Creationism, that mark the modern trend in Spanish-American poetry.

In making the translations, I have tried to steer a middle course between the literal prose translation and the poetical paraphrase. Undoubtedly, the prose translation gives the closest approximation to the poet's meaning, as in Butcher and Lang's rendering of the *Odyssey;* but, as those distinguished translators themselves say in their preface: "Without the music of the verse, only half the truth about Homer can be told." The same holds true of modern Spanish-American poetry. The modern poet—and particularly the Parnassian—insists no less than Homer on the music of his verse; and it is but fair that the translator should attempt to reproduce some of the effect at which the poet aimed. The poetical paraphrase, however, of which Fitzgerald's translation of the *Rubáiyát* of Omar Khayyám is probably the most brilliant example, involving as it does an actual recasting of the poetic material, demands of the translator an endowment of poetic genius to which I can make no claim. I offer, therefore, as close and accurate a rendering of the original as the idiom of the English language permits, setting forth the poet's thought without extenuation on the one hand or "padding" on the other. The plainness of speech of some of these writers may prove disconcerting to the reader, for the Spanish-American poet knows little of the reticence to which we are accustomed in English poetry; but any toning down would give a distorted impression of the poet; and, as Chaucer observes:

> The wordes moote be cosyn to the dede.

As for "padding," unless it is very carefully and very sparingly used, it may inject so many of the translator's peculiarities as to obscure the personality of the poet he translates.

As far as possible, I have tried to retain the rhythmical and musical qualities of the original. In general, I have adopted what seemed the nearest equivalent to its metrical form. Thus, for example, for the octosyllable, the simplest of Spanish verse-forms, I have used the English ballad meter; for the Spanish Alexandrine (fourteen syllables), the iambic pentameter. *El ruego* I have turned into blank verse, as this seemed better suited to the highly emotional and dramatic quality of Gabriela Mistral's poem. In *Leyendo a Silva,* a long poem in rhymed Alexandrines, I have discarded the rhymes, because in a long poem these might have involved too much distortion of the poet's meaning; but I have preserved as far as possible the rhythmic movement of Valencia's verse. Where the original makes use of assonance, I have felt at liberty to use either rhyme or blank verse, adopting whichever seemed most fitting.

More elusive than either the meaning or the metrical form is the spirit of the different poets, for Darío, Herrera y Reissig, Chocano, and Pezoa Véliz are as diverse in their mood and utterance as Tennyson, Browning, Kipling, and Masefield; and success or failure in conveying these differences to the reader must be the final test of the value of these as of other translations.

The Commentary is intended to serve a double purpose. It aims at elucidation of the text where that has appeared necessary. Biographical matter has been reduced to a minimum, and has been introduced only where it seemed helpful to an understanding of the poems or of the relation of a poet to the movement to which his work belongs. In the Commentary, also, I have tried to illustrate by detailed reference the general ideas outlined in the Introduction.

I should like to acknowledge my indebtedness to Miss Refugio Gaxiola-Tays for assistance in preparing the manuscript and to Professor Arturo Torres-Ríoseco for many valuable suggestions.

G. D. C.

THE MODERNIST TREND IN SPANISH-AMERICAN POETRY

INTRODUCTION

THE MODERNIST MOVEMENT in Spanish-American poetry was not an isolated phenomenon, but had its counterpart in France, Italy, and Spain as well as in Germany, England, and the United States. It developed when the Romantic movement began to lose its force and ceased to satisfy the aesthetic aspirations of the more ardent poetic spirits of the latter half of the nineteenth century.

In Spanish-American countries this development was less pronounced than elsewhere, for there Romanticism never took a great hold. It has been pointed out by Menéndez y Pelayo that, so far as Romanticism was the expression of the individualistic revolt against the rigidity of the classical school, it could be, and was, transplanted to America, though in the majority of writers it was the worst extravagances of their models (Byron, Hugo, Espronceda, and Zorrilla) that were most successfully imitated. To the other element in European Romanticism, that based on historic lore and traditions which had come down from medieval times, there was nothing corresponding in America, inasmuch as the traditions of the modern Mexican or Peruvian, for example, were European and had no living roots in the history or legends of the vanished Aztecs or Incas. Moreover, there were in America none of the Gothic cathedrals and feudal castles that served as inspiration for romantic dreams in Europe; hence there could not possibly exist that mysterious interpenetration of landscape and history which forms one of the greatest charms of Romantic poetry in Europe.[1]

Although in this last observation Menéndez y Pelayo seems to attach too great importance to mere externals (for the cathedrals and feudal castles existed before the tide of Romanticism rose, and are still there, high and dry, when it has long since receded), the main idea is sound, and, incidentally, exposes the futility of attempts like those of José Santos Chocano to found a new Americanism on the legends of the aborigines. There is, however, another fact that contributed to the weakness of the Romantic move-

---

[1] Menéndez y Pelayo, *Historia de la poesía hispanoamericana* (Madrid, 1893), 1:125–126.

ment in Spanish America. By the time the works of the European Romantics began to be known in Spanish America, the great task of emancipation from the Spanish yoke had everywhere, except in Cuba, been completed. Liberty had been achieved. As an inspiring watchword, Liberty had no longer the same appeal. The various states had settled down to adjust their mutual jealousies and consolidate their gains, and poetry for the time being became the handmaiden of successive petty dictators.

As far as poetry was concerned, the middle part of the nineteenth century was an age of mediocrity, and Spanish America a paradise of the poetaster—whose name was Legion. "In fact," says Menéndez y Pelayo, "the production is becoming excessive; and in Central America, as in all parts of America, the tares smother the wheat."[2]

This author, though precluded by the scope of his work from discussing the productions of authors still alive at the date of writing (1893), points out[3] the emergence of a brilliant group of writers, no longer following Victor Hugo but cherishing other artistic ideals, in whom seemed to predominate the taste of the French Parnassians and certain Italian poets. From this group he singles out Rubén Darío, whose *Azul* had shortly before drawn from the distinguished Spanish critic, Juan Valera, an appreciative review[4] (published in *La Nación,* Buenos Aires). This emphasizes the important fact that Modernism in Spanish America was not a spontaneous growth on American soil. Darío, while still in his teens, and employed in the Biblioteca Nacional at Managua, had read widely in Spanish literature both ancient and modern, and had also fallen under the spell of Victor Hugo. Coming to Chile in 1886, he was befriended by Pedro Balmaceda, who placed at Darío's disposal his library of modern French literature. Here, in the works of Baudelaire, Catulle Mendès, and Verlaine, he found even more congenial inspiration, the influence of which, as was observed by Valera, is to be seen in *Azul.* In this respect, however, Darío was not unique; rather he was typical of a number of young writers, for example, Julián del Casal, Manuel Gutiérrez Nájera, and José Asunción Silva, whose minds were turning in the same direction. Modernism was in the air; and that Darío is regarded as the leader of the movement means not that he was its initiator, but that by the force of his exceptional genius he gave it an impetus and prestige without which it might have made little headway.

---

[2] Menéndez y Pelayo, *op. cit.,* pp. 211–212.   [3] *Ibid.,* p. 167.
[4] Juan Valera, *Cartas americanas* (Madrid, 1889).

What then is Modernism? Miguel de Unamuno, in his Preface to the poems of José Asunción Silva, finds a difficulty in defining it.

> No sé bien [he writes] qué es eso de los modernistas y el modernismo, pues llaman así cosas tan diversas y hasta opuestas entre sí, que no hay modo de reducirlas a una común categoría. No sé lo que es el modernismo literario, pero en muchos de los llamados modernistas, en los más de ellos, encuentro cosas que encontré antes in Silva. Sólo que en Silva me deleitan y en ellos me hastían y enfadan.

But where native angels feared to tread in 1908, when the Modernist movement was at its height and feelings were strong, even an alien commentator may offer an opinion now that the movement has become part of history and may be viewed with the necessary detachment. Modernism may be described as the literary expression of that mood of unrest and of dissatisfaction with the prevailing worship of material success that marked the last few years of the nineteenth century. The young idealist of those days felt himself a spirit thrown by fate into an environment to which he did not belong. He had a soul above the sordid aims of his fellow-men, and his art and his ideals were things beyond their comprehension. In the midst of an unsympathetic democracy he was an aristocrat, "singing hymns unbidden" and unheeded—if not treated with contempt. Finding little sympathy in the world of men, and having none of the missionary zeal that would have converted them to his way of thinking, he naturally turned away and found solace in a world of the imagination. Thus Darío retired, figuratively, to his "ivory tower," and Herrera y Reissig shut himself up, not only metaphorically but also physically, in his "torre de los panoramas." Holding himself aloof from the world of reality, the poet went in pursuit of a vague and fugitive phantom of absolute beauty; and in keeping with his temperament he sought it not in the lives of ordinary men but in an imaginary realm of his own creation, about as far from reality as it was possible to go. In this same quest for beauty, the poet clothed his dreams in language and imagery so remote and unfamiliar as to be reminiscent of the Culteranismo of the seventeenth century.

Accepting in its fullest sense the dictum of Verlaine, "De la musique avant toute chose," as the governing principle of his work, the poet employed rhymes, skilfully varied rhythms, vowel music, and artful alliteration in such a way that all combined to produce the emotional effect of fine music. He claimed complete independence, adopting such innovations as the Romantic poets of the preceding generation had introduced, and experimenting freely with new forms and with older forms revived. Blank verse was not regarded with much favor, though Darío used it. Rhyme was considered essential; Lugones in one of his early prefaces actually asserted that it was indispensable, and that unrhymed verse was merely the refuge of those who lacked the power of rhyming. In spite of this, the feeling that rhyme limited the freedom of the poet led to its being gradually discarded. It led also to the increasing popularity of free verse, as in the work of Jaimes Freyre, and to this poet's attempt to find a formula to cover its vagaries. As for critics and the rules that criticism had deduced from the practice of past ages, they were treated with scant respect; the poet's own sense of beauty and his feeling for what was fitting to the occasion were the only criteria. Hence Darío declares, "Mi literatura es mía en mí"; Herrera y Reissig, "*Ego sum imperator*. Me incomoda que ciertos peluqueros de la crítica me hagan la barba"; and later, Huidobro, "El poeta es un pequeño Dios."

Another characteristic of the poetry of Modernism is its prevailing melancholy, a melancholy "compounded of many simples, extracted from many objects," but having its roots in the craving, particularly noticeable in Darío, Asunción Silva, and Valencia, to taste life to the uttermost. This, as Silva confesses in *De sobremesa,* led only to an acquaintance with life in its lowest dregs, to bitterness and despair.

It may be objected that many of these characteristics, if not all, can be found in earlier verse. To some extent this is true; but in the period from 1890 to 1910 they were combined in such proportions as to give to the work of this time a character that was entirely distinctive.

Modernism, as has been said above, was an outgrowth of the feeling of disquiet felt by certain of the more sensitive spirits in presence of the materialism of their immediate environment. The enthusiasm that accompanied the struggle for independence had passed away, and the energies of two generations had been given up to the development of the material resources of vast areas. With the great success that attended these efforts, a smug satisfaction arose, which is intelligible in a predominantly *bourgeois* population, but which tasted like Dead Sea fruit to those who felt that the soul as well as the body required nourishment. What culture there was in Spanish America was a reflection of that of eighteenth-century Spain, and it made little appeal to the younger generation. The poetry of the time, half Classical and half Romantic, had begun to pall. Its language, as infested with hackneyed terms and worn-out imagery as the "poetic diction" of the English poets of the eighteenth century that drew protest from Wordsworth, had ceased to have much real meaning; its artificiality and insincerity were too apparent.

It was natural, therefore, that aspiring poets should turn to France, where writers like Baudelaire, Banville, Coppée, Gautier, Leconte de Lisle, Samain, Mallarmé, and Verlaine seemed to have given a new life to French poetry. There they found a naturalness, sincerity, and directness that were entirely new to them, and, having seen and admired these things, they set themselves to imitate the effects these writers had so successfully achieved.

This study of French poetry was not confined to any one region of Spanish America, but was carried on everywhere, from Mexico and Cuba to Chile and Argentina. In Mexico, Justo Sierra (1848–1912), though past the heyday of his youth, was a fervent admirer of these French writers, and traces of their influence may be seen in some of his poems (e.g., *Playeras*),[5] while his personal prestige gave weight to his counsel to the younger men about him that they should make these French writers their models. That his precept and example were not without effect is seen in the work of Gutiérrez Nájera. In Cuba, Julián del Casal (1863–1893) was writing in imitation of Baudelaire, Gautier, and Poe. (Poe had reached Spanish America in a French translation by Baudelaire, and had widespread influence.) In Colombia, José Asunción Silva was deeply imbued with the Modernist spirit; while, as we have seen, Darío, on his arrival in Santiago (Chile) in 1886, found himself among admirers of the new French school and himself became an ardent student.

Manuel Gutiérrez Nájera (1859–1895) is one of the outstanding poets of Mexico, though strictly speaking we cannot class him as a Modernist poet. He is sympathetic toward the new aesthetic ideas, and the clarity of his style may be regarded as one fruit of his study of European models; but in spirit he is Romantic. His famous poem, *La serenata de Schubert,* is as full of the color and feeling of romance as the music that inspired it; and his equally famous *La duquesa Job* shows, in addition to its vividness, a playful fancy and an intimately personal touch, for a parallel to which one searches in vain in any Modernist writer. These poems, and most of Nájera's poetry, were written before 1888, the "zero hour" of Modernism in Spanish America, and *De blanco,* his imitation of Gautier's *Symphonie en blanc majeur,* appeared in that year. The yearning for an early death, an idea recurrent in his poems that has been cited as a proof of his Modernism, seems hardly natural; that a youth of eighteen should write

---
[5] Quoted by Arturo Torres-Ríoseco in *Precursores del modernismo,* p. 51.

> Morir y joven: antes que destruya
> el tiempo aleve la gentil corona;
> cuando la vida dice aún: «soy tuya,»
> aunque sepamos bien que nos traiciona . . .

seems more like Romantic pose. The only great poem of Nájera that falls within the period we are discussing is *La corregidora* (1895), a magnificent piece of work, which in its brilliance of color and richness of music is equal to the best that the Parnassian school has produced. The *Revista azul,* which he founded in the year before his death, did much to popularize the Modernist point of view; but he himself can hardly be regarded as more than a precursor of Modernism.

In Julián del Casal (1863–1893), a Cuban poet, the approach to Modernism is much closer. Though in some of his poems, for example, *Tras la ventana,* the treatment is Romantic, in others it is definitely Modernist. The personal note is less pronounced than in Gutiérrez Nájera. He has the Parnassian gift of vivid artistic presentation. His experiments with unusual verse-forms, his affection for the macabre, that he inherits from Baudelaire, and his love for the exotic elegance of the Orient are all characteristics of later Modernist poetry. More striking still are his apparent distaste for the freshness and natural beauty of the open country and his preference for the artificial delights of town life:

> Más que la voz del pájaro en la cima
> de un árbol todo en flor, a mi alma anima
> la música armoniosa de una rima.
>   Nunca a mi corazón tanto enamora
> el rostro virginal de una pastora
> como un rostro de regia pecadora. . . .
>   —*En el campo.*

This is authentically Decadent or Modernist in tone, yet shows no trace of the feeling of intellectual aloofness that was so distinctive a feature of the fully developed Modernist school.

In the poetry of José Asunción Silva (1865–1896), this aloofness, this sense of belonging to a spiritual aristocracy, is much more marked. Asunción Silva is quite Modernist in spirit: he feels out of his element in a world of crass materialism, and from this arises the profound melancholy which pervades almost all that he has written. It is on this account that, in spite of the ironic tinge coloring much of his poetry, translations from his work are included in this selection of representative Modernist writers, and the bearing of his work on the Modernist movement is discussed in the Commentary.

A recent critic writes:

La poesía esencial—en el hombre y en la naturaleza—es simple, antigua y perdurable como un vasto manantial que no varía la esencia de sus aguas porque vayan a beberlas en el cuenco de sus manos, como los rústicos primitivos; o en ánforas helénicas, como los pulcros clásicos; o en cristales multiformes que irisa el sol, como los modernos. El manantial no ha variado: lo que ha ido cambiando es el procedimiento del hombre-artista; su manera de beber esa agua musical, los puntos de vista desde donde ha contemplado sus reflejos, sus iris, sus trasparencias.[6]

At present we are dealing with the Modernist poet and the "cristales multiformes" in which he is collecting this nectar of the gods. The Modernist poet is chiefly preoccupied with the beauty of the stream, its sparkle, its changing form and color, its music: these things he tries to reproduce in his poem; his treatment is objective. At this stage he is Parnassian. Later, his attitude becomes more subjective: he feels an intimate sympathy between himself and the spring; he reflects on its life-giving properties, and the meaning it may have for himself and for others. He finds in it a sympathy with the ebb and flow of his own emotions; he divines a message in its music and tries to interpret it. Thus he becomes in the best sense of the word a Symbolist. Perhaps he is conscious of a spirit indwelling in the spring, and is oppressed by a sense of mystery when he contemplates its origin. In this mood he becomes a Mystic, either in the older, religious sense, or generally in a sense that is more fitly described as aesthetic or pantheistic. Hence, within limits, it seems true that between Parnassianism and Symbolism the difference is less one of essence than of emphasis. In both there is the search for beauty as the main purpose; but while the Parnassian concentrates on the form of writing, the Symbolist is more concerned with the idea to be conveyed.

In choice of subject the Parnassian was less attracted by the beauty of outward nature than by the artificial products of civilization and the sensations these produced on his own mind. He aimed, moreover, at a much more subtle interpretation of these things than the earlier poets had attempted, a more delicate perception of their different aspects, and a rendering, more by suggestion than by actual naming or description, of the emotions they produced in himself. He accepted as a guiding principle the dictum of Verlaine, "De la musique avant toute chose"; and by ingenious rhyming and

---

[6] Francisco Donoso G., *Al margen de la poesía* (Paris, 1927), p. 61.

variations of rhythm, and by a harmonious interweaving of vowel sounds, he tried to give to his verses some of the emotional effect that the musician achieves by ingenuities of harmony and counterpoint. He frequently attempted, moreover, to reproduce in poetry some of the effect the painter secures by means of color. Thus Manuel Machado speaks with approval of

> esa transfusión del color a la palabra tan perseguida por los modernos escritores, esa *indelimitación entre las dos artes distintas* que ha sido a mi entender tan saludable a los poetas como peligrosa para los pintores.[7]

Some have even gone so far as to identify certain colors with certain vowels; but as the different exponents of this theory have been unable to agree upon which vowel is red, which yellow, this may be dismissed as mere eccentricity.

The Parnassian was most scrupulous in his choice of words. He rejected the inflated language as well as the time-worn metaphors of the feebler Romantics. He ignored the advice of Verlaine in this particular:

> Il faut aussi que tu n'ailles point
> Choisir tes mots sans quelque mépris....

He preferred the Master's practice to his precept. The search for "le mot propre," which Verlaine here seems to discourage, was one of the Parnassian's main concerns, and the injunction of Théophile Gautier was his guide to finding it:

> Sculpte, lime, cisèle,
> que ton rêve flottant
>   se scelle
> dans le bloc résistant;
>   —*L'Art,* from *Emaux et camées.*

and as the "floating dream" was the Parnassian's ideal, he consciously aspired to write

> la chanson grise
> Où l'Indécis au Précis se joint;

not the indefiniteness of the lazy or incompetent, however, but the exact degree of diffusion necessary to produce the required artistic effect. In other words, his aim was not an etching but a painting in pastel; therefore he substituted for the classical clarity an atmosphere of gloom and mystery, for loud imprecations the feeling of vague yearning.

---

[7] Manuel Machado, *La guerra literaria* (Madrid, 1914), p. 43.

> Ser claro no es ser fecundo
> si no hay otro don más raro:
> un arroyo cuando es claro
> indica que no es profundo.

Yet, though the Parnassian charged his poem with rich and exotic sensuous impressions, he was seldom able to stir great emotion in his readers. His art was beautiful but cold.

The Symbolist was not content with the objective viewpoint of the Parnassian, nor with his seeming coldness. He sought for something deeper, something that would touch the heart. For him the world was full of signs and wonders, if he could only read them. The germ of modern Symbolism (for Symbolism is no new thing in literature: it is as old, at least, as Ezekiel and the Song of Solomon) is to be found in a sonnet by Baudelaire, who, though in general a Parnassian, had in him the soul of a Symbolist.

> La Nature est un temple où de vivants piliers
> Laissent parfois sortir de confuses paroles;
> L'homme y passe à travers des forêts de symboles
> Qui l'observent avec des regards familiers.
>
> Comme de longs échos qui de loin se confondent
> Dans une ténébreuse et profonde unité,
> Vaste comme la nuit et comme la clarté,
> Les parfums, les couleurs et les sons se répondent.
>
> Il est des parfums frais comme des chairs d'enfants,
> Doux comme les haubois, verts comme les prairies,
> — Et d'autres, corrompus, riches et triomphants,
>
> Ayant l'expansion des choses infinies,
> Comme l'ambre, le musc, le benjoin et l'encens,
> Qui chantent les transports de l'esprit et des sens.
> —*Correspondances,* from *Les Fleurs du mal.*

This implies that for the poet there is an essential unity between the outer world of sense and the emotions of the human spirit. Fifty years earlier, Wordsworth had written:

> To me the meanest flower that blows can give
> Thoughts that do often lie too deep for tears;

but for him the external reality was merely the stimulus to his poetic musing. For the Symbolist there is an actual interpenetration of the poet's emotion with the object of his contemplation, as is illustrated in the following lines from Lugones:

> La emoción del amor que con su angustia
> de dulce enfermedad, nos desacerba,
> era el silencio de la tarde mustia
> y la piedad humilde de la hierba.
>
> Humildad olorosa y solitaria
> que hacia el lívido ocaso decaía,
> cual si la tierra, en lúgubre plegaria
> se postrase ante el cielo en agonía.
> —*Paseo sentimental*, from *El libro fiel*.

In Baudelaire's sonnet it is worth noting how the poet delights to mingle sensuous impressions of different kinds:

> Il est des parfums *frais* comme des chairs d'enfants,
> *Doux* comme les *haubois, verts* comme les prairies;

a practice carried to extravagance and absurdity by the later Symbolists and the various schools of the Vanguardia.

Thus the Symbolist, while seeking to find hidden meanings in the world about him and in the impressions it made on his own mind, employed all the arts of the Parnassian—rhyme, assonance, vowel music, and variations of rhythm—to give charm to his verse, and imagery rich in suggestion to give fascination to the idea and to stir an emotional response in the heart of his reader.

In the account of the Modernist movement in its two phases of Parnassianism and Symbolism as here set forth, the matter has been regarded in agreement with the ideals of its best exponents. It may be looked at otherwise, however, as by Silva Uzcátegui in the rôle of Devil's Advocate.[8] According to this critic, the French Modernists, Parnassians and Symbolists alike, were a crew of profligate idlers, dipsomaniacs, and degenerates, who passed their lives in the atmosphere of Parisian cafés reeking with the fumes of alcohol and tobacco, and, in their craving for publicity, were willing to do anything to astonish the world. Hence Parnassianism, which began as a protest against the exaggerated individualism and conventional language and imagery of the less gifted Romantics, quickly degenerated into a mere pursuit of fine language for its own sake, and gave way to Symbolism, which, aiming at the expression of deeper and more subtle shades of feeling and emotion, lost itself in labyrinths of complicated and exaggerated meta-

---

[8] R. D. Silva Uzcátegui, *Historia crítica del modernismo en la literatura castellana* (Barcelona, 1925).

phor intelligible only to the initiated—and perhaps not to them. The pursuit of the *nuance* and the *chanson grise* led to the thoughts of the writers becoming so enveloped in haze as to be unintelligible to the reader; and this indefinite manner of expression was due not to any profundity or remoteness in the thought, but to the fact that these writers were so habitually bemused with liquor that they were incapable of thinking clearly. Other symptoms of the malady that afflicted these Parisian Modernists and some of their admirers and imitators from beyond the Atlantic were their aversion to the beauty of outward nature, their morbid affection for the macabre, their immense pride coupled with their contempt for ordinary humanity, and the sensuality of their lives and writings.

Thus, by deliberately shutting his eyes to everything on the opposite side, and by quoting at great length from Max Nordau's *Degeneration,* Silva Uzcátegui makes out a fairly good case. But in all fairness it has to be recognized that not all these writers were profligate idlers, and that not all the poetry of Baudelaire, Coppée, Mallarmé, Gautier, and Verlaine was so insincere and exaggerated as Silva Uzcátegui would have us believe. They expressed their thoughts in their own way, as they were entitled to do, and they wrote much beautiful poetry, some of which "the world will not willingly let die." Moreover, the reader of poetry does not always demand the absolute clearness and precision of thought and language that one has a right to expect in a scientific treatise. A landscape bathed in the noonday sun has its attraction; but the same landscape veiled in the mists of morning, or flooded with moonlight, has still more, for it leaves scope for the imagination to people it with the shapes of fancy. The half-lights have their appeal; the glamour of the imagination is a natural craving of the human mind. "Doth any man doubt," asks Bacon, "that if there were taken out of men's minds vain opinions, false valuations, *imaginations as one would,* and the like, but it would leave the minds of a number of men poor shrunken things, full of melancholy and indisposition, and unpleasing to themselves?"

It is true that Verlaine was a highly neurotic subject from his earliest years, and that the alcoholic stimulants and sensual indulgence that seemed for the time to satisfy his craving only aggravated the disease. There seems to be sufficient evidence that Darío, with the same hereditary taint and the same acquired habits, could not in his later years write at all without the stimulus of alcohol, and that one of his most admired poems, *Salutación del optimista,* promised by the poet for a meeting of the Unión Iberoamericana de Madrid, was produced in two hours—after days of procrastination—but only when his friends had dosed him with liquor till he reached the stage of alcoholic somnambulism at which his enfeebled brain would function.[9] But these facts do not lessen the value of the work produced, nor prove Silva Uzcátegui's contention that the poet was helplessly at the mercy of heredity. Rather, they prompt the question, If, weakened though Darío was by dissolute living, he was able to produce beautiful work, what might he not have accomplished had his environment been more favorable?

Before passing on to consider the development of Modernism, it may be well to notice that not all the poets in Spanish America accepted the Modernist gospel. Many continued to write, and to write well, without following the new fashions, for example, María Enriqueta (María Enriqueta Camarillo de Pereyra) in Mexico, and Pedro Bonifacio Palacio, who wrote under the pseudonym Almafuerte, in Argentina.

The transition from Parnassianism to Symbolism can be observed clearly in the poetical work produced between 1888 and 1910. Darío's first important work, *Azul* (1888), is definitely Parnassian. In *Prosas profanas* (1896) we find both types of poem. The *Sinfonía en gris mayor* and *Friso* are Parnassian in manner; *El reino interior,* an allegory of the conflict between the flesh and the spirit, and *Era un aire suave* are Symbolist. Of the latter Darío says the heroine is "la Eulalia simbólica que ríe, ríe, ríe, desde el instante en que tendió a Adán la manzana paradisíaca."[10] So, in *Cantos de vida y esperanza* (1905), *Los cisnes, Canto de esperanza,* and *Canción de otoño en primavera* are markedly Symbolist. The same progress may be observed in Guillermo Valencia, for *Leyendo a Silva,* while an epitome of all the Parnassian's ambitions and yearnings, is at the same time a perfect example of Parnassian method; and *Los camellos* is an equally fine example of the Symbolist mood and manner. Jaimes Freyre is in general Parnassian, while Lugones and Herrera y Reissig are predominantly Symbolist, and, like the later Symbolists, in their anxiety for novelty of imagery to clothe their ideas, frequently become obscure or grotesque.

A notable characteristic of all these Modernist writers is their marked preference for the unfamiliar, the strange, the exotic—a symptom of their distaste for the actual world in which they found themselves. "Yo detesto la vida y el tiempo en que me tocó nacer," says Darío;[11] and to this we may trace his early fondness for the *Arabian Nights* and his later infatuation with the lakes and swans, the fauns and fountains, the courtiers and courtesans

---

[9] See Vargas Vila, *Rubén Darío* (Madrid, 1917), pp. 81–82.
[10] *Autobiography,* p. 136.   [11] *Prosas profanas,* Preface.

of an idealized eighteenth-century Versailles. Out of the same feeling sprang Valencia's leaning to the culture of the Orient and his latest work, *Catay*, a set of translations from the Chinese; and to it also may be attributed Jaimes Freyre's attempt to put new life and meaning into the Scandinavian myths and Wagnerian legends.

Apart from the "mental Gallicism" that Valera noticed in *Azul*, Darío's main influence on Spanish-American poetry was in the direction of freedom and variety in the metrical structure of his lines and strophes. Erwin K. Mapes, in his work, *L'Influence française dans l'oeuvre de Rubén Darío* (Paris, 1925), tries to prove that in most of his innovations (of which Lauxar[12] enumerates more than twenty) Darío was consciously influenced by French models. Torres-Ríoseco, on the contrary, points out[13] that there exist in earlier Spanish writers examples of those forms that Darío either revived or believed he had invented. He quotes the well-known passage from Darío's autobiography (pp. 33-34):

Allí [in the National Library, Managua] pasé largos meses leyendo todo lo posible, y entre todas las cosas que leí ¡horrendo referens! [Darío's Latin, not Virgil's] fueron todas las introducciones de la Biblioteca de Autores Españoles de Rivadeneira, y las principales obras de casi todos los clásicos de nuestra lengua. De allí viene que, cosa que sorprendiera a muchos de los que conscientemente me han atacado, el que yo sea en verdad un buen conocedor de letras castizas, como cualquiera puede verlo en mis primeras producciones publicadas.

Professor Coester, basing his opinion on another passage in the autobiography, tells us that Darío began to write verses when he was thirteen years old, and that, having drawn some attention by these juvenile verses, he was sent by his political friends to Managua with a letter of introduction to the President. In this way be procured an appointment in the National Library, where through "largos meses" he read the Spanish classics. But in Managua also, as Dr. Torres informs us (*op. cit.*, p. 8), he decided at the age of fourteen to get married, and his friends to prevent this gave him money and sent him off to Salvador. It is just possible, therefore, that there is a touch of exaggeration in the "largos meses" and the supposed extent of his reading, for, by 1911-1912, when he wrote his autobiography, his memory was not too reliable. Besides, even granting that Darío was a precocious child,

---

[12] Lauxar (Osvaldo Crispo Acosta), *Motivos de crítica hispanoamericanos* (Montevideo, 1914).

[13] Torres-Ríoseco, *Rubén Darío, Casticismo y Americanismo* (Harvard, 1931), Part II, Chap. II.

it is difficult to believe that his reading of the classics at such a tender age could have left much impression on his mind. Dr. Torres seems to imply that Darío's innovations were made with an actual consciousness of the sources from which they were derived. This seems unlikely. Even the passage in the Preface to *Cantos de vida y esperanza,* frequently quoted to prove Darío's acquaintance with the Spanish classics, proves nothing of the kind. He writes:

> Y mis aficiones clásicas encontraban un consuelo con la amistosa conversación de cierto joven maestro que vivía, como yo, en el hotel de las Cuatro Naciones; se llamaba, y se llama hoy, en plena gloria, Marcelino Menéndez y Pelayo. El fué quien, oyendo una vez a un irritado censor atacar mis versos del «Pórtico» a Rueda, como peligrosa novedad,
>
> >... y esto pasó en el reinado de Hugo,
> > emperador de la barba florida,
>
> dijo: «Esos son sencillamente los viejos endecasílabos de gaita gallega:
> > Tanto bailé con el ama del cura,
> > Tanto bailé que me dió calentura.»
>
> Y yo aprobé. Porque siempre apruebo lo correcto, lo justo y lo bien intencionado. Yo no creía haber inventado nada.

This does not necessarily mean that Darío was aware that the measure he employed in *Pórtico* had been used by other writers before him; indeed, it reads as if Darío regarded Menéndez y Pelayo's remark as a revelation.

The fact that he claimed as an invention of his own the sonnet written in lines of fourteen syllables (his first example was *Caupolicán,* published in *Azul*) points in the same direction. An earlier example of this sonnet form has been found in the work of Pedro Espinosa (1578–1650), but there is no proof that Darío knew anything about it.[14] The truth seems to be that in his wide but desultory reading of the Spanish classics certain rhythms that had long ceased to be popular had appealed to him. They had remained subconsciously stored in his mind, and, when the occasion arose, they came spontaneously to his pen and were committed to paper as if they were discoveries. This does not rule out the possibility that some of his innovations were made in conscious imitation of archaic forms; nor does it imply that every revival of archaic forms he made was worth the trouble.

Still, on the whole, it seems that in this matter of metrical innovation Darío owed more to his immediate French predecessors than to the Spanish

---

[14] This sonnet is printed in the *Historia de la literatura española,* by Hurtado and González Palencia (Madrid, 1921–1922), p. 587.

classics. It is a well established fact that he was extremely susceptible to his environment: witness his extraordinary change of front from *A Roosevelt* to the *Salutación al águila*. He was in contact with the most daring of the French innovators. In view of the kind of life he led, his continued study of the classics, if it did continue, can hardly have been other than spasmodic. Consequently, if he ever sought justification for his new methods, he would have found it near at hand rather than among the hazy recollections of his juvenile reading.

In the chapter to which reference has been made, Dr. Torres finds himself in a painful dilemma:

> Algunas veces termina el primer hemistiquio del verso con las llamadas palabras de relación, siempre inacentuadas naturalmente, de modo que en la lectura o se pone un acento forzado donde no existe, o se lee de una manera natural y en este caso el verso pierde una sílaba:
>
>> y la esmeralda de - esos pájaros-moscas . . .
>> es recordada por - mis íntimos sentidos . . .
>> en la tierra de los - diamantes y la dicha . . .
>> Mas el calor de ese - Brasil maravilloso . . .
>> Los delegados pan - americanos que . . .

These examples and the eight others quoted are from the *Epístola a la Sra de Lugones*. Written in 1906, this is probably the poorest poetry Darío ever wrote; in fact, some of the lines are indistinguishable from prose. The normal line is the Alexandrine of fourteen syllables, with the accent on the sixth syllable; but the poet takes all manner of liberties, writing lines of twelve, thirteen, and fifteen syllables, and displacing the ordinary accent and the position of the caesura at will. But he had examples in abundance in his favorite French writers. The classical French Alexandrine with the obligatory accent on the sixth syllable had already been modified, and Hugo had made systematic use of the "vers trimètre"; but the Parnassians had gone much farther, and in their writings lines like the following were common:

> Celles qui furent, familières, mes pensées . . .
> —Henri de Regnier, *Les Médailles d'argile*.
> Pour la femme et pour les enfants, mes bons amis . . .
> —François Coppée, *La Grève des forgerons*.
> Comme des merles dans l'épaisseur des buissons . . .
> —Leconte de Lisle, *Le Coeur de Hialmar*.

These are not classical Alexandrines, but in their context they are unobjectionable; and it is conceivable that Darío thought he might take equal liberty with the caesura in Spanish. For his cutting down of his lines to thirteen or twelve syllables, the most probable explanation is that by the time he wrote the *Epístola* his mental faculties were so much impaired that he was unable to count fourteen, or that, if he could, his reputation was so well established that the difference between thirteen and fourteen did not concern him.

In the lines from the *Epístola* quoted above, the effect is certainly inharmonious; but it is hardly fair to judge a poet by his worst writing. In some of his finer poems the rhythmical effects he attains by varying the position of the accents and of the caesura are very notable, and today do not sound strange, though they shocked his critics thirty years ago. The same phenomenon is observable in music: the dissonances that offended the ears of Beethoven's contemporaries are today accepted as perfectly valid means of musical expression. It seems that in metrics as in biology the principle of the survival of the fittest is at work. Not all the early measures were worth preserving, and it is not likely that all Darío's revivals will continue in use. The meter of *Pórtico*, for instance, is rather commonplace, like the ballad meter in English poetry; it requires the hand of a master like Darío or Coleridge to give it life.

> L'Art ne fait que des vers, le coeur seul est poète.

When all this has been said, it still remains true that Darío was a great poet. Unlike many of his imitators and followers, he had great range and versatility. His vocabulary was rich, and his power over the language remarkable. At his best, in the clarity of his style he is equal to the best of his contemporaries, while in the beauty of his imagery he surpasses most. His influence in both America and Spain has been immense, and, though present taste recoils from the artificiality and preciosity of some of his poems, enough of his work that has permanent value remains for the delight of generations to come.

Apart from Colombia, where Guillermo Valencia continued the evolution begun by Asunción Silva, the literary history of Spanish America centers round the personality of Darío. His stay in Chile (1886-1888) not only procured for him many friends, but also encouraged a group of young writers whose studies in French authors had taken the same direction as his own. Among these may be mentioned Abelardo Varela, Francisco Contreras, and Antonio Borquez Solar.

Still more important was his sojourn in Buenos Aires (1894-1898), for there he met Leopoldo Lugones and R. Jaimes Freyre, in collaboration with whom he founded the short-lived *Revista de América* for the propagation of the new ideas. Of the two, Jaimes Freyre was more strictly the Parnassian, though Symbolist tendency is observable here and there in his poems. More than any of his contemporaries he preserved the note of impersonality upon which the original Parnassians had insisted. In the work of Lugones the personal note is seldom absent, and the Symbolist becomes increasingly dominant. Moreover, in the desire for novelty Lugones has recourse to metaphors so remote from ordinary ways of thinking that his meaning becomes obscure. In fact, he seems to anticipate some of the later schools of the Vanguardia, in which the figure is valued not for its power to illustrate the poet's idea, but as a work of art by itself. Even in *Poemas solariegos,* his latest volume of verse (1928), in the poem *Los burritos,* where simplicity would have been entirely appropriate, he cannot resist the temptation to display his ingenuity; thus

>La trompa en que el pequeño jinete borda
>Quimeras entre dientes, cual sonoro pespunte,
>Con su aguja monótona y sorda
>Escande asimismo la copla transeunte,
>«¡Ca–ú–cúa, ca–ú–cúa!»

The same tendency is seen in the work of Herrera y Reissig, who, living in Montevideo only one hundred and twenty miles away, became an admirer of Darío and an ardent apostle of Modernism.

In Lugones, the attitude of rebellion against the conventions of society and normal ways of thinking appears in the sensuality that disfigures some of his poems, in the extravagance of his imagery, and in his deliberate interlarding of his poetic style with unfamiliar technical terms drawn from mathematics, medicine, physics, chemistry, natural history, and anthropology. These serve little purpose except to display the erudition of the author, and can only puzzle the reader unless he has a Greek lexicon and an encyclopedia at his elbow.

In Herrera y Reissig the revolt took another form. He seems to have adopted as his motto the line from Horace,

>Odi profanum vulgus et arceo,

and to have taken it literally, living the life of a recluse in his "torre de los panoramas." His language is often difficult and his meaning obscure; but one has the feeling in reading his poems that behind his contorted imagery there is real profundity of thought, besides the deep sense of the mystery of life that the poet is striving to convey to the reader.

Closely associated also with Darío, though not in Buenos Aires, was Amado Nervo, a Mexican, born in 1870. His early work, written before he met Darío, has the full flavor of the Symbolist school, with much of the pantheistic mysticism so often found in Symbolist writing. (See *La hermana agua*.) In Paris and Madrid, from 1902 to 1905, Darío and Nervo were much together, and it is evident that Nervo had a great admiration for Darío's work, especially for the delicacy and refinement of his poetic expression. At the same time, Nervo had so much original poetic genius that it would be unjust to class him as a follower of Darío, except in the narrowest chronological sense. It would be more accurate to say that they had poetic tastes, aims, and ideals in common, though the forms in which they gave them utterance are very different. In temperament also they show marked contrasts, the eroticism and morbid pessimism of Darío being far removed from Nervo's early sentimentalism and later quietism.

It is worthy of notice that, though Nervo lived till 1919, his poetical work shows no trace of the changes that had been observable in the work of some of his contemporaries more than ten years earlier. Though the diplomat in him remained the most charming and affable of men, the poet seemed to withdraw ever farther within himself and to find satisfaction in complete renunciation of all happiness coming from outside sources. Yet,

> while the tired waves, vainly breaking,
> Seem here no painful inch to gain,
> Far back, through creeks and inlets making,
> Comes silent, flooding in, the main.

In fact, while Darío was still at the height of his fame, important changes were already in progress, and are noticeable in the work of men who seemed the embodiment of all his most cherished ideals. In Lugones the transition to Realism is marked in *El solterón* (*Crepúsculos del jardín,* 1905), and still more in *Odas seculares* (1910). More surprising than that Lugones, living the full life of a man of the world, should make this departure is the fact that Herrera y Reissig, the recluse, living apart from and contemning his fellow-men, found inspiration in humble, rustic scenes, and was able to paint them with faithfulness and sympathy, as, for example, in *La cena*.

It is at this point that the significance of José Santos Chocano becomes apparent. *Alma América* (1906) and *Fiat lux* (1908) begin what may be called a crusade against the domination of American poetry by the prevailing taste of Paris. For Chocano, Paris was a Circe, bringing under her spell the brightest minds of America, and making them forgetful of their high calling, which ought to be to exalt the glory of their own land. In the variety and wonder of the American scene there was inspiration for any poet, and in some of Chocano's descriptive poems in the two volumes mentioned he proved his point. He went farther. He boasted that he was descended not only from the Spanish conquerors, but equally from the Incas they conquered; hence he held that the new American poetry ought to find its inspiration in the myths and legends that survived from the days before Pizarro. For this belief he is somewhat indebted to Darío, who, in the Preface to *Prosas profanas* (1896), wrote:

Si hay poesía en nuestra América, ella está en las viejas cosas: en Palenque y Utatlán, en el indio legendario, y en el inca, sensual y fino, y en el gran Moctezuma de la silla de oro.

This, however, ignores certain important considerations. The native races that had attained to any notable degree of culture by the beginning of the sixteenth century were nearly exterminated, and their culture was completely submerged by that of the conquerors. The descendants of the survivors, through three and a half centuries of slavery, peonage, and intermarriage, became so penetrated by Spanish customs and ways of thinking as to regard themselves almost as European in descent.

It is true that in certain remote areas, from Mexico to Patagonia, descendants of the aborigines lived on (e.g., in the State of Chiapas, Mexico); but these were backward races, as compared with the Aztecs or Incas, when Cortés landed, and they have advanced little since. To look for the beginnings of a new, living, national, or American poetry among these tribes is obviously useless, and to seek for such sources among the dry bones of archeological research in Incan, Aztec, or Mayan ruins is not likely to be much more fruitful.

The richer and more accessible parts of the continent have been settled by Europeans, and other races of mixed blood, for whom the legends of the ancient Incas, Aztecs, or Mayas have no real interest. There are important urban populations, moreover, with vigorous life pulsing in their veins, and with a cosmopolitan mentality as distinct from that of the aborigines as from that of Spain. It is from these vast, new populations that the poetry of an independent America is likely to arise. Darío believed that Chocano was the destined poet, for in the Prologue to *Alma América* he wrote:

Su musa es la representativa de nuestra cultura, de nuestra alma hispanoamericana actual. Lugones, Nervo, yo mismo, parecemos extranjeros. Y ante todo hay que ser de su tierra.

In these last remarks Darío was undoubtedly right: neither he nor his fellow-expatriate, Nervo, was markedly "de su tierra" (in spite of his *Canto a la Argentina*, etc.); and at the date of writing (1906) the work of Lugones had more affinity with Paris than with Buenos Aires.

Historically more important than Chocano is González Martínez, whose *Silenter* (1910) marks definitely the end of one period and the beginning of another. Up to this point, the Modernist movement had been fairly homogeneous; Parnassians and Symbolists alike had had Beauty as the object of their striving; "Art for Art's sake" was their motto, and, in general, the form of their writing was of greater importance than their matter. Indeed, serious-minded men began to feel that poetry had become mere elegant trifling. Thus González Martínez exclaims:

> Tuércele el cuello al cisne de engañoso plumaje
> que da su nota blanca al azul de la fuente
> *él pasea su gracia no más,* pero no siente
> el alma de las cosas ni la voz del paisaje.

This writer was among the first to call upon poets to realize the high seriousness of their mission, and to listen for and interpret to men the voice of Nature. He gives utterance to his aspiration in these lines:

> ¿Cuándo será la hora que trémulo ambiciono
> en que, rendida amante, con lánguido abandono
> me digas en voz baja tu divino secreto?

He is becoming tired of artificiality; life is real, and the mysteries surrounding it are still a challenge to the poet to attempt their solution. If the earlier period is correctly summed up in the phrase, the Quest for Beauty, the later may be briefly described as the Quest for Truth. Art is no longer an end in itself, but only a means to an end. Moreover, the Truth must be sought in life as the poet knows it, in the life of modern America. He must interpret its spirit of buoyancy, hope, enthusiasm, of fearless and whole-hearted appreciation of every sensuous experience of which the human mind is capable, the spirit appropriate in a people as young and full of vigor as is the present population of the Spanish-speaking republics. González Martínez has not grown to the full stature of the poet who shall supply this need. No single writer has yet done so: America still awaits her Shakespeare, her supreme interpreter.

Apart from his call for a new attitude and viewpoint for the poet, the most important contribution of González Martínez has been his insistence by precept and example on the necessity for simplicity and directness of expression. His early study of the French Parnassians, and his own acute, artistic sensibility have given to his verse great beauty of form, and have also kept it free from the grotesque imagery with which Lugones and Herrera y Reissig burdened even their best work.

This tendency toward greater simplicity and directness is carried still farther by Enrique Banchs, Pedro Prado, and Carlos Pezoa Véliz. In fact, it looks as if these writers had deliberately set themselves to remove from their writing every trace of rhetorical adornment, and to depend for their success on the emotional appeal of the subject-matter alone.

Other influences, besides, were at work. It was in the first decade of the twentieth century that the novels of Emile Zola and the poems of Verhaeren became widely known in Spanish America, and French translations of advanced European thinkers began to find eager readers there. Nietzsche's philosophy of revolt against the fashionable pessimism, the anarchism preached by Max Stirner (J. Kaspar Schmidt) and Mikhail Bakunin, and, still more, the grim realism of the tales of Dostoyevsky, Tolstoy, and Gorky wrought a notable change in the outlook of the younger writers. The swan of Darío as a poetic symbol ceased, like the dodo, to have more than a historical significance, and, at the impact of the new ideas, the "ivory tower" and the gilded palaces crumbled as at the shock of an earthquake. In their place we find a literature of the common life, of human passions in their stark reality, of sympathy for the poor and downtrodden, and of revolt against the cruelty and oppression under which they lived and suffered. This is the spirit that animates the poetry of Domingo Silva. "Perhaps I am a poet," he said, "but more than a poet I am a revolutionary."

This sympathy with the poor, and particularly with the women and the neglected children, also inspires the work of Gabriela Mistral (Lucila Godoy Alcayaga). With this there is combined in many of her poems the note of religious mysticism, so deep and poignant that it stands out in startling contrast with the merely sensuous ecstasy of her immediate predecessors. With the great tragedy of her life, this becomes mingled with tones of bitterness, the bitterness of a love denied its due fruition.

More representative than Gabriela Mistral of the urban life of Spanish America is another poetess, Alfonsina Storni. To her, outward nature—that is, the life of the open country—makes little appeal; but she has a real power of evoking pictures of the city, with its rushing traffic, its tall buildings and monotonous, rectangular streets, its parks and theaters. Behind all this, however, is the passion of love, not as a spiritual force suffused with religious feeling, but as a tumult of desire, urgent and unabashed. In this respect her work shows a certain affinity with that of her French contemporary, Madame de Noailles, and still more with that of the Chilean poet, Pablo Neruda. In the structure of her poems, Alfonsina Storni is a careful artist, using with skill and discretion the sonnet and other established stanza forms as well as blank verse and free verse. In the poetry of Neruda, on the contrary, passionate feeling breaks through all restraints, and his verse becomes chaotic. In it we see, already at an advanced stage, the disintegration that had been going on and had given rise to the different schools of the so-called Vanguardia.

Critics have attempted to explain this disintegration as an outcome of the Great War; but its beginnings were manifest before the war began. In 1909 a group of enthusiasts, with Filippo Tommaso Marinetti as their leader, met in Milan and set forth the main ideas of their new gospel of Futurism; and, because these ideas are the basis of most of the new poetical sects, it may not be out of place to summarize them here.[15]

We wish to sing [they declared] the love of danger, the habit of energy, of daring. The essential elements of our poetry are strength, audacity, rebellion, speed: an automobile in rapid motion is more beautiful than the *Victory* of *Samothrace*. We desire to destroy museums and libraries, to combat morality and all opportunist and utilitarian forms of cowardice. We shall sing the great multitudes harassed by labor, the pleasure of rebellion, the surge of revolutions in modern capitals, the nightly vibration of arsenals and mines under the glare of electric light, the railway stations swallowing their steaming serpents, the factories hanging from the clouds by their cables of smoke....

There are more of these "wild and hurling words," for the propaganda touches not only literature, but also morals, social institutions, religion, and politics. On the purely literary side, however, their proposals have more immediate interest, for some of these proposals have been adopted by the latest Spanish-American writers, for example, Vicente Huidobro. They demand the abolition of syntax, the use of verbs in the infinitive mood only. They would do away with adverbs and adjectives, using compound nouns instead; and they would replace the ordinary signs of punctuation by mathematical signs.

This movement of revolt had repercussions in France, England, the United States, and Spain. In its Spanish form it is known as Ultraism, and

---

[15] These views are fully developed in Marinetti's *Le Futurisme* (Paris, 1910).

has Guillermo de Torres as its leader. Ultraism emerged as a definite cult in 1919, and its principles as expounded by Torres in his *Literaturas europeas de vanguardia* (Madrid, 1926) show certain points of resemblance to those of Italian Futurism. The Ultraist disdains the simple image and seeks for the double or multiple image; that is, two or more metaphors are superimposed, or fused into one, not with the object of illustrating the matter under discussion, but of striking the imagination by the daring of the metaphor itself. The metaphor is the poem, and the poem is the metaphor, or a chain of metaphors, usually with some of the links of the chain omitted. As for adjectives, the Ultraist uses only those that are metaphors or contain an antithesis. Rhyme is entirely excluded, and, as a protest against the tyranny of the traditional rhythms, Ultraist poetry has no definite beat or movement. Connective words and phrases are suppressed, and punctuation is considered useless.

Much of the most modern poetry in Spanish America today is written on this model; the following, for example, by Guillermo Juan (an Argentine poet):

Iglesia

En los brazos de Cristo
candelabro sangriento
    ardían las heridas
Las velas floreciendo
formaban un jardín en el altar
Cristo izado en la cruz
igual que una bandera hecha jirones

Still more striking is the following by Nora Lange, another Argentine writer:

Iglesia

La iglesia es un murmullo de paz.
El silencio de sus estampas
    mira hacia fuera
    por las ventanas abiertas.
La luz se quema
    sollozando Ave Marías.
Una suavidad de sombra languidece
sobre la noche adolescente.
Los ojos de Cristo
    tiemblan un rezo
y sobre el crucifijo de sus brazos
he sollozado mis recuerdos.

In these poems there are touches of undeniable beauty, but it is open to question whether equal if not greater beauty could not have been attained by the older methods.

Another offshoot of Futurism is Cubism; a protest, in painting, against the photographic and microscopic realism of artists like Meissonier, and, in literature, against a similar realism in writers like Zola. The Cubist poet does not try to reflect the external reality that has suggested his poem, but presents the poetic equivalent forged by his own imagination. His poem does not develop any theme, but presents a series of notes and reflections apparently having no causal connection, but bound together by a certain analogy among the images. The images are supposed to be such as will produce the desired emotional effect in the reader's mind. In Spanish America, Cubism appears as Simplicism, as in the work of Alberto Hidalgo. (For examples, see *Indice de la nueva poesía americana*, Buenos Aires, 1926.)

The nadir is reached in Dadaism, which is the negation of all that poets anywhere and at any time have considered essential to their art. Dadaism has no ideals; it preaches no gospel. It asserts the vitality of the instant—in this respect accepting the main idea of Impressionism—but argues that, because life is chaotic, and poetry is life, poetry can be nothing but chaotic, and that only the spontaneous and natural expression of this chaos can have poetic value.

From Dadaism, which may be described as literary nihilism, there was bound to be a recoil. This is found in Creationism, of which the leading exponent is Vicente Huidobro, a Chilean poet who lived many years in Paris and has recently settled in Madrid. For the Creationist, it is the business of the poet to produce forms of beauty that will stir emotion in the reader. Such beauty, however, is not in nature, and the poet must not copy nature, but interpret it, creating in his poem an artistic whole which shall be a thing of beauty by itself, independent of the subject that gave the original suggestion. After all, this is nothing new: Darío's *La dulzura del ángelus* and Keats's sonnet *On First Looking into Chapman's Homer* owe their beauty and their emotional appeal much less to the objects that gave occasion for them than to the wealth of association that the poet supplies from his own imagination. In method, Creationism seems to have little to distinguish it from Ultraism or Cubism. It shows the same fusing of images, the same lack of continuity of thought, the same tendency to use intransitive verbs as if they were transitive, and the same disregard for punctuation. Examples of Creationist poems by Huidobro are here translated, and from a perusal of these the reader may be able to form his own opinion. One is tempted sometimes to wonder whether, after all, Huidobro and others of his school (for example, Pierre Reverdy) are not secretly having a joke at their readers' expense, if they are not merely playing for publicity. That this suspicion is justified seems more than probable when one finds printed, apparently in all seriousness, the following "poem":

> PAISAJE
> SE PASEARA EN LA TARDE POR RUTAS PARALELAS
> EL ÁRBOL
> ERA
> MÁS
> ALTO
> QUE LA MONTAÑA
> PERO LA
> MONTAÑA
> ERA TAN ANCHA   EL
> QUE TRASPASABA   RÍO
> LOS BORDES DE LA TIERRA   QUE
> CORRE
> SOBRE
> LOS
> PECES
> CUIDADO CON
> JUGAR SOBRE LA HIERBA
> ESTÁ RECIÉN PINTADA
> UNA CANCIÓN CONDUCE LOS CORDEROS AL ESTABLO[16]

It is a curious coincidence that at the end of the seventeenth century and the beginning of the eighteenth, when a movement toward correctness was gathering strength in England, there was an epidemic of writing of this kind, and ingenious persons were writing poems in patterns like eggs or pairs of wings. Dryden recommends it as a fitting exercise for MacFlecknoe (his enemy, Shadwell):

> ...choose for thy command
> Some peaceful province in Acrostic land,
> Where thou mayest wings display or altars raise,
> And torture one poor word a thousand ways.

Addison also discusses the matter, ironically, in one of his essays (*Spectator*, 58) as an example of "false wit." If there is anything in the idea that history

---

[16] *Indice de la nueva poesía americana* (Buenos Aires, 1926).

repeats itself, there may be ground here for believing that a reaction toward greater strictness of literary form is about due.

From a survey of the whole period certain general conclusions may be drawn, and these I shall now state very briefly. The most obvious is that the poetic production of the period is essentially lyrical. If, as has been indicated, there is much imitation of foreign models, there is also much genuine and original feeling which demands expression. The majority of the poems are short; and a very large number are in sonnet form, either because the compactness of the sonnet suits the poet who for the moment has only one definite idea to set forth, or because the richness of the Spanish language in rhyming-sounds makes it easy to give to such a composition an air of finished workmanship. But this partiality for short forms is probably also a sign of weakness, an indication that the poet, though he may be able to catch a fleeting moment of emotion, has not the inspiration for sustained flight. Thus, when the poet attempts a work of much greater length, he finds it difficult to maintain an equally high level throughout.

In spite of the enormous amount of verse produced since the publication of *Azul,* and the diversity of forms which that verse has assumed, there is a surprising lack of variety in the choice of subjects. Human experience and the world in which we live are infinitely varied; but this variety does not find adequate reflection in the poets of this period. With the exception of Darío and perhaps Lugones, they have a very restricted range. The modern poet, like the cricket,

> preludia su solo monótono
> en la única cuerda que está en su violín.

Many of these poems deal with the emotion of love, and, as we might expect in a people filled with the exuberance of youth, they illustrate more fully the physical than the spiritual aspect of this emotion: they celebrate the sorrows, raptures, and despair of the lover seeking a personal satisfaction, not the desire to forget self in another, which is the primal motive of all the other forms of love, from friendship and maternal love to love of country, of mankind, of ideas, and of God. Of love in this wiser, steadier, graver, and less selfish sense the poets of this period know little. This narrowness of outlook is apparent in another respect. Life is not one long funeral procession; nor do we always wear mourning, though we know that "all that lives must die." But with these Spanish-American poets the thought of death is an obsession. Professor Ortega y Gasset puts the matter perhaps a little bluntly when he says, "El español siente la vida como un universal dolor de muelas."

Still, the truth of his observation is amply borne out in the present collection; for, as will be perceived, the atmosphere is one of gloom; life is regarded as almost unrelieved tragedy; only one poem, *El día que me quieras,* by Amado Nervo, seems to have been written by a man who was really happy. And this is no coincidence; it is typical of the period. Whether this melancholy was always the outcome of a highly refined sensibility (the "hyperaesthesia" that Darío claimed as his own), and not a mere literary pose, like Espronceda's lamentations over his "lost illusions," is open to question.

It will have been observed that the movement we have been considering extends over the period of the Great War; but, surprising as it may appear to English readers, the war seems to have left little or no trace on the poetry of Spanish America. To the war has been attributed the emergence of many conflicting schools of poetical activity; but, as is evident from what has already been said and from a perusal of even the few poems here translated, the tendencies of which these modern developments were the outcome were already perceptible before the war began. Among the poems of the more outstanding writers of the period I have found only one poem dealing directly with the war, and that a rather feeble satire on Kaiser Wilhelm by Arturo Capdevila (not published till 1928). It seems incredible that, while Europe was agonizing in what looked like her death-struggle, the poets of Spanish America had no ears for her cry and drew no inspiration from her sacrifice. Nero fiddling while Rome was burning was only a mild antetype.

As for the most modern schools, it is obvious that they arise from a desire to present the truth as the poet sees it. But truth is many sided, a gem of many facets, of which the "advanced" poet sees only one. The Futurist detests the artificiality of the Modernist. Poetry, he declares, must be absolutely sincere, and unrestrained by any mere convention; and in this he is right. The Cubist and the Simplicist insist on the most unadorned expression of the poetic idea; and when the idea is truly poetic, there is much to be said for this. The Realist feels, with Pope, that "the proper study of mankind is man," man and the grim struggle that makes up this life; and here again we must admit there is substantial truth. With the Dadaist we acknowledge that at times life seems chaotic, though it seems like an abdication of human reason to accept this fact as the basis for poetry. As for the Creationist's insistence on the supremacy of the imagination in poetry, this is nothing new. More than three centuries ago Shakespeare declared,

> The lunatic, the lover, and the poet
> Are of imagination all compact;

and experience since then has only confirmed what he said. When the essentials of poetry have thus been so fully analyzed—and the process of analysis can hardly go farther—the time seems propitious for a new synthesis; and in the latest work of Torres-Ríoseco, Pablo Neruda, and Jorge Luis Borges there seem to be emerging the elements from which a new American poetry will be evolved.

Writing of England in 1644, Milton observed that

where there is much desire to learn, there of necessity will be much arguing, much writing, many opinions; for opinion in good men is knowledge in the making.

With only slight adaptation this passage may be taken to represent the state of affairs poetical in Spanish America today. For the desire to master the secrets of the poetic art is not confined to any one state, or class of society. There is much arguing, much writing and experimenting; and many opinions are being canvassed under the aegis of Liberty, "which is the nurse of all great wits." If ever there was a soil favorable to the production of a work of supreme genius, it is there. Moreover, in these Latin-American republics, quite as much as in the United States, a fusion of the most diverse races and types is going on to an extent unequaled anywhere else in the world; and it is not fantastic to expect that within a measurable time a new type will be evolved, with a new culture that may surpass anything hitherto known. In much of the criticism appearing in Spanish-American reviews today the note of expectancy is distinctly perceptible. Darío, describing the land of his dreams, tells how there

> la eterna Vida sus semillas siembra,
> y brota la armonía del gran Todo;

and the critics argue in this manner: To the solidity of reasoning that Rome inherited from Greece and handed on to her children, Italy added brilliant imagination; Spain, power of idealistic exaltation; France, the sense of form; England, practical wisdom; and Germany, profundity of thought. Is it not possible, then [they ask], that in Spanish America, where all these diverse elements are so rapidly blending, Darío's dream may become a reality, and that a new and complete synthesis may emerge, in which sensibility, intelligence, imagination, and will, on the spiritual side, uniting with power, grace, and beauty on the physical, will produce a harmony comparable only to the culture of Ancient Greece?

Genius, however, is incalculable, both in its manifestations and in the time and place of its appearance. The wind bloweth where it listeth. Of old the

Jews scoffed and said, "Can any good thing come out of Nazareth?" and fifty years ago men may have asked as contemptuously, "Can any great poet come out of Nicaragua?" But on neither occasion was skepticism justified of her children. It may be well, therefore, since prophecy is a notoriously hazardous form of speculation, to leave the answering of the critics' question to the judgment of posterity.

How near the Spanish Americans have come to the realization of their dream the reader may judge from a perusal of the selection of poems here translated. He may find little trace of supreme genius, but in any event he will have gained some insight into the mind of the Spanish-American peoples—an important step toward international understanding and good will.

Part Two

TRANSLATIONS

NOCTURNO III

Una noche,
Una noche toda llena de murmullos, de perfumes y de música de alas;
una noche
en que ardían en la sombra nupcial y húmeda las luciérnagas fantásticas,
a mi lado lentamente, contra mí ceñida toda, muda y pálida,
como si un presentimiento de amarguras infinitas
hasta el más secreto fondo de las fibras te agitara,
por la senda florecida que atraviesa la llanura
caminabas;
y la luna llena
por los cielos azulosos, infinitos y profundos esparcía su luz blanca,
y tu sombra,
fina y lánguida,
y mi sombra,
por los rayos de la luna proyectadas,
sobre las arenas tristes
de la senda se juntaban,
y eran una,
y eran una,
y eran una sola sombra larga,
y eran una sola sombra larga,
y eran una sola sombra larga....

Esta noche
solo; el alma
llena de las infinitas amarguras y agonías de tu muerte,
separado de ti misma por el tiempo, por la tumba y la distancia,
por el infinito negro
donde nuestra voz no alcanza,
mudo y solo
por la senda caminaba....
Y se oían los ladridos de los perros a la luna,
a la luna pálida,
y el chirrido
de las ranas....

NOCTURNE

One night,
A night all full of murmurs, of perfumes, of the music of wings,
A night
In whose nuptial and humid shade burned the fantastic glowworms,
Slowly by my side, in close embrace, silent and pale,
As if some presentiment of infinite sorrow
Shook to their secret depths the fibers of thy being,
Along the flower-decked path that crossed the plain
Thou walkedst;
And the full moon
Shed over the heavens of deep and boundless blue its silvery light,
And thy shadow,
Languid and fine,
And my shadow,
Thrown by the moonbeams
Over the dreary sand
Of the path, were joined together,
And were one,
And were one long shadow....

Tonight,
Alone; my soul
Filled with infinite bitterness and agony by thy death,
Parted from thee by time, and distance, and the tomb,
By the black infinitude
Whither no voice of ours can reach,
Silent and alone
Along that path I walked....
The sound of dogs was heard baying the moon,
The pallid moon,
And the croak
Of the frogs....

Sentí frío. Era el frío que tenían en tu alcoba
tus mejillas y tus sienes y tus manos adoradas,
entre las blancuras níveas
de las mortuorias sábanas.
Era el frío del sepulcro, era el hielo de la muerte,
era el frío de la nada.

Y mi sombra
por los rayos de la luna proyectada,
iba sola,
iba sola,
iba sola por la estepa solitaria;
y tu sombra esbelta y ágil,
fina y lánguida,
como en esa noche tibia de la muerta primavera,
como en esa noche llena de murmullos, de perfumes y de música de alas,
se acercó y marchó con ella,
se acercó y marchó con ella,
se acercó y marchó con ella.... ¡Oh las sombras enlazadas!
¡Oh las sombras de los cuerpos que se juntan con las sombras de las almas!
¡Oh las sombras que se buscan en las noches de tristezas y de lágrimas! ...

I felt a chill. It was the chill that in thy chamber laid its hold
Upon thy cheeks, thy temples, and thy lovely hands,
      Amid the snowy whiteness
      Of thy winding-sheet.
It was the chill of the tomb, the freezing chill of death,
      The chill of nothingness.

      And my shadow,
  Thrown forward by the moonbeams,
      Walked alone,
      Walked alone,
  Walked alone over the solitary plain;
  And thy shadow lithe and nimble,
      Languid and fine,
As on that lush, warm night of the spring that's dead,
That night all full of murmurs, of perfumes, and the music of wings,
  Approached and walked with mine,
  Approached and walked with mine,
  Approached and walked with mine.... Oh, shades entwined!
Oh, shades of the body that unite with shadows of the soul!
Oh, shades that seek each other in the nights of sadness and of tears!

ÉGALITÉ

*Juan Lanas, el mozo de esquina,
es absolutamente igual
al Emperador de la China:
los dos son un mismo animal.

Juan Lanas cubre su pelaje
con nuestra manta nacional;
el gran magnate lleva un traje
de seda verde excepcional.

Del uno cuidan cien dragones
de porcelana y de metal;
el otro cuenta sus girones
triste y hambreado en un portal.

Pero si alguna mandarina
siguiendo el instinto sexual
al potentado se avecina
en el traje tradicional

que tenía nuestra madre Eva
en aquella tarde fatal
en que se comieron la breva
del árbol del bien y del mal,

y si al mismo Juan una Juana
se entrega de un modo brutal
y palpita la bestia humana
en un solo espasmo sexual,

Juan Lanas, el mozo de esquina,
es absolutamente igual
al Emperador de la China:
los dos son un mismo animal.

---

* Juan Lanas—a simpleton, a useless, pliant fellow.

EQUALITY

John Lanas, the boy at the corner,
Is every whit as good
As the Emperor of China:
Of the same animal brood.

John Lanas covers his body
With our common, homely cloak;
The great man wears a green silk
Gown, beyond common folk.

One's guarded by a hundred dragons
Of metal and china ware;
Famished and sad, the other counts
His rags in his gateway lair.

But if some highborn lady
Feeling the surge of sex
To this potentate finds entrance,
And with just such dress bedecks

Herself as Mother Eve had
That fatal afternoon,
When she ate from the tree of knowledge
Its fruit of bane and boon,

And if to this John some Jane
Gives herself in brute surrender,
And the beast in her is aquiver
With a hot lust to engender,

John Lanas, the boy at the corner,
Is every whit as good
As the Emperor of China:
Of the same animal brood.

YO SOY AQUEL

Yo soy aquel que ayer no más decía
el verso azul y la canción profana,
en cuya noche un ruiseñor había
que era alondra de luz por la mañana.

El dueño fuí de mi jardín de sueño,
lleno de rosas y de cisnes vagos;
el dueño de las tórtolas, el dueño
de góndolas y liras en los lagos;

y muy siglo diez y ocho y muy antiguo
y muy moderno; audaz, cosmopolita;
con Hugo fuerte y con Verlaine ambiguo,
y una sed de ilusiones infinita.

Yo supe de dolor desde mi infancia,
mi juventud... ¿fué juventud la mía?
Sus rosas aún me dejan su fragancia—
una fragancia de melancolía....

Potro sin freno se lanzó mi instinto,
mi juventud montó potro sin freno;
iba embriagada y con puñal al cinto;
si no cayó, fué porque Dios es bueno.

En mi jardín se vió una estatua bella;
se juzgó mármol y era carne viva;
un alma joven habitaba en ella,
sentimental, sensible, sensitiva.

Y tímida ante el mundo, de manera
que encerrada en silencio no salía,
sino cuando en la dulce primavera
era la hora de la melodía....

Hora de ocaso y de discreto beso;
hora crepuscular y de retiro;
hora de madrigal y de embeleso,
de «¡Te adoro!», de «¡Ay!» y de suspiro.

I AM THE MAN

I am the man who only yesterday
Spoke forth in "Azure" verse and song "Profane,"
For whom by night a nightingale would sing,
By morning light a lark take up the strain.

Now in my garden of dreams with roses filled
And errant swans, myself I master make;
The master of the turtledoves, and lord
Of lyres, and gondolas that skim the lake;

And very eighteenth-century, antique,
Yet modern; bold, a true cosmopolite,
Like Hugo strong, ambiguous like Verlaine,
And thirsting for illusions infinite.

Even from childhood I have suffered pain;
My youth... but what of youth was ever mine?
Its roses leave with me their fragrance still—
A fragrance, but of sadness deep the sign....

Like colt unbridled dashed my instinct forth;
My youth mounted this colt unbridled, free;
Drunken rode out, a dagger at my belt;
And if I fell not, 'twas God's care for me.

A lovely statue in my garden stood;
Marble it seemed, yet seemed like flesh to live;
A youthful spirit had its dwelling there,
Sensible, sentimental, sensitive.

So timid 'twas before the world, that never
It left the silence of its cloister'd pale,
Unless in dulcet springtime at the hour
When sweet harmonious music would prevail...

Hour of the sunset and the kiss discreet,
Hour of the twilight, and of soft retiring;
Hour of the madrigal and ravishment,
Worship or woe in the lover's soul inspiring.

Y entonces era en la dulzaina un juego
de misteriosas gamas cristalinas,
un renovar de notas del Pan griego
y un desgranar de músicas latinas,

   con aire tal y con ardor tan vivo,
que a la estatua nacían de repente
en el muslo viril patas de chivo
y dos cuernos de sátiro en la frente.

Como la Galatea gongorina
me encantó la marquesa verleniana,
y así juntaba a la pasión divina
una sensual hiperestesia humana;

   todo ansia, todo ardor, sensación pura
y vigor natural; y sin falsía,
y sin comedia y sin literatura....
Si hay un alma sincera, ésa es la mía.

La torre de marfil tentó mi anhelo;
quise encerrarme dentro de mí mismo,
y tuve hambre de espacio y sed de cielo
desde las sombras de mi propio abismo.

Como la esponja que la sal satura
en el jugo del mar, fué el dulce y tierno
corazón mío, henchido de amargura
por el mundo, la carne y el infierno.

Mas, por gracia de Dios, en mi conciencia
el Bien supo elegir la mejor parte;
y si hubo áspera hiel en mi existencia,
melificó toda acritud el Arte.

Mi intelecto libré de pensar bajo,
bañó el agua castalia el alma mía,
peregrinó mi corazón, y trajo
de la sagrada selva la armonía.

Then came a playful music from the flute,
Strange crystal notes that through the gamut ran,
Scattering abroad tunes of the Latin muse,
Renewing harmonies of Grecian Pan,

With air so light, and ardor so alive
That to the statue all at once were born
On its virile limbs the nimble feet of a goat;
On either side of its brow, the satyr's horn.

As Góngora's Galatea charmed me once,
So Verlaine's marchioness was mistress mine;
Thus hyperaesthesia, sensual and human,
Was joined in me to passion all divine;

Then all was yearning, ardor, pure sensation,
And natural strength, deception none to fear,
No comedy, no trace of literature....
Mine was a soul, if any was, sincere.

The ivory tower tempted my eager longing;
I sought within myself to find seclusion,
Hungered for space, thirsted for light of heaven
On my abysmal depths of dark illusion.

My gentle, tender heart was like the sponge
That salt sea-water saturates with brine,
And by the world, the flesh, the devil, made
To swell with bitter feeling past confine.

But, thanks to God, my conscience aiding me,
The Good prevailed to choose the better part;
And if my life has tasted bitter gall,
All bitterness was sweetened still by Art.

My intellect I saved from thoughts debased,
Castalian streams washed clear my soul's dark mood;
My heart went forth on pilgrimage, and brought
Celestial harmony from the sacred wood.

¡Oh, la selva sagrada! ¡Oh, la profunda
emanación del corazón divino
de la sagrada selva! ¡Oh, la fecunda
fuente cuya virtud vence al destino!

Bosque ideal que lo real complica,
allí el cuerpo arde y vive, y Psiquis vuela;
mientras abajo el sátira fornica,
ebria de azul deslíe Filomela

perla de ensueño y música amorosa
en la cúpula en flor del laurel verde,
hipsipila sutil liba en la rosa,
y la boca del fauno el pezón muerde.

Allí va el dios en celo tras la hembra,
y la caña de Pan se alza del lodo;
la eterna Vida sus semillas siembra,
y brota la armonía del gran Todo.

El alma que entra allí debe ir desnuda,
temblando de deseo y fiebre santa,
sobre cardo heridor y espina aguda:
así sueña, así vibra y así canta.

Vida, luz y verdad, tal triple llama
produce la interior llama infinita;
el Arte puro como Cristo exclama:
Ego sum lux et veritas et vita.

Y la vida es misterio, la luz ciega
y la verdad inaccesible asombra;
la adusta perfección jamás se entrega,
y el secreto Ideal duerme en la sombra.

Por eso ser sincero es ser potente.
De desnuda que está, brilla la estrella;
el agua dice el alma de la fuente
en la voz de cristal que fluye d'ella.

Oh, sacred wood! Oh, emanation deep
That issues from the heart divine that beats
In the sacred wood! Oh, fountain rich in grace
And virtue that even destiny defeats!

Oh, wood ideal with the real commingled!
The body there has life, the soul has wings;
While underneath the lustful satyr plays,
Drunk with the azure, Philomela sings

Her pearly dreams of music amorous
Under the blossoming dome of laurel green,
The cunning hypsipila sucks the rose,
The faun's mouth gnaws the teat with tooth obscene.

With ardor there the god pursues the female,
And the reeds of Pan rise lofty from the slime;
Eternally Life there her seed is sowing;
There springs the harmony of the Whole, sublime.

The soul that enters there must naked go,
Trembling with sacred fever and desire,
O'er stinging thistle and sharp piercing thorn:
So shall he dream, sing, vibrate like a lyre.

Life, light, and truth—this glowing trinity
Springs from the infinite, interior flame;
Christ said: "I am the light, the truth, the life";
And Art, if pure, may make an equal claim.

Life is mysterious, and light makes us blind,
Truth inaccessible leaves us dismayed;
Austere perfection never yields to search,
The Ideal slumbers in the secret shade.

And hence I hold, sincerity is power.
'Tis nakedness gives brilliance to the star;
The water sends the fountain's spirit forth
With voice of crystal clearness flowing far.

Tal fué mi intento, hacer del alma pura
mía una estrella, una fuente sonora,
con el horror de la literatura
y loco de crepúsculo y de aurora.

Del crepúsculo azul que da la pauta
que los celestes éxtasis inspira,
bruma y tono menor—¡toda la flauta!
y Aurora, hija del Sol—¡toda la lira!

Pasó una piedra que lanzó una honda;
pasó una flecha que aguzó un violento.
La piedra de la honda fué a la onda,
y la flecha del odio fuése al viento.

La virtud está en ser tranquilo y fuerte;
con el fuego interior todo se abrasa;
se triunfa del rencor y de la muerte,
¡y hacia Belén... la caravana pasa!

EL CISNE

Fué en una hora divina para el género humano.
El Cisne antes cantaba sólo para morir.
Cuando se oyó el acento del Cisne wagneriano
fué en medio de una aurora, fué para revivir.

Sobre las tempestades del humano oceano
se oye el canto del Cisne; no se cesa de oír,
dominando el martillo del viejo Thor Germano
o las trompas que cantan la espada de Argantir.

¡Oh Cisne! ¡Oh sacro pájaro! Si antes la blanca Helena
del huevo azul de Leda brotó de gracia llena,
siendo de la Hermosura la princesa inmortal,

bajo tus blancas alas la nueva Poesía
concibe en una gloria de luz y de armonía
la Helena eterna y pura que encarna el ideal.

Such has been my intent, to make my soul
Pure as a star, sonorous as a stream,
Abhorring all that smacked of literature,
And mad for twilight and the morning beam.

For azure twilight setting forth the scale
That does celestial ecstasies inspire,
Its mist and tone subdued—for it the flute!
For Dawn, Sol's daughter—all the power of the lyre!

There passed a stone that hurtled from a sling;
An arrow passed whetted by cruel hand.
The hurtling stone went harmless to the sea,
And down the wind the shaft by hatred fanned.

True virtue lies in strength with quietness;
The inner fire will all things vivify;
We triumph over rancor, over death,
To Bethlehem then ... the caravan passes by!

THE SWAN

In an hour divine it happened for the human race.
Of old the Swan would sing only when death was near;
But when the Wagnerian Swan was heard, the night gave place
To dawn, and then a finer life began to appear.

Above the storms that o'er our mortal ocean chase
Was heard the song of the Swan; we never cease to hear
It dominate the ancient Thor's Teutonic mace,
Or the trumpets loud that sing the sword of Argantir.

O Swan! O sacred bird! if erst Helena fair
From the blue egg of Leda burst with graces rare
To be princess immortal of Beauty still, though real,

The new Poetic Art under thy wings of white
Shall now conceive, in glory of harmony and light,
The Helen, eternal, pure, embodying the ideal.

BLASÓN

El olímpico cisne de nieve
Con el ágata rosa del pico
Lustra el ala eucarística y breve
Que abre al sol como un casto abanico.

En la forma de un brazo de lira
Y del asa de un ánfora griega
Es su cándido cuello, que inspira
Como prora ideal que navega.

Es el cisne, de estirpe sagrada,
Cuyo beso, por campos de seda,
Ascendió hasta la cima rosada
De las dulces colinas de Leda.

Blanco rey de la fuente Castalia,
Su victoria ilumina el Danubio;
Vinci fué su barón en Italia;
Lohengrín es su príncipe rubio.

Su blancura es hermana del lino,
Del botón de los blancos rosales
Y del albo toisón diamantino
De los tiernos corderos pascuales.

Rimador de ideal florilegio
Es de armiño su lírico manto,
Y es el mágico pájaro regio
Que al morir rima el alma en un canto.

El alado aristócrata muestra
Lises albos en campo de azur,
Y ha sentido en sus plumas la diestra
De la amable y gentil Pompadour.

Boga y boga en el lago sonoro
Donde el sueño a los tristes espera,
Donde aguarda una góndola de oro
A la novia de Luis de Baviera.

BLAZON

Olympian-proud and white as snow,
With rosy agate beak, the swan
Makes his short stainless wings to glow
That open sunward a chaste fan.

His neck is curved like arm of lyre
Or handle of a Grecian vase,
And, glittering white, seems to inspire
Like ship that sails ideal ways.

This is the swan of brood sublime
That, over silken fields, to kiss
Even Leda's blushing cheek, would climb
Her sweetly moulded charms, to bliss.

White monarch of the Castalian spring,
On the Danube is his triumph seen;
O'er Vinci in Italy he was king,
His fair young prince is Lohengrin.

No linen can surpass his whiteness,
Nor white buds on the early rose,
Nor diamond-glittering fleece his brightness
That tender lambs in spring disclose.

Maker of songs as yet unheard,
In singing robes of ermine dressed,
This royal and mysterious bird
When dying sings his soul to rest.

The fleurs-de-lis on a field of blue
By this winged patrician are displayed;
The hand of Pompadour so true
He has felt on his plumes in kindness laid.

He oars his way on the sounding lake
Where dreams for saddened souls abide,
Where a golden shallop waits to take
Bavarian Louis' destined bride.

Dad, Condesa, a los cisnes cariño,
Dioses son de un país halagüeño,
Y hechos son de perfume, de armiño,
De luz alba, de seda y de sueño.

SINFONÍA EN GRIS MAYOR

El mar como un vasto cristal azogado
refleja la lámina de un cielo de zinc;
lejanas bandadas de pájaros manchan
el fondo bruñido de pálido gris.

El sol como un vidrio redondo y opaco
con paso de enfermo camina al cenit;
el viento marino descansa en la sombra
teniendo de almohada su negro clarín.

Las ondas que mueven su vientre de plomo
debajo del muelle parecen gemir.
Sentado en un cable, fumando su pipa,
está un marinero pensando en las playas
de un vago lejano brumoso país.

Es viejo ese lobo. Tostaron su cara
los rayos de fuego del sol del Brasil;
los recios tifones del mar de la China
le han visto bebiendo su frasco de gin.

La espuma impregnada de yodo y salitre
ha tiempo conoce su roja nariz,
sus crespos cabellos, sus biceps de atleta,
su gorra de lona, su blusa de dril.

En medio del humo que forma el tabaco
ve el viejo el lejano brumoso país,
adonde una tarde caliente y dorada
tendidas las velas partió el bergantín....

Give love then, Countess, to the swans,
Gods of a land with charm that teems;
Of perfume made, with ermine fans,
Of dawning light, of silk and dreams.

A SYMPHONY IN GRAY

The ocean like some mirror-surface vast
Reflects the zinc-hued sky that dims the day;
By distant flocks of birds a blot is cast
Upon the burnished background, pallid gray.

The sun with face of glass, opaque and round,
Paces the zenith like a man outworn;
The sea-wind seeks the shade and rest profound,
Making a pillow of his sable horn.

The waves that writhe their leaden forms here seem
To groan beneath the pier among its piles.
Upon a cable seated, in a dream
A sailor smoking thinks of far-off isles,
Where vague and misty all the landscape smiles.

An old sea-wolf; the hot Brazilian sun
Has bronzed his face with rays of darting fire;
In Chinese seas the bellowing typhoon
Has seen him drink his gin despite its ire.

The sea-foam charged with niter and iodine
Long years has known his shining ruddy nose,
His crispy locks, his muscles big and fine,
His woolen cap, the blouse of drill he shows.

Amid the clouds of pipe-smoke upward rolled
The old man sees that distant, misty shore,
Whither one sultry eve 'neath skies of gold
His bark with all sails set put forth of yore.

La siesta del trópico. El lobo se aduerme.
Ya todo lo envuelve la gama del gris;
parece que un suave y enorme esfumino
del curvo horizonte borrara el confín.

La siesta del trópico. La vieja cigarra
ensaya su ronca guitarra senil,
y el grillo preludia su solo monótono
en la única cuerda que está en su violín.

FRISO

Cabe una fresca viña de Corinto
Que verde techo presta al simulacro
Del Dios viril, que artífice de Atenas
En intacto pentélico labrara,
Un día alegre, al deslumbrar el mundo
La harmonía del carro de la Aurora,
Y en tanto que arrullaban sus ternezas
Dos nevadas palomas venusinas
Sobre rosal purpúreo y pintoresco,
Como olímpica flor de gracia llena,
Ví el bello rostro de la rubia Eunice.
No más gallarda se encamina al templo
Canéfora gentil, ni más riente
Llega la musa a quien favor prodiga
El divino Sminteo, que mi amada
Al tender hacia mí sus tersos brazos.
Era la hora del supremo triunfo
Concedido á mis lágrimas y ofrendas
Por el poder de la celeste Cipris,
Y era el ritmo potente de mi sangre
Verso de fuego que al propicio numen
Cantaba ardiente de la vida el himno.
Cuando mi boca en los bermejos labios
De mi princesa de cabellos de oro
Licor bebía que afrentara al néctar.

The tropic afternoon the sea-wolf sleeps,
All things are merged in changing hues of gray;
A soft yet mighty brush appears to sweep
The curved horizon's boundary away.

The locust through the tropic afternoon
Teases his ancient hoarse guitar to sing;
And the cricket starts his one monotonous tune
On his violin that has but a single string.

FRIEZE

   Close by the cool shade of a Corinth vine
That forms a green roof o'er the virile god
Whose image some artificer of Athens
From marble of Pentelicus had wrought,
One joyous day, when from Aurora's car
Harmonious sounds came forth to wake the world,
And while two snow-white doves of Venus' train
Murmured their tender notes among the roses
Blushing and picturesque, as 'twere some flower
Filled to o'erflowing with Olympian grace,
I saw the beauteous face of fair Eunice.
More joyously no gentle basket-bearer
E'er to the temple went, more laughingly
The muse did never come to him on whom
Divine Apollo would his favors shower,
Than my belovèd, as her smooth, white arms
She stretched toward me.
   It was the hour when to my offered vows
And tears, by Venus' power, triumph supreme
Had come, and the pulsing torrent in my veins
Was a song of fire that poured forth ardently
To the auspicious deity the hymn of life.
But as my mouth drank from the crimson lips
Of my princess whose locks were all of gold
The liquor that leaves pale the gods' own nectar,

Por el sendero de fragantes mirtos
Que guía al blanco pórtico del templo,
Súbitas voces nuestras ansias turban;
Lírica procesión al viento esparce
Los cánticos rituales de Dionisio,
El evohé de las triunfales fiestas,
La algazara que enciende con su risa
La impúber tropa de saltantes niños,
Y el vivo son de músicas sonoras
Que anima el coro de bacantes ebrias.
En el concurso báquico el primero,
Regando rosas y tejiendo danzas,
Garrido infante, de Eros por hermoso
Émulo y par, risueño aparecía.
Y de él en pos las ménades ardientes,
Al aire el busto en que su pompa erigen
Pomas ebúrneas; en la mano el sistro,
Y las curvas caderas mal veladas
Por las flotantes, desceñidas ropas,
Alzaban sus cabezas que en consorcio
Circundaban la flor de Citerea
Y el pámpano fragante de las viñas.
   Aun me parece que mis ojos tornan
Al cuadro lleno de color y fuerza:
Dos robustos mancebos que los cabos
De cadenas metálicas empuñan,
Y cuyo porte y músculos de Ares
Divinos dones son, pintada fiera
Que felino pezón nutrió en Hircania,
Con gesto heroico entre la turba rigen;
Y otros dos un leopardo cuyo cuello
Gracias de Flora ciñen y perfuman,
Y cuyos ojos en las anchas cuencas
De furia henchidos sanguinosos giran.
Pétalos y uvas el sendero alfombran,
Y desde el campo azul do el Sagitario

Along the pathway decked with fragrant myrtles
That to the white gate of the temple led,
Came sudden voices to disturb our raptures;
A lyric rout came, scattering to the breeze
The ritual chants to Dionysus sung,
The evohe of his triumphal festivals,
The merriment that troops of innocent boys
Inspire with their laughter as they leap along,
And the lively notes of music, loud, sonorous,
That animate the bacchantes' reeling choir.
Next, smiling, there appeared a fair young child,
For beauty Cupid's rival and his peer;
And after him the flaming Maenad sisters,
Free to the air their breasts, that raise to view
The pomp of ivory apples, in their hands
The sistrum, and their curving, shapely loins
But thinly veiled by flowing garments free;
They carried high their heads round which the flower
Of Venus and the fragrant tender leaves
Of the vine, as if in wedlock joined, were bound.
  And yet from these my eyes appear to turn
To a picture rich in color and in strength:
Two lusty youths, who hold with iron grasp
The ends of metal chains, and in their bearing
And muscles as of Mars show gifts divine,
Drive through the throng with bold heroic mien
A painted beast in far Hyrcania nursed
On feline breast; two others lead a leopard
Whose neck is perfumed and adorned with blooms,
The gifts of Flora, and whose blood-red eyes
Swollen with fury in deep wide sockets roll;
The path is carpeted with flowers and grapes,
And from the fields of azure, where the Archer

De coruscantes flechas resplandece,
Las urnas de la luz la tierra bañan.
　Pasó el tropel. En la cercana selva
Lúgubre resonaba el grito de Atis,
Triste pavor de la inviolada ninfa.
Deslizaba su paso misterioso
El apacible coro de las Horas.
Eco volvía la acordada queja
De la flauta de Pan. Joven gallardo,
Más hermoso que Adonis y Narciso,
Con el aire gentil de los efebos
Y la lira en las manos, al boscaje
Como lleno de luz se dirigía.
　Amor pasó con su dorada antorcha.
　Y no lejos del nido en que las aves,
Las dos aves de Cipris, sus arrullos
Cual tiernas rimas a los aires dieran,
Fuí más feliz que el luminoso cisne
Que vió de Leda la inmortal blancura,
Y Eunice pudo al templo de la diosa
Purpúrea ofrenda y tórtolas amables
Llevar el día en que mi regio triunfo
Vió el Dios viril en mármol cincelado
Cabe la fresca viña de Corinto.

CANCIÓN DE OTOÑO EN PRIMAVERA

¡Juventud, divino tesoro,
ya te vas para no volver!
Cuando quiero llorar, no lloro,
y a veces lloro sin querer....

Plural ha sido la celeste
historia de mi corazón.
Era una dulce niña, en este
mundo de duelo y aflicción.

Resplendent with his flashing arrows shines,
The urns of light pour brightness on the earth.
  The rout has gone. In the forest near at hand
Resounded Attis' weird and mournful cry,
The plaintive terror of the inviolate nymph.
The Hours in peaceful choir mysteriously
With gliding motion passed upon their way;
And to the tuneful and complaining flute
Of Pan came Echo's answer. Then a swain,
More debonair, more beauteous than Adonis
And Narcissus, with the mild and gentle air
Of young Athenians, in his hands the lyre,
His way directed to the wood all full
Of light. And Love too passed with golden torch.
  Thus, near the nest where Venus' sacred birds
Their murmurs gave to the air, like tender rhymes,
I felt myself more happy than the gleaming swan
That gazed on Leda's white immortal radiance;
And to the goddess' temple my Eunice
Might bear her purple gift and gentle doves,
That day the god beheld my royal triumph,
That virile god in marble chiseled out
Close by the cool shade of the Corinth vine.

AN AUTUMN SONG IN SPRING

  O Youth, divinest of treasures,
No more to return thou art fled;
When I fain would weep, I weep not,
And oft tears unwillingly shed!

  A varied tale, though a heavenly,
Has my heart's life-story been.
The first was a sweet maid, joyous,
In a world of grief and teen.

Miraba como el alba pura;
sonreía como una flor.
Era su cabellera obscura
hecha de noche y de dolor.

Yo era tímido como un niño.
Ella, naturalmente, fué,
para mi amor hecho de armiño,
Herodías y Salomé....

¡Juventud, divino tesoro,
Ya te vas para no volver!
Cuando quiero llorar, no lloro,
y a veces lloro sin querer....

La otra fué más sensitiva,
y más consoladora y más
halagadora y expresiva,
cual no pensé encontrar jamás.

Pues a su continua ternura
una pasión violenta unía.
En un peplo de gasa pura
una bacante se envolvía...

En sus brazos tomó mi ensueño
y lo arrulló como a un bebé...
Y le mató, triste y pequeño,
falto de luz, falto de fe....

¡Juventud, divino tesoro,
te fuiste para no volver!
Cuando quiero llorar, no lloro,
y a veces lloro sin querer....

Otra juzgó que era mi boca
el estuche de su pasión;
y que me roería, loca,
con sus dientes el corazón,

She looked with the pure eyes of dawning,
Her smile had the grace of a flower.
Her tresses had the blackness
Of grief and the midnight hour.

I was as shy as a child is.
She, naturally, played
Herodias and Salome
With my love like ermine made.

O Youth, divinest of treasures,
No more to return thou art fled;
When I fain would weep, I weep not,
And oft tears unwillingly shed!

The next I found more soothing,
More flattering and more kind;
Her like for depth of feeling
I never thought to find.

For with tenderness enduring
Strong passion she combined;
Her peplus, gauze of the purest,
A bacchante raging behind . . .

Her arms embraced my illusion,
Crooned over it as a child . . .
And killed it, sad and a weakling,
Of light and of faith beguiled. . . .

O Youth, divinest of treasures,
No more to return thou art fled;
When I fain would weep, I weep not,
And oft tears unwillingly shed!

Another judged that my lips were
But the cradle for her passion;
That her teeth might gnaw my heartstrings
In wildly fatuous fashion,

poniendo en un amor de exceso
la mira de su voluntad,
mientras eran abrazo y beso
síntesis de la eternidad;

y de nuestra carne ligera
imaginar siempre un Edén,
sin pensar que la Primavera
y la carne acaban también....

¡Juventud, divino tesoro,
ya te vas para no volver!
Cuando quiero llorar, no lloro,
y a veces lloro sin querer....

¡Y las demás! En tantos climas,
en tantas tierras, siempre son,
si no pretextos de mis rimas,
fantasmas de mi corazón.

En vano busqué a la princesa
que estaba triste de esperar.
La vida es dura. Amarga y pesa.
¡Ya no hay princesa que cantar!

Mas a pesar del tiempo terco,
mi sed de amor no tiene fin;
con el cabello gris, me acerco
a los rosales del jardín....

¡Juventud, divino tesoro,
ya te vas para no volver!
Cuando quiero llorar, no lloro,
y a veces lloro sin querer....

¡Mas es mía el Alba de Oro!

Placing in love without limits
The object of her desiring,
For a heaven complete a kiss,
An embrace, and no more requiring;

Believing an Eden forever
Our weak, fickle flesh will lend,
Nor thinking that like the Springtime
Flesh too must come to an end....

O Youth, divinest of treasures,
No more to return thou art fled;
When I fain would weep, I weep not,
And oft tears unwillingly shed!

The rest—in so many countries,
In so many varied climes—
Were but figments of my fancy,
If not pretexts for my rhymes.

In vain I've sought for the princess
Who was sad with waiting so long.
Life is hard; it embitters, depresses;
There's princess no more for my song.

But in spite of all life's hardness,
My thirst for love has no end;
With my hair turned gray, my footsteps
To the garden of roses I bend....

O Youth, divinest of treasures,
No more to return thou art fled;
When I fain would weep, I weep not,
And oft tears unwillingly shed!

But mine is the Golden Dawn!

MÍA

Mía: así te llamas.
¿Qué más harmonía?
Mía: luz del día,
Mía: rosas, llamas.

¡Qué aroma derramas
En el alma mía
Si sé que me amas,
¡Oh Mía! ¡Oh Mía!

Tu sexo fundiste
Con mi sexo fuerte,
Fundiendo dos bronces.

Yo triste, tu triste...
¿No has de ser entonces
Mía hasta la muerte?

PARA UNA CUBANA

Poesía, dulce y mística,
Busca a la blanca cubana
Que se asomó a la ventana
Como una visión artística.

Misteriosa y cabalística,
Puede dar celos a Diana,
Con su faz de porcelana
De una blancura eucarística.

Llena de un prestigio asiático,
Roja, en el rostro enigmático,
Su boca púrpura finge,

Y al sonreírse ví en ella
El resplandor de una estrella
Que fuese alma de una esfinge.

MINE

Mine: so thou'rt called; what name
Could more harmonious be?
Mine! the day's light I see;
Mine! a rose, a flame.

What sweet aroma came
To fill my soul from thee
When I knew thou loved'st me!
Mine! ever mine, the same!

Sex made to sex response,
Thy weakness to my strength,
Two metals fused to bronze.

I am sad; thou too, at length...
But does not fate design
That even till death thou'rt mine?

FOR A CUBAN LADY

O Poesy, sweet spirit mystic,
Seek out the Cuban maiden fair,
Who looked from her window with the air
Of a vision most artistic.

Mysterious she, and cabalistic,
Diana's envy she might dare,
For her face with porcelain might compare,
Suffused with whiteness eucharistic.

Filled with enchantment Asiatic,
The red of her countenance enigmatic
About her lips to purple sinks,

And as she smiled, I saw a gleam,
Such star-like splendor, one might deem
It was the spirit of a sphinx.

MARGARITA

¿Recuerdas que querías ser una Margarita
Gautier? Fijo en mi mente tu extraño rostro está,
cuando cenamos juntos, en la primera cita,
en una noche alegre que nunca volverá.

Tus labios escarlatas de púrpura maldita
sorbían el champaña del fino baccarat;
tus dedos deshojaban la blanca margarita:
«Sí..no..; sí..no..,» ¡y sabías que te adoraba yá!

Después, ¡oh flor de histeria! llorabas y réias;
tus besos y tus lágrimas tuve en mi boca yo;
tus risas, tus fragancias, tus quejas, eran mías.

Y en una tarde triste de los más dulces días,
la Muerte, la celosa, por ver si me querías,
¡como a una margarita de amor, te deshojó!

LOS TRES REYES MAGOS

—Yo soy Gaspar. Aquí traigo el incienso.
Vengo a decir: La vida es pura y bella.
Existe Dios. El amor es inmenso.
Todo lo sé por la divina Estrella!

—Yo soy Melchor. Mi mirra aroma todo.
Existe Dios. El es la luz del día.
La blanca flor tiene sus pies en lodo,
y en el placer hay la melancolía!

—Soy Baltasar. Traigo el oro. Aseguro
que existe Dios. Él es el grande y fuerte.
Todo lo sé por el lucero puro
que brilla en la diadema de la Muerte.

—Gaspar, Melchor y Baltasar, callaos.
Triunfa el amor y a su fiesta os convida.
Cristo resurge, hace la luz del caos
y tiene la corona de la Vida!

MARGARITA

Dost thou remember how thou fain would'st be
A Margaret Gautier? I recall the trace,
When first we supped, of strangeness on thy face,
That joyous night—whose like we ne'er shall see.

Thy scarlet-purple lips with perverse glee
Drank up the fine champagne, and, for a space,
"Yes..., No...," thou said'st, sending in silver chase
The daisy's petals; yet knew'st that I loved thee!

And then, hysteria's flower, thou'dst laugh and cry,
Mingle thy kisses and thy tears with mine;
I knew them mine, thy fragrance, smile, and sigh.

And one sad eve, our sweetest day gone by,
Death, jealously, thy love for me to try,
Snatched, like the daisy's bloom, thy form benign!

THE KINGS OF THE EAST

Gaspar am I. Hither I incense bring.
I come to say that life is pure and bright,
That love's unmeasured, and that God is King.
All this I know by yon star's holy light.

And Melchior I. My myrrh sheds fragrance round.
God reigns; he is the very light of day.
The white flower sinks its roots in slimy ground,
And melancholy grows 'mid pleasures gay.

I, Balthasar, bring gold; my task, to assure
That God doth reign, that He is strong and great.
This know I by yon gleaming planet pure,
That Death wears sparkling in his crown of state.

Nay, Gaspar, Melchior, Balthasar; be still.
Love triumphs, bids you come his feast to share.
The risen Christ with light will Chaos fill,
And holds the crown of Life for you to wear.

LA DULZURA DEL ÁNGELUS

La dulzura del ángelus matinal y divino
que diluyen ingenuas campanas provinciales
en un aire inocente a fuerza de rosales,
de plegaria, de ensueño de virgen y de trino

de ruiseñor, opuesto todo al rudo destino
que no cree en Dios... El áureo ovillo vespertino
que la tarde devana tras opacos cristales
por tejer la inconsútil tela de nuestros males,

todos hechos de carne y aromados de vino...
Y esta atroz amargura de no gustar de nada,
de no saber adónde dirigir nuestra prora

mientras el pobre esquife en la noche cerrada
va en las hostiles olas huérfano de la aurora...
(¡Oh, suaves campanas entre la madrugada!)

SALUTACIÓN DEL OPTIMISTA

Inclitas razas ubérrimas, sangre de Hispania fecunda,
espíritus fraternos, luminosas almas, ¡salve!
Porque llega el momento en que habrán de cantar nuevos himnos
lenguas de gloria. Un vasto rumor llena los ámbitos; mágicas
ondas de vida van renaciendo de pronto;
retrocede el olvido, retrocede engañada la muerte;
se anuncia un reino nuevo, feliz sibila sueña,
y en la caja pandórica de que tantas desgracias surgieron
encontramos de súbito, talismánica, pura, riente,
cual pudiera decirla en sus verso Virgilio divino,
la divina reina de luz, la celeste Esperanza!

Pálidas indolencias, desconfianzas fatales que a tumba
o a perpetuo presidio, condenastéis al noble entusiasmo,
ya veréis el salir del sol en un triunfo de liras,
mientras dos continentes, abonados de huesos gloriosos,

THE ANGELUS

The sweetness of the angelus divine
That simple rustic bells diffuse each morn
In an air of innocence, of roses born,
Of prayers, of virgin dreams, and rapture fine

Of nightingale, opposed to fate malign
That fears not God... The evening's golden skein
Coiled up behind the night's dark crystal bourne
To spin the seamless web of our lot forlorn,

With flesh inwoven, and scented all with wine...
And the bitterness of finding joy in naught,
Of knowing not whither to steer our way

While the poor bark in night's deep darkness caught
Makes fight against the billows, orphan'd of day...
(Oh, soothing of the bells by morning brought!)

THE OPTIMIST'S SALUTATION

Famous and fruitful races, blood of Spain the prolific,
Spirits fraternal, souls all luminous, greeting!
Now the moment has come for glorious tongues to be singing
Hymns that are new. Vast rumors the air are filling; and magical
Waves of life each moment are rising around us;
Backward retires oblivion, and death deluded sinks backward;
Now a new reign is announced, a joy-bringing sybil is dreaming,
And in the box of Pandora from which so much evil has issued,
All of a sudden we find, like a talisman, modest and smiling,
Such as Virgil divine in poetic strains might have sung her,
Gleaming divine, light's queen, Hope, spirit celestial!

Pallid indolence, fatal mistrust, that condemned to extinction,
Sent to prison perpetual men dower'd with noble enthusiasm,
Now shall you see the sun arise in lyrical triumph,
While two continents, fertilized by the bones of the heroes,

del Hércules antiguo la gran sombra soberbia evocando,
digan al orbe: la alta virtud resucita
que a la hispana progenie hizo dueña de siglos.

   Abominad la boca que predice desgracias eternas;
abominad los ojos que ven sólo zodíacos funestos;
abominad las manos que apedrean las ruinas ilustres,
o que la tea empuñan o la daga suicida.
Siéntense sordos ímpetus en las entrañas del mundo,
la inminencia de algo fatal hoy conmueve la tierra;
fuertes colosos caen, se desbandan bicéfalas águilas,
y algo se inicia como vasto social cataclismo
sobre la faz del orbe. ¿Quién dirá que las savias dormidas
no despierten entonces en el tronco del roble gigante
bajo el cual se exprimió la ubre de la loba romana?
¿Quién será el pusilánime que al vigor español niegue músculos
y que al alma española juzgase áptera y ciega y tullida?
No es Babilonia ni Nínive enterrada en olvido y en polvo,
ni entre momias y piedras reina que habita el sepulcro,
la nación generosa, coronada de orgullo inmarchito
que hacia el lado del alba fija las miradas ansiosas,
ni la que tras los mares en que yace sepulta la Atlántida,
tiene su coro de vástagos, altos, robustos y fuertes.

   Únanse, brillen, secúndense tantos vigores dispersos;
formen todos un solo haz de energía ecuménica.
Sangre de Hispania fecunda, sólidas, ínclitas razas,
muestren los dones pretéritos que fueron antaño su triunfo.
Vuelva el antiguo entusiasmo, vuelva el espíritu ardiente
que regará lenguas de fuego en esa epifanía.
Juntas las testas ancianas ceñidas de líricos lauros
y las cabezas jóvenes que la alta Minerva decora,
así los manes heroicos de los primitivos abuelos,
de los egregios padres que abrieron el surco prístino,
sientan los soplos agrarios de primaverales retornos
y el rumor de espigas que inició la labor triptolémica.

   Un continente y otro renovando las viejas prosapias,
en espíritu unidos, en espíritu y ansias y lengua,

Raising the mighty and haughty shade of Hercules ancient,
Tell to the world that again is reviving the eminent virtue
That brought to the offspring of Spain the lordship of centuries.

   Treat with disdain the lips that foretell misfortunes unending;
Hate those eyes that foresee but events in disastrous recurrence;
Down with the hands that are raised to stone the ruins illustrious,
Or that grasp the torch, or the dagger of suicide.
Dull reverberations are felt in earth's deepest recesses;
Something fatal today is moving and threatening the world;
Powerful colossi fall, and the two-headed eagles are sundered;
Something now is beginning, some cataclysm vast for society
Over earth's face; and who shall say that the sap that is sleeping
Will not awaken then in the trunk of the oak tree gigantic,
Under which the she-wolf of Rome gave her udder for suckling?
Who shall the puny soul be, to deny strong thews to the Spaniard,
To say that the Spanish soul is blinded, wingless, and faded?
This is no Babylon, Nineveh, buried in dust and oblivion,
Nor is she queen among mummies and stones, inhabiting sepulchers,
This generous nation wearing a crown of pride unfading,
She who turns to the region of daybreak her looks of anxiety,
Nor she who beyond the ocean, in which lies the buried Atlantis,
Gathers the circle around her of children, tall, vigorous, powerful.

   Let them unite, and, shining, and working each with the other,
Make of their scattered forces a center of power ecumenical.
Blood of Spain the prolific, these strong, illustrious races,
Let them display their pristine gifts, that once were their triumph,
Bring back again their ancient enthusiasm, their ardor of spirit,
So that tongues of fire shall descend in this newer epiphany.
Bring together the ancient brows surrounded with laurels poetic,
Bring the youthful poets that lofty Minerva has honored;
Thus the heroic shades of our ancestors back through the ages,
Shades of preëminent parents who opened the earliest furrow,
May feel in a breath from the fields the signs of the springtime returning,
And hear the rustle of cornstalks begun by their labors in husbandry.

   Thus both continents, giving new life to lines old and ancestral,
One in heart, united in spirit and longing and language,

ven llegar el momento en que habrán de cantar nuevos himnos.
La latina estirpe verá la gran alba futura
en un trueno de música gloriosa; millones de labios
saludarán la espléndida luz que vendrá del Oriente,
Oriente augusto en donde todo lo cambia y renueva
la eternidad de Dios, la actividad infinita.
Y así sea Esperanza la visión permanente en nosotros,
ínclitas razas ubérrimas, sangre de Hispania fecunda!

A ROOSEVELT

Es con voz de la Biblia, o verso de Walt Whitman,
que habría que llegar hasta ti, cazador!
Primitivo y moderno, sencillo y complicado,
con un algo de Wáshington y cuatro de Nemrod!
Eres los Estados Unidos,
eres el futuro invasor
de la América ingenua que tiene sangre indígena,
que aun reza a Jesucristo y aun habla en español.

Eres soberbio y fuerte ejemplar de tu raza;
eres culto, eres hábil; te opones a Tolstoy.
Y domando caballos, o asesinando tigres,
eres un Alejandro-Nabucodonosor.
(Eres un Profesor de Energía
como dicen los locos de hoy.)

Crees que la vida es incendio,
que el progreso es erupción;
que en donde pones la bala
el porvenir pones.
    No.

Los Estados Unidos son potentes y grandes.
Cuando ellos se estremecen hay un hondo temblor
que pasa por las vértebras enormes de los Andes.
Si clamáis se oye como el rugir del león.
Ya Hugo a Grant lo dijo:—Las estrellas son vuestras.—

See the moment approaching when the songs they sing shall be new songs;
The Latin race shall behold the magnificent dawn of the future
In a thunder of glorious music; the lips of the millions
Shall greet the refulgent light that shall come from the Orient,
Orient august, where all suffers change and renewal
Through the being eternal of God and his boundless activity;
Thus may the vision of Hope remain forever among us,
Races illustrious and fruitful, blood of Spain the prolific!

TO ROOSEVELT

With a Hebrew prophet's voice or a verse from Walt Whitman,
'Tis thus we must approach you, hunter!
Primitive yet modern, simple yet complex,
With one part Washington and four parts Nimrod,
You are the United States,
You are the future invader
Of that ingenuous America of native blood,
That prays to Jesus still and still speaks Spanish!

You are proud and strong and typical of your race;
Cultured and clever, firmly opposed to Tolstoy.
In breaking horses and in killing tigers
You are an Alexander-Nebuchadnezzar.
(You are a professor of the strenuous life,
As fools say nowadays.)

You hold that life is a fire,
And progress an eruption;
That where your guns can reach,
There you control the future.
        No.

The United States indeed are great and powerful;
They shake themselves, and a deep tremor rocks
The enormous ridges of the Andes to their base.
Once Hugo said to Grant: "The stars are yours."

(Apenas brilla, alzándose, el argentino sol
y la estrella chilena se levanta...) Sois ricos.
Juntáis al culto de Hércules el culto de Mammón;
y alumbrando el camino de la fácil conquista,
la Libertad levanta su antorcha en Nueva-York.

   Mas la América nuestra, que tenía poetas
desde los viejos tiempos de Netzahualcoyotl,
que ha guardado las huellas de los pies del gran Baco;
que el alfabeto pánico en un tiempo aprendió;
que consultó los astros, que conoció la Atlántida,
cuyo nombre nos llega resonando en Platón;
que desde los remotos momentos de su vida
vive de luz, de fuego, de perfume, de amor;
la América del grande Moctezuma, del Inca,
la América fragante de Cristóbal Colón,
la América católica, la América española,
la América en que dijo el noble Guatemoc:
—Yo no estoy en un lecho de rosas—; esa América
que tiembla de huracanes y que vive de amor,
hombres de ojos sajones y alma bárbara, vive.
Y sueña. Y ama, y vibra; y es la hija del Sol.
Tened cuidado. ¡Vive la América española!
Hay mil cachorros sueltos del León español.
Se necesitaría, Roosevelt, ser, por Dios mismo,
el riflero terrible y el fuerte cazador
para poder tenernos en vuestras férreas garras.

   Y, pues contáis con todo, falta una cosa: ¡Dios!

(For, rising but then, the sun of the Argentine
Scarce shone; the Chilean star had barely risen ...)
You're rich; to that of Hercules you join the cult of Mammon;
And, illumining the path that leads to easy conquest,
Liberty rears her torch above New York.

    But our America, in which from the far-off days
Of Netzahualcoyotl poets have sung,
Which still preserves the footprints of great Bacchus,
And learned long since the alphabet of Pan,
Which reads the stars, and knew the great Atlantis
Whose fame resounding reaches us from Plato;
This, our America, from the first has lived, and lives
On light and fire, on perfume and on love,
The land of Moctezuma, of the Inca,
Fragrant still with the memory of Columbus,
America Catholic, America Spanish,
America in which the noble Guatemoc said:
"I'm on no bed of roses"; this America,
That rocks with hurricanes, and lives by love,
Ye men of Saxon eyes and barbarous souls, she lives,
Dreams, loves, vibrates, is daughter of the Sun;
Beware, for Spanish America still lives;
The Spanish Lion has a thousand cubs.
'Twere needful, Roosevelt, to be, for God himself,
The terrible rifleman and the hunter strong,
Ever to keep us in your iron grasp.

    And you think all's yours: you still lack one thing—God!

SALUTACIÓN AL ÁGUILA

> May this grand Union have no end.
> —Fontoura Xavier

Bien vengas, mágica Águila de alas enormes y fuertes,
a extender sobre el Sur tu gran sombra continental,
a traer en tus garras, anilladas de rojos brillantes,
una palma de gloria del color de la inmensa esperanza,
y en tu pico la oliva de una vasta y fecunda paz.

Bien vengas, oh mágica Águila, que amara tanto Walt Whitman,
quien te hubiera cantado en esta olímpica jira,
Águila que has llevado tu noble y magnífico símbolo
desde el trono de Júpiter hasta el gran continente del Norte.

Ciertamente, has estado en las rudas conquistas del orbe.
Ciertamente, has tenido que llevar los antiguos rayos.
Si tus alas abiertas la visión de la paz perpetúan,
en tu pico y tus uñas está la necesaria guerra.

¡Precisión de la fuerza! ¡Majestad adquerida del trueno!
Necesidad de abrirle el gran vientre fecundo a la tierra,
para que en ella brote la concreción de oro de la espiga
y tenga el hombre el pan con que mueve su sangre.

No es humana la paz con que sueñan ilusos profetas;
la actividad eterna hace precisa la lucha;
y desde tu etérea altura tú contemplas, divina Águila,
la agitación combativa de nuestro globo vibrante.

Es incidencia la Historia. Nuestro destino supremo
está más allá del rumbo que marcan fugaces las épocas.
Y Palenque y la Atlántida no son más que momentos soberbios
con que puntúa Dios los versos de su augusto Poema.

Muy bien llegada seas a la tierra pujante y ubérrima
sobre la cual la Cruz del Sur está, que miró Dante,
cuando siendo Mesías impulsó en su intuición sus bajeles,
que antes que los del sumo Cristóbal supieron nuestro cielo.

SALUTATION TO THE EAGLE

> May this grand Union have no end.
> —Fontoura Xavier

Welcome, magical Eagle, with wings enormous and powerful,
Spreading over the South thy shadow, great, continental,
Bringing to us in thy talons, red rings sparkling and brilliant,
Palms that speak of glory, in hue like the hope that is boundless,
And in thy beak the olive of peace both widespread and fruitful.

Welcome, O magical Eagle, so deeply beloved by Walt Whitman,
Who, on this feast Olympian, loud would have sounded thy praises;
Eagle, thou who hast brought thy noble, magnificent symbol
Down from Jupiter's throne to the continent great to the Northward.

Truly, thou hast been there, in the midst of the rudest of conquests;
True, thou hast had to bear the age-old flash of the lightning.
And, if thy open wings hold visions of peace still before us,
Yet in thy beak and claws are the symbols of justified warfare.

Force, a thing of necessity! Majesty gained from the thunder!
Needful it is that the fruitful womb of the earth be opened,
That from it may arise the golden ears of the harvest,
Giving to man the bread he needs for full-blooded movement.

Nowise human the peace that is dreamt of by prophets deluded;
Men's never-ending activity needs must compel them to struggle;
Thou, looking down from ethereal heights, O heavenly Eagle,
Seest the combat and turmoil with which the earth itself trembles.

History is but an episode. Truly our ultimate destiny
Lies far beyond the boundaries marked by the flight of the ages;
Even Atlantis, Palenque, are merely the glorious moments
God has employed as points in the verse of this noblest of poems.

Welcome indeed art thou to this land of abundance and energy,
Under the Southern Cross with its four stars looked on by Dante,
When, as Messiah, with bold intuition he pushed on his vessels,
Scanning our southern skies, still unknown to the noble Columbus.

E Pluribus Unum! ¡Gloria, victoria, trabajo!
Tráenos los secretos de las labores del Norte,
y que los hijos nuestros dejen de ser los retores latinos,
y aprendan de los yanquis la constancia, el vigor, el carácter.

Dinos, Águila ilustre, la manera de hacer multitudes
que hagan Romas y Grecias con el jugo del mundo presente,
y que, potentes y sobrias, extiendan su luz y su imperio,
y que, teniendo el Águila y el Bisonte y el Hierro y el Oro,
tengan un áureo día para darle las gracias a Dios.

Águila, existe el Cóndor. Es tu hermano en las grandes alturas.
Los Andes le conocen y saben que, cual tú, mira al Sol.
May this grand Union have no end! dice el poeta.
Puedan ambos juntarse, en plenitud, concordia y esfuerzo.

Águila, que conoces desde Jove hasta Zaratustra
Y que tienes en los Estados Unidos tu asiento,
que sea tu venida fecunda para estas naciones
que el pabellón admiran constelado de bandas y estrellas.

¡Águila, que estuviste en las horas sublimes de Patmos,
Águila prodigiosa, que te nutres de luz y de azul,
como una cruz viviente, vuela sobre estas naciones,
y comunica al globo la victoria feliz del futuro!

Por algo eres la antigua mensajera jupiterina;
Por algo has presenciado cataclismos y luchas de razas;
por algo estás presente en los sueños del Apocalipsis;
por algo eres el ave que han buscado los fuertes imperios.

¡Salud, Águila! Extensa virtud a tus inmensos revuelos,
reina de los azures, ¡salud! ¡gloria! ¡victoria y encanto!
¡Que la Latina América reciba tu mágica influencia
y que renazca un nuevo Olimpo, lleno de dioses y de héroes!

¡Adelante, siempre adelante! ¡Excelsior! ¡Vida! ¡Lumbre!
¡Que se cumpla lo prometido en los destinos terrenos,
y que vuestra obra inmensa las aprobaciones recoja
del mirar de los astros, y de lo que Hay más Allá!

E Pluribus Unum! Symbol of glory, victory, labor!
Bring us the secrets that stimulate men in the North to endeavor;
Grant that our sons of the Latin race cease to be mere rhetoricians,
Learning instead from the Yankees constancy, vigor, and character.

   Teach us, illustrious Eagle, to nourish a race multitudinous,
Rivaling Rome and Greece with the rising power of the present,
So that, powerful yet temperate, spreading their light and their influence,
They with the Eagle and Bison, and treasures of Gold and of Iron,
Thanks may render, one golden day, to God for his bounty.

   High on the mighty peaks is the Condor, thy brother, O Eagle,
Gazing like thee at the Sun, as the Andes that know him acknowledge.
"May this grand Union have no end," are the words of the poet;
Grant that united they both may abound in vigor and harmony.

   Jove, Zarathustra alike, have given to thee of their wisdom;
Thou who didst take the United States for the seat of thy dwelling,
May thy coming be fruitful, a blessing for each of the nations,
Nations that look with admiring eyes on the star-spangled banner.

   Eagle, thou who wert present in hours sublime upon Patmos,
Eagle, portentous, that liv'st in the light and azure of heaven,
Wing thy flight, like a living crucifix, over these nations,
Scattering over the earth triumphant joy for the future.

   Not for naught wert thou the ancient envoy of Jupiter;
Not for naught hast thou witnessed racial struggles and cataclysms;
Not for naught didst thou haunt the dreams of the Apocalypse;
Not for naught art the bird sought after by vigorous empires.

   Hail to thee, Eagle! More power and space to thy sweeping gyrations!
Queen of the azure! Glory and victory, skill to enchant us!
Long may Latin America thrive by thy magical influence,
Giving life to a new Olympus of gods and of heroes!

   Onward, ever onward and upward! Life ever glowing!
May the promises made be fulfilled in the lot of the nations,
And may thy mighty labors meet with true approbation
Won from the stars above and whatever there may be beyond them!

COBARDÍA

Pasó con su madre. ¡Qué rara belleza!
¡Qué rubios cabellos de trigo garzul!
¡Qué ritmo en el paso! ¡Qué innata realeza
de porte! Qué formas bajo el fino tul....

Pasó con su madre. Volvía la cabeza:
¡me clavó muy hondo su mirada azul!

Quedé como en éxtasis....
                    Con febril premura,
—¡Síguela!—gritaron cuerpo y alma al par.
... Pero tuve miedo de amar con locura,
de abrir mis heridas, que suelen sangrar,
¡y no obstante toda mi sed de ternura,
cerrando los ojos, la dejé pasar!

EL DÍA QUE ME QUIERAS

El día que me quieras tendrá más luz que junio;
la noche que me quieras será de plenilunio,
con notas de Beethoven vibrando en cada rayo
sus inefables cosas,
y habrá juntas más rosas
que en todo el mes de mayo.

Las fuentes cristalinas
irán por las laderas
saltando cantarinas,
el día que me quieras.

El día que me quieras, los sotos escondidos
resonarán arpegios nunca jamás oídos.
Éxtasis de tus ojos, todas las primaveras
que hubo y habrá en el mundo, serán cuando me quieras.

COWARDICE

   She passed with her mother. What beauty so rare!
What looks all aglow with the wheat's burnished gold!
What rhythm in her step! How innate her air
So royal! What lines 'neath the tulle's soft fold!

   She passed with her mother; turned toward me, and there
Blue eyes pierced my heart to a depth untold!

   I stood there enraptured....
                      Quick, fever'd, the cry,
"Yes, follow her!" burst from both body and soul.

   ... But I feared the mad path of rash loving to try,
And opening old wounds not so quickly made whole;
And in spite of my yearning beyond all control,
I shut close my eyes, and let her pass by!

WHEN THOU LOV'ST ME

   The day when thou shalt love me will be brighter far than June;
The night thou lov'st me will be filled with splendors of the moon,
With music of Beethoven vibrating in each ray
Things no tongue can declare.
And more roses will be there
Than in all the month of May.

   The sparkling crystal fountains
Aleaping down the mountains
Will rush with songs of glee
That day when thou lov'st me.

   That day when thou lov'st me, the woods and hidden dells
Will ring with harmonies from unimagined bells.
All the springtimes of the world that were or are to be
Shall be the ecstasy of thine eyes when thou lov'st me.

Cogidas de la mano, cual rubias hermanitas,
luciendo golas cándidas, irán las margaritas
por montes y praderas
delante de tus pasos, el día que me quieras....
Y si deshojas una, te dirá su inocente
postrer pétalo blanco: *¡Apasionadamente!*

Al reventar el alba del día que me quieras,
tendrán todos los tréboles cuatro hojas agoreras,
y en el estanque, nido de gérmenes ignotos,
florecerán las místicas corolas de los lotos.

El día que me quieras será cada celaje
ala maravillosa, cada arrebol miraje
de las Mil y Una Noches, cada brisa un cantar,
cada árbol una lira, cada monte un altar.

El día que me quieras, para nosotros dos
cabrá en un solo beso la beatitud de Dios.

«TEL QU'EN SONGE»

Ayer vino Blanca;
me miró en silencio,
y era más misteriosa que otras veces:
como se ven las cosas en los sueños....

Larga, largamente
me sonrió; pero
con la rara expresión con que sonríen
las bocas que miramos en los sueños....

¡Qué melancolías
en sus ojos negros!
Esas melancolías indecibles
que entristecen los rostros en los sueños....

Me miró y se fué
con paso ligero,
más ligero que nunca: con el paso
con que andan los fantasmas en los sueños....

—*En voz baja.*

And hand in hand, like maids with golden hair
And snowy necks, the marguerites will fare
Up hills and o'er the lea
Before thy feet, the day that thou lov'st me....
Pluck leaf from leaf, the last in simple fashion
With petal white shall answer, "Yes, with passion!"

And when dawn breaks, that day when thou lov'st me,
The clovers all will show four leaves for joy to thee;
And on the lake, the teeming nest of life unknown,
The lotus-flower will burgeon forth its mystic crown.

That day when thou lov'st me, each cloudy fleece
Will be a magic wing, a mirage endowed
With wonders of the Thousand Nights, each breeze a song,
Each tree a lyre, each mount an altar strong.

That day when thou lov'st me, why, God's own bliss
For us will be sublimed into one single kiss.

AS IN A DREAM

Yesterday came Blanca;
Silent she looked at me,
And more mysterious seemed than e'er before:
As are the things that in our dreams we see....

Slowly, very slowly
She deigned to smile on me,
But with expression rare, like that of those
Whose lips enwreathed with smiles in dreams we see....

What melancholy gazed
From her dark eyes on me!
The melancholy that no words can tell
Saddening the faces that in dreams we see....

She looked on me, and went
Away with step so free,
So light—none lighter ever was—a step
Like that of phantoms which in dreams we see....

SI TÚ ME DICES:—¡VEN!

Si tú me dices: —¡Ven!— lo dejo todo.
No volveré siquiera la mirada
para mirar a la mujer amada....
Pero dímelo fuerte, de tal modo,
que tu voz, como toque de llamada,
vibre hasta en el más íntimo recodo
del ser, levante al alma de su lodo
y hiera el corazón como una espada.

Si tú me dices: —¡Ven!— todo lo dejo.
Llegaré a tu santuario casi viejo,
y al fulgor de la luz crepuscular;
mas he de compensarte mi retardo,
difundiéndome, ¡oh Cristo!, como un nardo
de perfume sutil, ante tu altar.

NO TODOS...

No todos los muertos contemplan a Dios.
¿Tú piensas que basta morir para ver
ese gran misterio del que vas en pos?
¿que el velo de Isis habrás de romper?
¡Iluso creer!
No todos los muertos contemplan a Dios!

En cambio, las almas austeras y grandes,
en vida—si saben «subir»—le verán,
como ven el alba florecer los Andes,
¡cuando aún los llanos en la noche están!

IF THOU SAY'ST "COME"

If Thou say'st "Come," I will leave all for Thee.
I shall not even stay to turn my eyes
On her whose love holds me with strongest ties....
But speak the word so loudly that in me
Thy voice, like a stirring peal of bells, may rise,
Vibrating to my inmost depths, and be
A power, from mire to set my spirit free,
And sword-like strike the soul that heedless lies.

If Thou say'st "Come," I will relinquish all.
And, as the twilight shades begin to fall,
Almost an old man to Thy shrine I'll falter;
But for my tardy coming I'll atone,
Sublimed to spirit, like a lily blown,
In subtle perfume round Thy holy altar!

NOT ALL WHO DIE...

Of those who die not all behold God's face.
Think'st thou thou needest but to die to see
The mystery thou long hast sought to trace?
That the veil of Isis will be rent for thee?
    Delusion vain!
Of those who die not all behold God's face!

Rather instead, those souls austere and grand,
Who here have learned to soar, shall Him behold,
As Andes peaks see morning light expand
While shades of night the valleys still enfold.

DELICTA CARNIS

Carne, carne maldita que me apartas del cielo,
carne tibia y rosada que me impeles al vicio:
ya rasgué mis espaldas con cilicio y flagelo
por vencer tus impulsos, y es en vano; ¡te anhelo
a pesar del flagelo y a pesar del cilicio!

Crucifico mi cuerpo con sagrados enojos,
y se abraza a mis plantas Afrodita la impura;
me sumerjo en la nieve, mas la templan sus ojos;
me revuelco en un tálamo de punzantes abrojos,
y sus labios lo truecan en deleite y ventura.

Y no encuentro esperanza, ni refugio ni asilo,
y en mis noches, pobladas de febriles quimeras,
me persigue la imagen de la Venus de Milo,
con sus lácteos muñones, con su rostro tranquilo
y las combas triunfales de sus amplias caderas....

¡Oh Señor Jesucristo, guíame por los rectos
derroteros del justo; ya no turben con locas
avideces la calma de mis puros afectos
ni el caliente alabastro de los senos erectos,
ni el marfil de los hombros ni el coral de las bocas!

DELICTA CARNIS

Flesh, flesh accursed, that keep'st me far from Heaven,
Flesh, warm and ruddy, that drivest me to sin;
With lash and hair shirt have I seared my shoulders
To quell thy promptings—and in vain: despite
The lash and hair shirt still I yearn for thee!

With pains devout I crucify my body,
And Aphrodite clings impure to my feet;
I plunge myself in snow, but her eyes melt it;
I toss on a bridal couch of stinging thistles,
And her lips change it to delight and joyance.

I find no hope, no haven, nor place of refuge,
And in the night with fever'd visions haunted
Venus de Milo's image still pursues me,
With her white truncated limbs, her tranquil features,
The curves triumphant of her ample loins....

Lord Jesus Christ, in the straight paths of the just
Be Thou my guide; with mad desires no longer
May the warm alabaster of the swelling breasts,
Or the marble shoulders, or the lips of coral
Disturb the quiet of my pure affections.

LA MONTAÑA

Desde que no persigo las dichas pasajeras,
muriendo van en mi alma temores y ansiedad;
la Vida se me muestra con amplias y severas
perspectivas, y siento que estoy en las laderas
de la montaña augusta de la Serenidad....

Comprendo al fin el vasto sentido de las cosas;
sé escuchar en silencio lo que en redor de mí
murmuran piedras, árboles, ondas, auras y rosas...
Y advierto que me cercan mil formas misteriosas
que nunca presentí.

Distingo un santo sello sobre todas las frentes;
un divino *me fecit Deus,* por dondequier,
y noto que me hacen signos inteligentes
las estrellas, arcanos de las noches fulgentes,
y las flores, que ocultan enigmas de mujer.

La Esfinge, ayer adusta, tiene hoy ojos serenos;
en su boca de piedra florece un sonreír
cordial, y hay en la comba potente de sus senos
blanduras de almohada para mis miembros, llenos
a veces de la honda laxitud del vivir.

Mis labios, antes pródigos de versos y canciones,
ahora experimentan el deseo de dar
ánimo a quien desmaya, de verter bendiciones,
de ser caudal perenne de aquellas expresiones
que saben consolar....

Finó mi humilde siembra; las mieses en las eras
empiezan a dar fruto de amor y caridad;
se cierne un gran sosiego sobre mis sementeras;
mi andar es firme....
                    ¡Y siento que estoy en las laderas
de la montaña augusta de la Serenidad!

THE MOUNTAIN

Since I have ceased to follow fleeting pleasures,
The fears and troubles of my soul die day by day;
Life shows itself to me in grave perspectives
And wider, and I feel that now I stand
On the slopes of the stately mount, Serenity....

At length I understand the depth of meaning
In things; silent, can hear what round about me
The stones and trees, waves, roses, winds are saying;
I feel around me a thousand forms mysterious
I never felt before.

On each brow a sacred seal I can distinguish;
A stamp divine, "God made me," everywhere,
And note that for me the stars show symbols full
Of meaning, mysteries of the nights refulgent,
And the flowers that keep a woman's secrets hidden.

The Sphinx, of old austere, now looks serene;
Upon her stony mouth there blooms a smile
That heartens, and on her breasts' proud curvature
A pillowed softness for my limbs that feel
At times deep weariness of life.

My lips, of late profuse with songs and verses,
Experience now a new desire to give
Courage to fainting souls, to scatter blessings,
To be a treasure house forever filled
With the words that can console....

My humble sowing is done; on the floors the harvests
Are yielding fruits of charity and love;
Over my sown land hovers a great calm;
My step is firm....
        And I feel that now I stand
On the slopes of the stately mount, Serenity!

EN PAZ

Artifex vitae, artifex sui

Muy cerca de mi ocaso, yo te bendigo, Vida,
porque nunca me diste ni esperanza fallida
ni trabajos injustos, ni pena inmerecida;

porque veo al final de mi rudo camino
que yo fuí el arquitecto de mi propio destino;
que si extraje las mieles o la hiel de las cosas,
fué porque en ellas puse hiel o mieles sabrosas;
cuando planté rosales, coseché siempre rosas.

...Cierto, a mis lozanías va a seguir el invierno:
¡mas tú no me dijiste que Mayo fuese eterno!

Hallé sin duda largas las noches de mis penas;
mas no me prometiste tú sólo noches buenas;
y en cambio tuve algunas santamente serenas....

Amé, fuí amado, el sol acarició mi faz.
¡Vida, nada me debes! ¡Vida, estamos en paz!

AT PEACE

Artifex vitae, artifex sui

I bless thee, Life, my sun now all but set,
For false hope never hast thou given me yet;
Nor toils nor pain unmerited I've met;

For, now the rough road's past, I can detect
'Twas I that was my own fate's architect;
That if from things bitter or sweet I drew,
Their gall or honey to myself was due:
From rosebush planted always roses grew.

... Winter, indeed, will end my proud endeavor;
Thou never said'st that May should last forever!

Long, doubtless, have I found the nights of pain;
That nights should all be good thou ne'er didst feign;
Through others still in saintly calm I've lain....

I've loved, been loved, the sun has kissed my face.
Naught dost thou owe me, Life! We are at peace!

AETERNUM VALE

Un Dios misterioso y extraño visita la selva.
Es un Dios silencioso que tiene los brazos abiertos.
Cuando la hija de Thor espoleaba su negro caballo,
le vió erguirse, de pronto, a la sombra de un añoso fresno.
    Y sintió que se helaba su sangre
ante el Dios silencioso que tiene los brazos abiertos.

De la fuente de Imer, en los bordes sagrados, más tarde,
la Noche a los dioses absortos reveló el secreto;
el Águila negra y los Cuervos de Odín escuchaban,
y los cisnes que esperan la hora del canto postrero;
    y a los dioses mordía el espanto
de ese Dios silencioso que tiene los brazos abiertos.

En la selva agitada se oían extrañas salmodias;
mecía la encina y el sauce quejumbroso viento;
el bisonte y el alce movían las ramas espesas,
y a través de las ramas espesas huían mugiendo.
    En la lengua sagrada de Orga
despertaban del canto divino los divinos versos.

Thor, el rudo, terrible guerrero que blande la maza,
—en sus manos es arma la negra montaña de hierro,—
va a aplastar, en la selva, a la sombra del árbol sagrado,
a ese Dios silencioso que tiene los brazos abiertos.
    Y los dioses contemplan la maza rugiente
que gira en los aires y nubla la lumbre del cielo.

    *   *   *   *   *   *

Ya en la selva sagrada no se oyen las viejas salmodias,
ni la voz amorosa de Freya cantando a lo lejos;
agonizan los dioses que pueblan la selva sagrada,
y en la lengua de Orga se extinguen los divinos versos.
    Solo, erguido a la sombra de un árbol,
hay un Dios silencioso que tiene los brazos abiertos.

ETERNAL FAREWELL

A strange, mysterious God visits the woodland,
A silent God who holds his arms outstretched.
The daughter of Thor, as she spurred her sable steed,
Saw him suddenly rise in the shade of an agèd ash-tree,
      And felt her blood congeal
Before this silent God who holds his arms outstretched.

And later, by the sacred marge of Imer's spring,
Night told the secret to the astounded gods;
The swarthy Eagle and the Crows of Odin heard,
And the swans that wait to sing the final song;
      And the gods were seized with dread
Of this silent God who holds his arms outstretched.

In the quaking wood unwonted strains were heard;
A rumbling wind made oaks and willows shake;
The elk and bison swayed the ponderous branches,
And through the heavy brushwood vanished roaring.
      In Orga's consecrated tongue
Burst forth the sacred strains of the song divine.

Grim warrior, Thor, who brandishes the mace,
—He wields as weapon the gloomy mountain of iron,—
Goes forth to crush, in the shade of the sacred tree,
The silent God who holds his arms outstretched.
      And the gods behold the mace, which groans
As it whirls in the air and dims the light of heaven.

* * * * * *

In the sacred wood the old strains are heard no more,
Nor Freya's amorous voice in the distance singing;
Agonizing are the gods of the sacred wood,
And the lays divine of Orga now are quenched.

      Alone, erect in the shadow of a tree,
There stands a silent God who holds his arms outstretched.

PÓRTICO

Villano, trovador, fraile o guerrero,
Con hoz, breviario, bandolín o espada,
Fuera hermoso vivir en la pasada
Heroica edad de corazón de acero.

Fuera hermoso ¡en verdad! Si fraile austero
Ver a Dios con extática mirada;
Llevar por la Esperanza constelada
Y la Fe, el alma, si infeliz pechero.

Si trovador, en el feudal castillo
Cantar guerras y amor, al suave brillo
De los ojos de hermosa castellana;
Combatir, si guerrero, noche y día,
Asaltar, lanza en mano, una abadía,
O acuchillar la hueste musulmana!
—*Medioevales.*

EL ALBA

Las auroras pálidas,
Que nacen entre penumbras misteriosas,
Y enredados en las orlas de sus mantos
Llevan girones de sombra,
Iluminan las montañas,
Las crestas de las montañas, rojas;
Bañan las torres erguidas,
Que saludan su aparición silenciosa,
Con la voz de sus campanas
Soñolienta y ronca;
Ríen en las calles
Dormidas de la ciudad populosa,
Y se esparcen en los campos
Donde el invierno respeta las amarillentas hojas.
Tienen perfumes de Oriente

THE PORTAL

How beautiful it would be if one could feel
Oneself a churl or minstrel, priest or knight,
With sickle, prayer-book, lute or swordblade bright
Of an age heroic, with a heart of steel!

'Twere sweet indeed, if monk austere, to kneel
And see God's face, enraptured with the sight;
If an unhappy soul, with starry light
Of Hope and Faith, the mind in peace to seal;

If minstrel, in the feudal baron's keep
To sing of love and war, under the deep
Soft brilliance of the lovely lady's eye;

If warrior, to fight by night or day,
To assault an abbey, lance in hand, or slay
The hosts of Saracens that Christ deny.

DAWN

Those pallid dawns,
That come to birth amid half-lights mysterious,
And tangled in the fringes of their mantles
Bear with them shreds of darkness,
Illuminate the mountains,
The crests of the mountains, fiery red;
They bathe the lofty towers,
Which greet their silent appearing
With the voice of their bells
Dreamy and hoarse;
They laugh in the sleeping streets
Of the crowded city,
And scatter over the fields
Where winter pays respect to the yellowing leaves.
They hold the perfumes of the Orient,

Las auroras;
Los recojieron al paso, de las florestas ocultas
De una extraña Flora.
Tienen ritmos y músicas harmoniosas,
Porque oyeron los gorjeos y los trinos de las aves
Exóticas.

　Su luz fría,
Que conserva los girones de la sombra,
Enredóse, vacilante, de los lotos
En las anchas hojas.
Chispeó en las aguas dormidas,
Las aguas del viejo Ganges, dormidas y silenciosas;
Y las tribus de los árabes desiertos,
Saludaron con plegarias a las pálidas auroras.
Los rostros de los errantes bedüinos
Se bañaron con arenas ardorosas,
Y murmuraron las suras del Profeta
Voces roncas.

Tendieron las suaves alas
Sobre los mares de Jonia,
Y vieron surgir a Venus
De las suspirantes olas.

　En las cimas,
Donde las nieblas eternas sobre las nieves se posan,
Vieron monstruos espantables
Entre las rocas,
Y las crines de los búfalos que huían
Por la selva tenebrosa.
Reflejaron en la espada
Simbólica,
Que a la sombra de una encina
Yacía, olvidada y polvorosa.

　Hay ensueños,
Hay ensueños en las pálidas auroras....
Hay ensueños,

These dawns;
They have culled them, as they passed, from hidden forests
Of a strange Flora.
And they bring rhythmic and harmonious music,
For they have heard the trills and warbling notes of birds
Exotic.

   Their chilly light,
Preserving still the pennants of the dark,
Has waveringly enmeshed itself
In the broad leaves of the lotus;
It has sparkled over the sleeping waters,
The silent, sleeping water of the ancient Ganges;
And the tribes of desert Arabs
Have greeted with their prayers those pallid dawns;
Those wandering Bedouins
Have bathed their faces with the burning sands,
And their rough voices have murmured
The words of the Prophet.

They have spread their quiet wings
Over the Ionian waters,
And have seen Venus arise
From the sighing waves.

   On the peaks,
Where clouds forever rest upon the snow,
They have seen dreadful monsters
Among the rocks,
And the manes of the buffaloes that fled
Through the gloom of the forest.
They have pondered over the sword
Symbolic,
That under the shadow of an oak
Lies dusty and forgotten.

   There are dreams,
Dreams in those pallid dawns....
There are dreams

Que se envuelven en sus girones de sombra....
Sorprenden los amorosos
Secretos de las nupciales alcobas,
Y ponen pálidos tintes en los labios
Donde el beso dejó huellas voluptuosas....

Y el Sol eleva su disco fulgurante,
Sobre la tierra, los aires y las suspirantes olas.

LAS VOCES TRISTES

Por las blancas estepas
Se desliza el trineo;
Los lejanos aullidos de los lobos
Se unen al jadëante resoplar de los perros.

Nieva.
Parece que el espacio se envolviera en un velo,
Tachonado de lirios
Por las alas del cierzo.

El infinito blanco...
Sobre el vasto desierto
Flota una vaga sensación de angustia,
De supremo abandono, de profundo y sombrío desaliento.

Un pino solitario
Dibújase a lo lejos,
En un fondo de brumas y de nieve
Como un largo esqueleto.

Entre los dos sudarios
De la tierra y el cielo,
Avanza en el Naciente
El helado crepúsculo de invierno....

That mingle with their tattered shreds of night...
They startle with surprise
The amorous secrets of the nuptial bower,
And bring a shade of pallor to the lips
Where kisses have left their voluptuous flush behind...

   And the Sun lifts his disk resplendent
Over the earth, the air, and the sighing waves.

THE MOURNFUL VOICES

   Over the snowy steppe
The sledge glides on;
The distant howling of the wolves
Mingles with the panting breath of the dogs.

   It snows.
The wide expanse seems shrouded in a veil
Sprinkled with lilies
By the wings of the north wind.

   Whiteness illimitable...
Over the boundless desert
Floats a vague sensation of uneasiness,
Of extreme abandonment, of depression deep and somber.

   A solitary pine
Is outlined in the distance
On a background of fog and snow,
Like some lank skeleton.

   Between the sepulchral shrouds
Of earth and sky,
Advances in the East
The freezing twilight of the winter dawn....

EL SOLTERÓN

I

Largas brumas violetas
flotan sobre el río gris,
y allá en las dársenas quietas
sueñan oscuras goletas
con un lejano país.

El arrabal solitario
tiene la noche a sus pies,
y tiembla su campanario
en el vapor visionario
de ese paisaje holandés.

El crepúsculo perplejo
entra a una alcoba glacial,
en cuyo empañado espejo
con soslayado reflejo
turba el agua del cristal.

El lecho blanco se hiela
junto al siniestro baúl,
y en su herrumbrada tachuela
envejece una acuarela
cuadrada de felpa azul.

En la percha del testero,
el crucificado frac
exhala un fenol severo,
y sobre el vasto tintero
piensa un busto de Balzac.

La brisa de las campañas,
con su aliento de clavel,
agita las telarañas
que son inmensas pestañas
del desusado cancel.

THE BACHELOR

I

   Long clouds of violet mist
Float over the river gray,
And there at the quiet quays
The dark-hulled vessels dream
Of a country far away.

   The lonely suburb holds
About its feet the night,
And in the dream-like air
Of this Dutch landscape rare
Quivers the bell tower's height.

   The uncertain twilight enters
A chamber cold as ice,
And on the tarnished mirror
With slant reflections troubles
The moisture's dim device.

   By an evil-looking trunk
A bed stands white and cold,
And on its rusty nail
A water color, in a blue
Plush frame, hangs, growing old.

   The dress coat in the closet
Crucified on its rack
Smells heavy with carbolic;
And over the bulky inkstand
Is a pensive bust, Balzac.

   The breeze that comes from the plains
With its fragrance of carnation,
Over the unused screen
Blows spiders' webs, eyelashes
Vast, into agitation.

Allá por las nubes rosas
las golondrinas, en pos
de invisibles mariposas,
trazan letras misteriosas
como escribiendo un adiós.

En la alcoba solitaria,
sobre un raído sofá
de cretona centenaria,
junto a su estufa precaria
meditando un hombre está.

Tendido en postura inerte
masca su pipa de boj,
y en aquella calma advierte
¡qué cercana está la muerte
del silencio del reloj!

En su garganta reseca
gruñe una biliosa hez,
y bajo su frente hueca
la verdinegra jaqueca
maniobra un largo ajedrez.

¡Ni un gorjeo de alegrías!
¡Ni un clamor de tempestad!
Como en las cuevas sombrías
en el fondo de sus días
bosteza la soledad.

Y con vértigos extraños
en su confusa visión
de insípidos desengaños,
ve llegar los grandes años
con sus cargas de algodón.

There the swallows, chasing
Through clouds of rosy hue
The butterflies invisible,
Trace characters mysterious
As if writing an adieu.

In the solitary chamber
On a sofa badly worn,
With its cretonne ages old,
A man is meditating
Close to a stove forlorn.

Reclining in lifeless posture,
He chews on his boxwood pipe,
And in that stillness ponders
How near is the clock's silence
To being of death the type.

In his dry throat a bilious
Phlegm gives groans of distress,
And under his hollow brows
A dark-green megrim plays
A long-drawn game of chess.

He hears no joyous warble,
Nor ever a tempest's roar!
The solitude yawns idly
As in the gloomy caverns
Of forgotten days of yore.

And, with vertigo amazing
In vision misbegotten
Of futile disillusion,
He sees the long years coming,
His hair gone white as cotton.

II

A inverosímil distancia
se acongoja un violín,
resucitando en la estancia
como una ancestral fragancia
del humo de aquel esplín.

Y el hombre piensa. Su vista
recuerda las rosas té
de un sombrero de modista...
El pañuelo de batista...
Las peinetas...el corsé....

Y el duelo en la playa sola:—
Uno...dos...tres...Y el lucir
de la montada pistola...
y el son grave de la ola
convidando a bien morir.

Y al dar a la niña inquieta
la reconquistada flor
en la persiana discreta,
sintióse héroe y poeta
por la gracia del amor.

Epitalamios de flores
la dicha escribió a sus pies,
y las tardes de colores
supieron de esos amores
celestiales....Y después....

Ahora una vaga espina
le punza en el corazón,
si su coqueta vecina
saca la breve botina
por los hierros del balcón;

II

At some incredible distance
Complains a violin,
Reviving in the chamber
As 'twere an ancient fragrance
From the fume of that fit of spleen.

And the man thinks on. His vision
Recalls the pale tea-roses
In the hat of a dainty milliner...
Her fine lawn kerchief...her combs...
The corset her waist that encloses....

And the duel on the lonely beach—
One...two...three...And the gleam
Of the pistol raised to shoot...
And the solemn call of the wave
To a death that was worth esteem.

And, handing the anxious maiden
The struggle's hard-won flower
By the window blinds discreet,
He felt himself hero, poet,
Through love's own gracious power.

And flowery nuptial songs
Joy at his feet did pen,
And the evenings rich with color
Had knowledge of these amours
That heavenly seemed....And then....

Now some vague thing pricks him
And rankles in his heart,
If through the bars at her window
Her neat shoe his neighbor pushes
With wily, coquettish art;

y si con voz pura y tersa,
la niña del arrabal
en su malicia perversa,
temas picantes conversa
con el canario jovial;

surge aquel triste percance
de tragedia baladí:
la novia... la flor... el lance...
veinte años cuenta el romance.
Turguenef tiene una así.

¡Cuán triste era su mirada,
cuán luminosa su fe
y cuán leve su pisada!
¿Por qué la dejó olvidada?...
¡Si ya no sabe por qué!

III

En el desolado río
se agrisa el tono punzó
del crepúsculo sombrío,
como un imperial hastío
sobre un otoño de gro.

Y el hombre medita. Es ella
la visión triste que en un
remoto nimbo descuella;
es una ajada doncella
que le está aguardando aún.

Vago pavor le amilana,
y va a escribirle, por fin,
desde su informe nirvana...
la carta saldrá mañana
y en la carta irá un jazmín.

And if the girl of the streets there
With pure voice smooth and airy,
With perverse malice prompted
Discusses piquant stories
With her jovial canary,

The tragic scene arises,
Sad, futile, turned amiss:
The girl...the flower...the duel...
A twenty years' romance—
Turgénev has one like this.

How luminous her faith was;
How sad the look in her eye;
How tripping light her footstep!
Why left he her forgotten?
May she even now know why?

III

Over the river deserted
The darkening twilight tones
From crimson turn to gray,
As dimmed a silken autumn
An emperor's wearied groans.

She is the vision doleful—
The man sits meditating—
That in a cloud looms dimly,
A maid much overburdened,
Who still for him is waiting.

Disquiet vague unmans him;
He'll write to her, even though
From his confused Nirvana...
In the note he must send tomorrow
A jasmine-flower shall go.

La pluma en sus dedos juega;
ya el pliego tiene el doblez;
y su alma en lo azul navega.
A los veinte años de brega
va a escribir *tuyo* otra vez.

No será trunca ni ambigua
su confidencia de amor
sobre la vitela exigua.
¡Si esa carta es muy antigua!...
Ya está turbio el borrador.

Tendrá su deleite loco,
blancas sedas de amistad
para esconder su ígneo foco.
La gente reirá un poco
de esos novios de otra edad.

Ella, la anciana, en su leve
candor de virgen senil,
será un alabastro breve.
Su aristocracia de nieve
nevará un tardío abril.

Sus canas, en paz suprema,
a la alcoba sororal
darán olor de alhucema,
y estará en la suave yema
del fino dedo el dedal.

Cuchicheará a ras del suelo
su enagua un vago frú-frú,
¡y con qué afable consuelo
acogerá el terciopelo
su elegancia de bambú!...

Así está el hombre soñando
en el aposento aquel,
y su sueño es dulce y blando;
mas la noche va llegando
y aun está blanco el papel.

He plays with the pen in his fingers;
Already the sheet has the fold;
And his spirit sails in the blue.
After twenty years of struggle
He will write, "I am thine," as of old.

No short or doubtful message
Shall his love-revealing be
On the scanty sheet of parchment...
How very old this note is!...
His rough draft blurred he can see.

He'll have his fill of wild pleasures,
But, to hide his consuming flame,
The white silk garment of friendship.
The people will laugh a little
At these elderly lovers' game.

The agèd dame, pure-minded,
With the senile virgin's glow
Will be a slight alabaster.
Her silvered aristocracy
Will, like late April, snow.

In her nun-like room, from her tresses,
In peace supreme will linger
The lavender's sweet smell.
And the thimble will be there, too,
On her soft and delicate finger.

On the floor her skirt will rustle
With a whispering, vague frou-frou;
And with what genial comfort
The velvet will enclose her
And her elegance of bamboo!...

Thus is the man still dreaming
In that room so dim and dank;
And his dream is sweet and pleasant;
But now the night is coming—
And the paper still is blank.

Sobre su visión de aurora,
un tenebroso crespón
los contornos descolora,
pues la noche vencedora
se le ha entrado al corazón.

Y como enturbiada espuma,
una idea triste va
emergiendo de su bruma:
¡qué mohosa está la pluma!
¡la pluma no escribe ya!

A LOS GANADOS Y LAS MIESES

... Aldabeaba el chubasco en los postigos,
llorando los lamentos de la honda
noche exterior deshecha en aguacero
sobre la pampa bostezada en sombra.
Adentro, junto a la pared, se oía
en un cacharro el canto de una gota;
pero las altas vigas afirmaban
con una recta solidez de eslora,
aquel amparo de la paz interna
cuya seguridad satisfactoria,
parece que la vela concentrara
en su yema de luz quieta y metódica.
Y la madre pensaba en las ovejas
recién paridas, que caminan solas
en incesante marcha por los campos
cuando las lluvias frías las acosan,
al azar de la ráfaga empapada,
con doliente humildad unas tras otras;
las pobres con sus hondos lagrimales
de vieja rubia, son tan lastimosas...
 —Tendremos mortandad en los corderos,
decía su palabra previsora.
Y a poco rato, el padre, confirmando

Over his dawn-bright vision
Dark, crape-like shadows roll,
Discoloring the landscape,
For night, the overwhelming,
Has entered into his soul.

And as scum rises turbid,
A sad thought waxes stronger,
Emerging from the gloom:
How rusty the old pen is!
This pen will write no longer!

TO THE CATTLE AND HARVEST FIELDS

The squall knocked loudly at the outer doors,
Voicing the lamentations of the night
Without, profound, dissolved in beating rain
Over the pampa yawning in the gloom.
Within, close by the wall one heard the song
Of drops that fell into an earthen jar,
But the lofty roof-beams, like a vessel's deck
For straight solidity, ensured protection
For that domestic peace, whose unconcern
The candle seemed to concentrate in its yolk
Of light so quiet and methodical.
And the mother's thoughts turned to the new-born lambs
That wander lonely with incessant march,
Grieving but meek, the one behind the other
Through the fields, when freezing rains molest
And drenching blasts bring troubles unforeseen;
Poor beasts, that with their tear ducts faded gold
And sunken deep, so move the heart to pity...
"We'll have disease and death among the sheep,"
Her warning words announced. And, after a space,
The father, with an air of resignation
Grave as became his age, enlarged upon

la resignación grave de sus horas,
ampliaba el parecer de la consorte
con palabras escasas y juiciosas.
 —Allá por el 63, en tiempo
de Mitre.... Y los recuerdos de su crónica
en la barba entrecana resumían
la evidencia inherente de las cosas.
 —Al fin no se han de derretir (bromeaba
por animar) como esas de las monjas,
las crespas ovejitas de confite
que eran industria conventual de Córdoba.

DESDÉN

Si tan sólo una caricia
De tus ojos consiguiera,
Precio digno de tal gloria
La vida me pareciera.

Si con mortal puñalada
Tu rencor me hiriese un día,
Por padecer de tu mano
Contento sucumbiría.

Pero lo que de seguro
Va a darme muerte angustiada,
Es que para mí no seas
Caricia ni puñalada.

The opinion of his spouse with words that were
Sparing but wise: "Back there in sixty-three,
In Mitre's* time..." and reminiscences
From his life's story, issuing from the beard
Grown gray, confirmed the evidence inherent
In things as they are. "And after all," he joked
To keep their courage up, "these beasts won't melt
Like those the nuns make"—comfits crisp, fashioned
Like little sheep, a convent industry
In Córdoba.

DISDAIN

If but one single kindly look
From your eyes I might obtain,
Not life itself a price would seem
Too great such prize to gain.

If rancor on your part should strike
With fatal poniard blow,
Were't yours the hand that brought the pain,
Content to death I'd go.

But what assuredly will give
A painful death I could not brook
Is that for me you neither have
The poniard stroke nor kindly look.

---

* Bartolomé Mitre (1821–1906), Argentine author and statesman; President, 1862–1868.

LIED DE LA BOCA FLORIDA

Al ofrecerte una rosa
El jardinero prolijo,
Orgulloso de ella dijo
No existe otra más hermosa.

A pesar de su color,
Su belleza y su fragancia,
Respondí con arrogancia:
Yo conozco una mejor.

Sonreíste tú a mi fiero
Remoque de paladín....
Y regresó a su jardín
Cabizbajo el jardinero.

THE LAY OF THE ROSY LIPS

The gardener plucked a lovely rose,
And, offering it to thee,
He, vainly talkative, declared:
No finer rose can be.

And yet, despite its gorgeous hue,
Its beauty and fragrance rare,
I answered him with haughty mien:
I know a rose more fair.

Thou smiledst at my proud reply,
My mocking, knightly wit....
The gardener back to his garden went
Crestfallen, as was fit.

LEYENDO A SILVA

Vestía traje suelto de recamado viso
en voluptuosos pliegues de un color indeciso,

y en el diván tendida, de rojo terciopelo,
sus manos, como vivas parásitas de hielo,

sostenían un libro de corte fino y largo,
un libro de poemas delicioso y amargo.

De aquellos dedos pálidos la tibia yema blanda
rozaba tenuemente con el papel de Holanda

por cuyas blancas hojas vagaron los pinceles
de los más refinados discípulos de Apeles:

era un lindo manojo que en sus claros lucía
los sueños más audaces de la Crisografía:

sus cuerpos de serpiente dilatan las mayúsculas
que desde el ancho margen acechan las minúsculas,

o trazan por los bordes caminos plateados
los lentos caracoles, babosos y cansados.

Para el poema heroico se vía allí la espada
con un león por puño y contera labrada,

donde evocó las formas del ciclo legendario
con sus torres y grifos un pincel lapidario.

Allí la dama gótica de rectilínea cara
partida por las rejas de la viñeta rara;

allí las hadas tristes de la pasión excelsa:
la férvida Eloísa, la suspirada Elsa.

Allí los metros raros de musicales timbres:
ya móviles y largos como jugosos mimbres,

ya diáfanos, que visten la idea levemente
como las albas guijas un río transparente.

READING SILVA

She wore a flowing garment, embroidered, translucent,
In voluptuous folds of changing color uncertain,

And, as she reclined on a divan of crimson velvet,
Her hands, like parasites clinging, ice-cold yet living,

Sustained a volume long-shaped and daintily fashioned,
A book of poems of mingled sweet and bitter.

The soft, warm tips of those pale and delicate fingers
Toyed lightly with the pages of fine Dutch paper,

O'er whose white leaves the vagrant brush had traveled
Of great Apelles' most distinguished pupils;

A fair collection, the vacant spaces gleaming
With the boldest visions of the illuminator's art:

The capitals dilate their serpent bodies;
The minuscules watching snare them from the margin;

Or, along the edges, leaving a trail of silver,
Slow-moving snails go, wearied out and slimy.

The sword is there, fit sign for the poem heroic,
With a lion for hilt and figures wrought on the scabbard,

Where the delicate brush of the artist with towers and griffins
Had evoked the figures drawn from the cycle of legends.

The Gothic lady was there with face rectilinear,
Set apart by the trellis-bars of the fine vignetting;

And there the mournful phantoms of passion excelling:
The fervid Eloise, and Elsa so longed-for.

There the exotic measures of musical concord,
Some long and slow of movement, like branches of willow,

Some diaphanous, clothing the meaning lightly,
As a river pellucid revealing the glistening pebbles.

Allí la Vida llora y la Muerte sonríe
y el Tedio, como un ácido, corazones deslíe.... 30

Allí, cual casto grupo de núbiles Citeres,
cruzaban en silencio figuras de mujeres

que vivieron sus vidas, invioladas y solas
como la espuma virgen que circunda las olas:

la rusa de ojos cálidos y de bruno cabello
pasó con sus pinceles de marta y de camello,

la que robó al piano en las veladas frías
parejas voladoras de blancas armonías

que fueron por los vientos perdiéndose una a una
mientras, envuelta en sombras, se atristaba la luna... 40

Aquesa, el pie desnudo, gira como una sombra
que sin hacer ruído pisara por la alfombra

de un templo... y como el ave que ciega el astro diurno
con miradas nictálopes ilumina el Nocturno,

do al fatigado beso de las vibrantes clines
un aire triste y vago preludian dos violines....

La luna, como un nimbo de Dios, desde el Oriente
dibuja sobre el llano la forma evanescente

de un lánguido mancebo que el tardo paso guía,
como buscando un alma, por la pampa vacía. 50

Busca a su hermana; un día la negra Segadora
—sobre la mies que el beso primaveral enflora—

abatiendo sus alas, sus alas de murciélago,
hirió a la virgen pálida sobre el dorado piélago,

que cayó como un trigo.... Amiguitas llorosas
la vistieron de lirios, la ciñeron de rosas;

céfiro de las tumbas, un bardo israelita
le cantó cantos tristes de la raza maldita

Life is there weeping, and Death seems smiling,
While Ennui, like an acid, corrodes the heartstrings.

Like some chaste group of nubile Cythereas,
There slowly passed in silence figures of women

Who had lived their lives, inviolate and lonely,
As the virgin foam that caps the ocean breakers.

The Russian with burning eyes and dark-brown tresses
Passed with her brushes of sable and of camel,

She who from the piano, in the chill night-watches,
Drew flying chords of pure white harmonies,

That one by one went fading on the breezes,
While sadly, veiled in clouds, the moon was waning...

With naked foot she circles, like a shadow
That, making not a sound, might tread the carpet

Of a temple floor... and like the owl, day-blinded,
With night-loving eyes sheds light upon the Nocturne,

Where to the quivering bow's fatigued caress
Two violins give forth a vague, sad tune....

    The moon, like a nimbus of God, as it shines from the eastward,
Projects on the plain the shadow evanescent

Of a languid youth who guides his sluggish paces
O'er the empty prairie, as seeking for some lost spirit.

He seeks his sister; for once the grim black Reaper,
—On the fields which the kiss of Spring had decked with flowers,—

Sweeping on baleful wings, like bats' wings noiseless,
Struck, mid the sea of gold, at the pallid virgin,

Who fell like a cornstalk.... Friends very dear to her
Covered her body with lilies, decked her with roses;

Like a zephyr come from the tombs, a Hebrew melodist
Sang for her the sad lays of the race accursed,

a ella, que en su lecho de gasas y de blondas,
se asemejaba a Ofelia mecida por las ondas:

por ella va buscando su hermano entre las brumas,
de unas alitas rotas las desprendidas plumas,

y por ella.... —Pasemos esta doliente hoja
que mi ser atormenta, que mi sueño acongoja,—

dijo entre sí la dama del recamado viso
en voluptuosos pliegues de color indeciso,

y prosiguió del libro las hojas volteando,
que ensalza en áureas rimas de son *calino* y blando

los perfumes de Oriente, los vívidos rubíes
y los joyeles mórbidos de sedas carmesíes.

Leyó versos que guardan como gastados ecos
de voces muertas; cantos a ramilletes secos

que hacen crujir, al tacto, cálices inodoros;
metros que reproducen los gemibundos coros

de las locas campanas que en Día de Difuntos
despiertan con sus voces los muertos cejijuntos,

lanzados en racimos entre las sepulturas
a beberse la sombra de sus noches oscuras....

...Y en el diván tendida, de rojo terciopelo,
sus manos, como vivas parásitas de hielo,

doblaron lentamente la página postrera
que, en gris, mostraba un cuervo sobre una calavera...

y se quedó pensando, pensando en la amargura
que acendran muchas almas; pensando en la figura

del bardo, que en la calma de una noche sombría,
puso fin al poema de su melancolía:

¡exangüe como un mármol de la dorada Atenas,
herido como un púgil de itálicas arenas,

As she lay on her couch of silken lace and muslin,
Resembling Ophelia borne up and rocked by the water.

For her through the mists the brother still goes searching—
For the scattered feathers of her broken wings,

And for her.... "Let us turn this page with its mournful story,
Which wrings my soul and fills my dreams with sadness,"

So spoke the lady in garment embroidered, translucent,
With voluptuous folds of changing color uncertain,

And went on slowly turning over the pages
That praised in golden rhymes with sound endearing

The perfumes of the Orient, brilliant rubies,
And jewels delicate on silks of crimson.

Verses she read that keep the fading echoes
Of voices dead; cantos to withered nosegays

Whose scentless calyxes a touch makes rustle;
Measures that brought to life the groaning chorus

Of the frenzied bells that in the DAY OF THE DEAD
Waken with their peal the frowning departed,

To stalk in somber bands among the sepulchers
And drink the gloom of their dark hours nocturnal....

... And as she reclined on the divan of crimson velvet,
Her hands like icy parasites, but living,

Turned over languidly the last of the pages
Which showed, in gray, above a skull, a raven...

And she remained in thought, deep thought of the sorrow
That cleanses many a soul; she thought of the face

Of the bard, who in the stillness of a gloomy midnight
Brought to an end the poem of his suffering:

All bloodless as a marble from golden Athens,
Like a fighter wounded in some Roman arena,

unió la faz de un Numen dulcemente atediado
a la ideal belleza del estigmatizado!... 90

Ambicionar las túnicas que modelaba Grecia,
y los desnudos senos de la gentil Lutecia;

pedir en copas de ónix el ático nepentes;
querer ceñir en lauros las pensativas frentes;

ansiar para los triunfos el hacha de un Arminio;
buscar para los goces el oro del triclinio;

amando los detalles, odiar el Universo;
sacrificar un mundo para pulir un verso;

querer remos de águila y garras de leones
con que domar los vientos y herir los corazones; 100

para gustar lo exótico que el ánimo idolatra
esconder entre flores el áspid de Cleopatra;

seguir los ideales en pos de Don Quijote
que en el Azul divaga de su rocín al trote;

esperar en la noche las trémulas escalas
que arrebaten ligeras a las etéreas salas;

oír los mudos ecos que pueblan los santuarios,
amar las hostias blancas, amar los incensarios

(poetas que diluyen en el espacio inmenso
sus ritmos perfumados de vagaroso incienso); 110

sentir en el espíritu brisas primaverales
ante los viejos monjes y los rojos misales;

tener la frente en llamas y los pies entre lodo;
querer sentirlo, verlo y adivinarlo todo:

eso fuiste, ¡oh poeta! Los labios de tu herida
blasfeman de los hombres, blasfeman de la vida,

modulan el gemido de las desesperanzas,
¡oh místico sediento que en el raudal te lanzas!...

He combined the look of a deity wearied but happy
With the ideal beauty of the Crucified! ...

To long for the raiment Greece was wont to model,
And the flaunting breasts of exquisite Lutetia;

To seek in flagons of onyx the Attic nepenthe,
To wreathe about the pensive brow with laurel;

For triumphs, to yearn for the battle-axe of Hermann;
For pleasure, to seek the ease of the gold triclinium;

In love with details, to hate the Universe,
To sacrifice a world to polish a couplet;

To covet the eagle's pinions, the claws of the lion,
With which to tame the winds, to wound the spirit;

In hope to taste the exotic, the soul's dear idol,
To hide Cleopatra's asp among the flowers;

To follow after ideals with Don Quixote,
Who vaguely courses the blue on his ambling charger;

To await in hope by night those tremulous scales
That carry one lightly away to the halls ethereal;

To hear the voiceless echoes that people the churches,
To love the Host all white, to love the censers

(Poets they, through the shrine's wide space diffusing
With rhythmic swing the scent of dreamy incense);

To feel in the soul the breezes of the springtime
In the presence of ancient monks with their red missals;

To have the brow inflamed, the feet mud-planted;
To aspire to feel, see, guess the truth of all things:

Such thou wert, poet; thy wounds, made eloquent,
Blaspheme all men, call human life accursed,

Ring changes on the groan of deep despair.
Oh, mystic thirst that drove thee to the torrent!

¡Oh Señor Jesucristo! por tu herida del pecho,
¡perdónalo! ¡perdónalo! ¡desciende hasta su lecho

de piedra a despertarlo! Con tus manos divinas
enjuga de su sangre las ondas purpurinas...

Pensó mucho: sus páginas suelen robar la calma;
sintió mucho: sus versos saben partir el alma;

¡amó mucho!; circulan ráfagas de misterio
entre los negros pinos del blanco cementerio...

No manchará su lápida epitafio doliente:
tallad un verso en ella, pagano y decadente,

digno del crespo Adonis en muerte de Afrodita:
un verso como el hálito de una rosa marchita,

que llore su caída, que cante su belleza,
que cifre sus ensueños, ¡que diga su tristeza!...

¡Amor!, dice la dama del recamado viso,
en voluptuosos pliegues de color indeciso.

¡Dolor!, dijo el poeta: los labios de su herida
blasfeman de los hombres, blasfeman de la vida,

modulan el gemido de la desesperanza;
fué el místico sediento que en el raudal se lanza;

su muerte fué la muerte de una lánguida anémona,
se evaporó su vida como la de Desdémona;

ebrio del vino amargo con que el dolor embriaga
y a los fulgores trémulos de un cirio que se apaga...

¡Así rindió su aliento, bajo un sitial de seda,
el último nacido del viejo Cisne y Leda!

O Jesus Christ, Lord, by Thy breast once wounded,
Forgive him, oh, forgive! To his stony bed

Descend; wake him again; with Thy hand divine
Make clean the waves stained purple with his blood . . .

For he thought much: his pages raise disquiet;
And much he felt: his verses cleave the spirit;

And much he loved! Mysterious emanations
Haunt the black pines of the dead-white cemetery . . .

   His tomb no mourning epitaph shall tarnish:
Grave there a verse for him, pagan, decadent,

Worthy of Venus mourning her fair Adonis,
A verse like the scent that breathes from a rose that's faded,

That shall weep his end, proclaim in song his beauty,
Recount his dreams, and tell again his sadness! . . .

   Love! says the lady in vesture fine, embroidered,
With voluptuous folds of changing color uncertain.

Grief! said the poet: his wounds, made eloquent,
Blaspheme all men, call human life accursèd,

Ring changes on the groan of deep despair;
'Twas the mystic thirst that drove him to the torrent.

Like that of a languid anemone was his death,
His life was quenched like that of Desdemona;

With the bitter wine of grief intoxicated,
His light went out like the flickering flame of a candle . . .

Thus he yielded his breath, 'neath a throne of silk,
The latest born of the ancient Swan and Leda!

LOS CAMELLOS

Dos lánguidos camellos, de elásticas cervices,
de verdes ojos claros y piel sedosa y rubia,
los cuellos recogidos, hinchadas las narices,
a grandes pasos miden un arenal de Nubia.

Alzaron la cabeza para orientarse, y luego
el soñoliento avance de sus vellosas piernas
—bajo el rojizo dombo de aquel cenit de fuego—
pararon, silenciosos, al pie de las cisternas....

Un lustro apenas cargan bajo el azul magnífico,
y ya sus ojos quema la fiebre del tormento:
tal vez leyeron, sabios, borroso jeroglífico
perdido entre las ruinas de infausto monumento.

Vagando taciturnos por la dormida alfombra,
cuando cierra los ojos el moribundo día,
bajo la virgen negra que los llevó en la sombra,
copiaron el desfile de la Melancolía.

Son hijos del Desierto: prestóles la palmera
un largo cuello móvil que sus vaivenes finge,
y en sus marchitos rostros que esculpe la Quimera
¡sopló cansancio eterno la boca de la Esfinge!

Dijeron las Pirámides que el viejo sol rescalda:
—Amamos la fatiga con inquietud secreta—
y vieron desde entonces correr sobre una espalda,
tallada en carne viva, su triangular silueta.

Los átomos de oro que el torbellino esparce
quisieron en sus giros ser grácil vestidura,
y unidos en collares por invisible engarce
vistieron del giboso la escuálida figura.

Todo el fastidio, toda la fiebre, toda el hambre,
la sed sin agua, el yermo sin hembras, los despojos
de caravanas...huesos en blanquecino enjambre...
todo en el cerco bulle de sus dolientes ojos.

THE CAMELS

With supple necks and clear green eyes, with hair
Tawny and smooth like silk, with heads held back
And nostrils wide, two camels with an air
Of languor pace the Nubian desert's track.

They raise their heads to find their course, then halt
The dreamy progress of their hairy limbs—
Beneath the red dome of that fiery vault—
Mute, at the cisterns' base, as daylight dims....

Scarce five years laboring 'neath the rich deep blue,
Their eyes already burn with fever'd pain;
Wise, they have read perhaps, though lost to view,
The secret signs these ruins accursed contain.

Across the sleepy carpet of the sand
They move, as dying day must close its eyes
'Neath the swarthy virgin's shadow-bringing hand,
And Melancholy's march they actualize.

The desert's sons, to them the palm has lent
The long and mobile necks that feign its waving;
Eternal weariness the Sphinx has sent
Into each withered face, Chimera's graving.

The Pyramids sun-scorched of old declared,
"We love fatigue with secret care beset,"
And saw thenceforth how o'er one shoulder fared
In living flesh their triangular silhouette.

Those golden grains the tempest scatters wide
Would in their whirling form a vesture fair,
And, necklace-like strung on a thread unspied,
Adorn the hunchbacked, sorry figure spare.

All the vexation, fever, hunger, thirst
In a waterless waste where female there was none,
Débris of caravans—white heaps of bones accursed—
All throbbed upon their eyeballs woebegone.

Ni las sutiles mirras, ni las leonadas pieles,
ni las volubles palmas que riegan sombra amiga,
ni el ruido sonoroso de claros cascabeles
alegran las miradas al rey de la fatiga.

¡Bebed dolor en ellas, flautistas de Bizancio,
que amáis pulir el dáctilo al son de las cadenas;
sólo esos ojos pueden deciros el cansancio
de un mundo que agoniza sin sangre entre las venas!

¡Oh, artistas! ¡Oh, camellos de la llanura vasta
que vais llevando a cuestas el sacro Monolito!
¡Tristes de Esfinge! ¡Novios de la Palmera casta!
¡Sólo calmáis vosotros la sed de lo infinito!

¿Qué pueden los ceñudos? ¿Qué logran las melenas
de las zarpadas tribus cuando la sed oprime?
Sólo el poeta es lago sobre este mar de arenas,
sólo su arteria rota la Humanidad redime.

Se pierde ya a lo lejos la errante caravana
dejándome—camello que cabalgó el Excidio...—
¡cómo buscar sus huellas al sol de la mañana,
entre las ondas grises de lóbrego fastidio!

¡No! Buscaré dos ojos que he visto, fuente pura
hoy a mi labio exhausta, y aguardaré paciente
hasta que suelta en hilos de mística dulzura
refresque las entrañas del lírico doliente.

Y si a mi lado cruza la sorda muchedumbre
mientras el vago fondo de esas pupilas miro,
dirá que vió un camello con honda pesadumbre
mirando, silencioso, dos fuentes de zafiro....

No perfumed myrrh, nor tawny lion-skin,
Nor the talking palms that yield a friendly shade,
Nor the clear-tinkling bells with strident din
Can looks, where care is king, with joy pervade.

 Drink grief from them, Byzantine flautist, drink,
Who tune your dactyls to the clank of chains;
Those eyes alone can tell to what may sink
An agonizing world with bloodless veins!

 Thou artist! Camel of the vast expanse,
Who carriest on thy back the sacred sign,
Sad as the Sphinx, the chaste palm's own romance,
Thirst for the infinite to calm, is only thine!

 What help the horse's hoof, the shaggy mane
Of beasts with cruel claws, when thirst is sore?
The poet is the lake of this waste terrain,
His shed blood only can lost Man restore.

 The wandering caravan now is lost to sight;
And I am left—a camel, grief-pursued. . . .
How seek by morning's sun its tracks aright
Among those waves of dull distaste gray-hued?

 No! I will seek two eyes I've seen, a spring
My lips have drained today, and suffering wait
Till mystic-sweet in flowing streams it bring
Refreshing to the grieving lyrist's state.

 And if, while in those vague, deep eyes I peer,
Beside me there should pass the crowd of fools,
They'll say they saw a camel of mournful cheer
Gaze silently into two sapphire pools.

ALBA TRISTE

Todo fué así. Preocupaciones lilas
turbaban la ilusión de la mañana,
y una garza pueril su absurda plana
paloteaba en las ondas intranquilas.

Un estremecimiento de Sibilas
epilepsiaba a ratos la ventana,
cuando de pronto un mito tarambana
rodó en la obscuridad de mis pupilas.

«¡Adiós, adiós!» grité y hasta los cielos
el gris sarcasmo de su fino guante
ascendió con el rojo de mis celos.

Wagneriaba en el aire una corneja,
y la selva sintió en aquel instante
una infinita colisión compleja.

LA SOMBRA DOLOROSA

Gemían los rebaños. Los caminos
llenábanse de lúgubres cortejos;
una congoja de holocaustos viejos
ahogaba los silencios campesinos.

Bajo el misterio de los velos finos,
evocabas los símbolos perplejos,
hierática, perdiéndote a lo lejos
con tus húmedos ojos mortecinos.

Mientras unidos por un mal hermano,
me hablaban con suprema confidencia
los mudos apretones de tu mano,

manchó la soñadora transparencia
de la tarde infinita el tren lejano,
aullando de dolor hacia la ausencia.

A MOURNFUL DAWN

'Twas thus: preoccupations lilac-hued
Disturbed in me morning's illusion vain,
And a childish heron on his page inane
Made awkward strokes 'mid the waves' inquietude.

And Sibyls, shuddering, gave at times a rude,
Epileptic rattle to the window pane,
When all at once a whimsey, half-insane,
Upon my darkened eyeballs 'gan intrude.

"Good-bye, Good-bye," I cried; and to the skies
Gray sarcasm from her delicate glove ascended,
As did the red of jealousy from my eyes.

Wagnerian notes croaked forth a warning crow,
And the woodland felt as if o'er it impended
A cataclysm of final overthrow.

THE DOLEFUL SHADOW

The flocks went bleating homeward, and the ways
Were dense with mournful men and dames;
An agony of ancient ritual flames
Flooded the rural silence with their rays.

Beneath fine veils mysterious to the gaze
Thy breast perplexing symbols frames;
The far-off scene thy vision, priestess, claims,
Thy humid eyes fixed with a death-like glaze.

Thy unwelcome brother joined us, but thy hand
With silent pressures spoke meanwhile thy mind
With confidence supreme; and the dreamy land,

Transparent as the long daylight declined,
Was smudged by the distant train whose shrill command
Brings pain and separation to mankind.

LA CENA

Un repique de lata la merienda circula....
Aploma el artesano su crasura y secuestra
media mesa en canónicas dignidades de bula,
comiendo con la zurda, por aliviar la diestra....

Mientras la grey famélica los manjares adula,
en sabroso anticipo, sus colmillos adiestra;
y por merecimiento, casi más que por gula,
duplica su pitanza de col y de menestra....

Luego que ante el rescoldo sus digestiones hipa,
sumido en la enrulada neblina de su pipa,
arrullan, golosinas domésticas de invierno:

la Hormiga y Blanca Nieve, Caperuza y el Lobo....
Y la prole apollada, bajo el manto materno,
choca de escalofríos, en un éxtasis bobo.

LA GOTA AMARGA

Soñaban con la Escocia de tus ojos
verdes, los grandes lagos amarillos;
y engarzó un nimbo de esplendores rojos
la sangre de la tarde en tus anillos.

En la bíblica paz de los rastrojos
gorjearon los ingenuos caramillos,
un cántico de arpegios tan sencillos
que hablaban de romeros y de hinojos.

¡Y dimos en sufrir! Ante aquel canto
crepuscular, escintiló tu llanto....
Viendo nacer una ilusión remota,

callaron nuestras almas hasta el fondo.
Y como un cáliz angustioso y hondo
mi beso recogió la última gota.

SUPPER

A clatter of tin proclaims the evening meal....
The laborer sets his fat bulk down, and takes
The lion's share, like monks with the Pope's own seal;
Left hand relieving right, good speed he makes....

And as his hungry brood the victuals praise,
Sniffing the savory mess, he works his jaw,
And while his merit more than appetite he weighs,
Crams double soup and cabbage down his maw....

Then as he hiccoughs by the embers' glow,
And, sunk in pipe-smoke, nothing more can want,
The winter's lulling tales make murmur low,
Of Riding Hood and the Wolf, Snow White, and the Ant....
The children, chicken-like, their mother near,
Shudder with ecstasy and simple fear.

ANGUISH AND LOVE

Of the Scotland in thine eyes of green, the lakes
Immense and flushed with golden light were dreaming;
And in thy rings the blood of evening gleaming
A nimbus of red splendors round thee makes.

In the stubble-fields whose holy peace none breaks
The flutes were warbling notes free from all scheming,
A song in arpeggios, so artless seeming,
Of pilgrims kneeling, memories it wakes.

We suffered then! At that song in the fading light
Thy weeping twinkled like the stars at night.
Perceiving then a far illusion born,

Our spirits to their lowest depths were stilled;
And, as a chalice with deep anguish filled,
My kiss caught up the latest drop forlorn.

BLASÓN

Soy el cantor de América autóctono y salvaje:
mi lira tiene un alma, mi canto un ideal.
Mi verso no se mece colgado de un ramaje
con un vaivén pausado de hamaca tropical....

Cuando me siento Inca, le rindo vasallaje
al Sol, que me da el cetro de su poder real;
cuando me siento hispano y evoco el Coloniaje,
parecen mis estrofas trompetas de cristal.

Mi fantasía viene de un abolengo moro:
los Andes son de plata, pero el León de oro;
y las dos castas fundo con épico fragor.

La sangre es española e incaico es el latido;
¡y de no ser Poeta, quizás yo hubiese sido
un blanco Aventurero o un indio Emperador!

LAS PUNAS

Silencio y soledad.... Nada se mueve....
Apenas, a lo lejos, en hilera,
Las vicuñas con rápida carrera
pasan, a modo de una sombra leve.

¿Quién a medir esa extensión se atreve?
Sólo la desplegada cordillera,
que se encorva después a la manera
de un colosal paréntesis de nieve.

Vano será que busque la mirada
alegría de vívidos colores,
en la tristeza de la puna helada:

sin mariposas, pájaros, ni flores,
es una inmensidad deshabitada,
como si fuese un alma sin amores....

BLAZON

Of native, savage America I sing;
My lyre has a soul, my song a lofty aim.
Not like a hammock do my verses swing,
Slung from a tropic branch, with movement tame.

As Inca, I render to the Sun, my king,
Due homage, and his powerful scepter claim;
When forth, as Spaniard, colonial times I bring,
My lines like crystal trumpets seem to flame.

My fancy takes its form from Moorish mould:
The Andes are of silver, León of gold;
And these two have I fused with epic clamor.

The blood is Spanish, Incan its pulsation;
And were I not a Poet by vocation,
I'd wear the white Corsair's or red Chief's glamour.

THE FROZEN HEIGHTS

Silence and solitude.... No movement shows....
Far off, in single file, though hardly seen,
Vicuñas pass with rapid tread between
The steeps, like shades a light cloud throws.

Who shall measure the space these peaks enclose?
Only the winding mountain chain, I ween,
That curves upon itself in glittering sheen,
A huge parenthesis of eternal snows.

Vain, vain will be his search who hopes to find
The joy of vivid color meet his eyes
'Mid those icy peaks to sadness pale consigned;

Sans butterflies, and birds, and flowers' bright dyes,
It is a waste devoid of living kind,
As 'twere a soul that knew not love's sweet ties.

LOS ANDES

Cual se ve la escultórica serpiente
de Laoconte en mármoles desnudos,
los Andes trenzan sus nerviosos nudos
en el cuerpo de todo un Continente.

Horror dantesco estremecer se siente
por sobre ese tropel de héroes membrudos,
que se alzan con graníticos escudos
y con cascos de plata refulgente.

La angustia de cada héroe es infinita,
porque quiere gritar, retiembla, salta,
se parte de dolor..., pero no grita;

y sólo deja, extático y sombrío,
rodar, desde su cúspide más alta,
la silenciosa lágrima de un río....

CUACTHEMOC

Solemnemente triste fué Cuacthemoc. Un día
un grupo de hombres blancos se abalanzó hasta él;
y mientras que el imperio de tal se sorprendía,
el arcabuz llenaba de huecos el broquel.

Preso quedó; y el Indio, que nunca sonreía,
una sonrisa tuvo que se deshizo en hiel.
— ¿En dónde está el tesoro? — clamó la vocería;
y respondió un silencio más grande que el tropel....

Llegó el tormento.... Y alguien de la imperial nobleza
quejóse. El Héroe dijóle, irguiendo la cabeza:
— ¡Mi lecho no es de rosas! — y se volvió a callar.

En tanto, al retostarle los pies, chirriaba el fuego,
que se agitaba a modo de balbuciente ruego,
¡porque se hacía lenguas como queriendo hablar!

THE ANDES

The Andes, like the writhing, sculptured snakes
Of Laocoön, with their naked marble coils
Hold fast within their nervous knotted toils
The frame a whole vast continent that makes.

A horror such as Dante dreamed here shakes
The brawny hero host that now recoils
And, bright with silver casques no dimness spoils
And granite shields, a fresh uprising takes.

The anguish of each hero has no end,
For he would cry aloud, and leap and quiver,
Yet give no groan, though grief his frame should rend;

And in the ecstatic gloom that wraps his soul
Only permits a silent tear to roll
From his most exalted pinnacle—a river.

CUACTHEMOC

Solemnly sad was Cuacthemoc. One day
A band of white men burst on him, and, while
Surprised that such men had him 'neath their sway,
The harquebus had riddled through his shield.

A captive now; a smile then died away
In bitterness, on his face not used to smile.
"Where is your treasure hid?" then clamored they;
And silence, great as the uproar, naught revealed.

Torture was brought.... Some nobleman in dread
Complained. The hero raised his brow and said:
"My bed is not of roses,"—and was dumb.

But as it seared his feet, the fire would hiss,
Moved as to stuttering prayer with sounds amiss,
For it made tongues as if words yearned to come.

TRES NOTAS DE NUESTRA ALMA INDÍGENA

(A) ¡Quién Sabe!

Indio que asomas a la puerta
de esa tu rústica mansión:
¿para mí no tienes agua?
¿para mi frío, cobertor?
¿parco maíz para mi hambre?
¿para mi sueño, mal rincón?
¿breve quietud para mi andanza?...
— ¡Quién sabe, señor!

Indio que labras con fatiga
tierras que de otros dueños son:
¿ignoras tú que deben tuyas
ser, por tu sangre y tu sudor?
¿ignoras tú que audaz codicia
siglos atrás, te las quitó?
¿ignoras tú que eres el Amo?
— ¡Quién sabe, señor!

Indio de frente taciturna
y de pupilas sin fulgor:
¿que pensamiento es el que escondes
en tu enigmática expresión?
¿qué es lo que buscas en tu vida?
¿qué es lo que imploras a tu Dios?
¿qué es lo que sueña tu silencio?
— ¡Quién sabe, señor!

¡Oh Raza antigua y misteriosa,
de impenetrable corazón,
que sin gozar ves la alegría
y sin sufrir ves el dolor:
eres augusta como el Ande,
el Grande Océano y el Sol!
Ese tu gesto que parece
como de vil resignación

THREE NOTES OF OUR INDIGENOUS SPIRIT

(A) Who Knows?

"O Indian, looking from the doorway
Of this thy rustic dwelling-place,
For my thirst hast thou no water?
For the cold I feel, no covering?
Nor corn, though scanty, for my hunger?
Nor some odd corner I may dream in,
Some quiet respite from Life's chances?"
      "Ah, sir, who knows?"

"O Indian, thou who laborest hard
On fields that other masters own,
Dost thou not know that by thy blood
And sweat they should be thine by right?
Dost thou not know that ages since
Audacious greed snatched them from thee?
Dost thou not know thou art the master?"
      "Ah, sir, who knows?"

"O Indian, taciturn of brow,
And eyes in which no spark appears,
What is the thought that hidden lies
Behind thine enigmatic mask?
What is it that in life thou seek'st?
What is't thou pray'st for to thy God?
What is the dream thy silence hides?"
      "Ah, sir, who knows?"

"O ancient and mysterious race,
Whose heart remains impenetrable,
Who look on joy without enjoying
And without pain can look on suffering;
August you are, as are the Andes,
The Sun, and the wide-spreading Ocean!
This attitude of yours that seems
As if of cowardly resignation,

es de una sabia indiferencia
y de un orgullo sin rencor....
   Corre en mis venas sangre tuya,
y, por tal sangre, si mi Dios
me interrogase qué prefiero
— cruz o laurel, espina o flor,
beso que apague mis suspiros
o hiel que colme mi canción —
responderíale dudando:
               — ¡Quién sabe, señor!

   (B) Así será
   El joven indio comparece
ante el ceñudo Capataz:
—Tu padre ha muerto; y, como sabes,
en contra tuya y en pie están
deudas, que tú con tu trabajo
tal vez nos llegues a pagar....
Desde mañana, como es justo,
rebajaremos tu jornal. —
El joven indio abre los ojos
llenos de trágica humedad;
y, con un gesto desplicente
que no se puede penetrar,
dice, ensayando una sonrisa:
               — Así será....

   Clarín de guerra pide sangre.
Truena la voz del Capitán;
—Indio: ¡a las filas! Blande tu arma
hasta morir o hasta triunfar.
Tras la batalla, si es que mueres,
nadie de ti se acordará;
pero si, en cambio, el triunfo alcanzas,
te haré en mis tierras trabajar....
No me preguntes por qué luchas,
ni me preguntes dónde vas. —
Dócil el indio entra en las filas

Is one of wise indifference
And pride that harbors no resentment....
 'Tis yours the blood that fills my veins,
And, by that blood, if that my God
Should question me which I prefer—
The cross or the laurel, thorns or flowers,
The kiss that should assuage my sighs,
Or gall more than to fill my song—
Still doubting, I should answer him:
"O Lord, who knows?"

(B) So Let It Be

 The youthful Indian, summoned forth,
Appears before the frowning Foreman:
"Your father has died; and, as you know,
Standing against you on our books
Are his debts, which by your labor you
Perhaps in time may come to pay....
Hence, from tomorrow, as is just,
We shall reduce your daily wage."
The Indian youth looks up with eyes
That overflow with tragic tears,
And, with a gesture of displeasure,
Whose meaning none can penetrate,
Says, with a smile upon his lips:
"So let it be."

 War's clarion calls out for blood.
The Captain's voice like thunder shouts:
"Indian, to the ranks; and wield your sword
Till death or triumph is the end.
After the battle, if you die,
No soul will ever think of you;
But, if perchance you triumph win,
I'll have you labor in my fields....
And do not ask me why you fight,
And where you're going don't inquire."
In the ranks the Indian takes his place,

como un autómata marcial;
y sólo dice, gravemente:
               —Así será....

Mujer del indio: en ti los ojos
un día pone blanco audaz.
Charco de sangre... Hombre por tierra...
Junto al cadáver, un puñal...
Y luego el juez increpa al indio,
que se sonríe sin temblar:
—Quien como tú con hierro mata,
con hierro muere. ¡Morirás!—
Pone un relámpago en sus ojos
turbios el indio; y con faz
vuelta a los cielos, dice apenas:
               —Así será....

¡Oh Raza firme como un árbol
que no se agobia al huracán,
que no se queja bajo el hacha
y que se impone al pedregal!
Raza que sufre su tormento
sin que se oiga lamentar
(¿Rompió en sollozos Atahualpa?
¿Guatemocín?... ¿Caupolicán?...),
El «Dios lo quiere» de los moros
suena como este «Así será....»

¿Resignación? Antes orgullo
de quien se siente valer más
que la fortuna caprichosa
y que la humana crueldad....
Un filosófico desprecio
hacia el dolor acaso da
la herencia indígena a mi sangre,
pronta a fluir sin protestar;
y cada vez que la torpeza
de la Fortuna huye a mi afán,
y crueldades harto humanas

Docile, automaton for war,
And gravely utters only this:
>"So let it be."

O Indian's wife... on you one day
A shameless white has set his eyes.
A pool of blood... on the earth a man
Lies slain... beside the corpse a dagger...
And then the judge inveighs against
The Indian, who smiles but trembles not:
"Who uses sword to kill, like you,
Himself the sword shall kill: you die!"
In the Indian's troubled eyes a flash
Of lightning shows; and with his face
Upturned to heaven he softly breathes:
>"So let it be."

O Race, fast-rooted as an oak
That bends not to the hurricane,
That 'neath the axe makes no complaint
And holds its own on the stony slope!
A race that suffers torments rude,
Nor e'er was heard to utter groan
(Did Atahualpa burst in tears?
Guatemocín? Caupolicán?),
The Moors' refrain, "It is God's will,"
Sounds much like your "So let it be...."

Is't resignation? Rather pride
Of one who feels himself above
Capricious fate that Fortune sends,
Or the cruelty of human-kind....
My native heritage has given
Perhaps a philosophic scorn
Of pain to my blood, so prompt to flow
Without desire to make protest;
And every time my eager grasp
Has failed to catch dull Fortune's hand,
When all too human cruelties

niéganle el paso a mi Ideal,
y hasta la Vida me asegura
que nada tengo que esperar,
dueño yo siempre de mí mismo
y superior al bien y al mal,
digo, encogiéndome de hombros:
  — Así será....

(c) Ahí, no mas
Indio, que a pie vienes de lejos
(y tan de lejos que quizás
te envejeciste en el camino,
y aun no concluyes de llegar...),
detén un punto el fácil trote
bajo la carga de tu afán,
que te hace ver siempre la tierra
(en que reinabas siglos ha),
y dime en gracia a la fatiga,
¿en dónde queda la ciudad? —
Señala el Indio una ágil cumbre,
que a mi esperanza cerca está;
y me responde sonriendo:
  — Ahí, no más....

Espoleado echo al galope
mi corcel; y una eternidad
se me desdobla en el camino....
Llego a la cuesta; un pedregal
en que monótonos los cascos
del corcel ponen su chis-chas....
Gano la cumbre; y, por fin, ¿qué hallo?
aridez, frío y soledad....
Ante esta cumbre hay otra cumbre:
y después de ésa, ¿otra no habrá?
—Indio, que vives en las rocas
de las alturas y que estás
lejos del valle y las falacias
que la molicie urde sensual,

Forbid advance to my Ideal,
And even Life itself declares
That I have nothing here to hope for,
Yet always master of my soul
Superior to both good and ill,
I shrug my shoulders, and I say:
                    "So let it be."

  (c) WHY, THERE; JUST OVER THERE
"O Indian, come on foot from far
(So very far thou hast come perhaps
That by the way thou hast grown old,
With, even yet, no end in sight ...),
A moment stay thy swinging gait
Enforced on thee by eagerness,
Which makes thee ever view the land
(Where centuries ago thou reigned'st),
And tell me, for I'm much fatigued,
Where is the city to be found?"
The Indian points to a lofty peak—
Close to my hoped-for goal it stands—
And, smiling, to me thus replies:
          "Why, there; just over there...."

  I spur my steed to the gallop and ride;
Eternity seems to unfold
Before me as I speed along....
I reach the slope, a stony ridge
On which, monotonous, the hoofs
Of the horse resound with noisy clang....
I gain the crest, and find at last—
Barrenness, cold, and solitude....
Beyond this peak is another peak;
And after that will there be no other?
"Indian, who livest amid the rocks
Of these high altitudes, and art
Far from the valley, and the falsehood
That sensual luxury entails,

¿quieres decirle a mi fatiga
en dónde queda la ciudad?—
El Indio asómase a la puerta
de su palacio señorial,
hecho de pajas que el Sol dora
y que desfleca el huracán;
y me responde sonriendo:
—Antes un río hay que pasar...
—¿Y queda lejos ese río?
　　　　　—Ahí, no más....

　Trepo una cumbre y otra cumbre
y otra... Amplio valle duerme en paz;
y sobre el verde fondo, un río
dibuja su S de cristal.
—Este es el río; pero ¿en dónde,
en dónde queda la ciudad?—
Indio que sube de aquel valle,
oye mi queja y, al pasar,
deja caer estas palabras:
　　　　　—Ahí, no más....

　¡Oh Raza fuerte en la tristeza,
perseverante en el afán,
que no conoces la fatiga
ni la extorsión del «mas allá»
—Ahí, no más...—encuentras siempre
cuanto deseas encontrar;
y, así, se siente, en lo profundo
de ese desprecio con que das
sabia ironía a las distancias,
una emoción de Eternidad!...

　Yo aprendo en ti—lo que me es fácil,
pues tengo el título ancestral—
a hacer de toda lejanía
un horizonte familiar;
y en adelante, cuando busque

Pray, tell me, wearied as I am,
Where is the city to be found?"
The Indian peeps out from the door
Of his palatial home manorial,
Made from straw by the sun turned gold,
And scattered abroad by the hurricane's force;
And, smiling meanwhile, thus replies:
"There's first a river you must cross..."
"And is that river far from here?"
    "Why, there; just over there...."

  I climb one steep and then another,
Another...a wide vale sleeps in peace,
And a river over its green expanse
Traces an S like crystal clear.
"This indeed is the river; but where,
Oh, where, I ask, does the city stand?"
An Indian from the valley climbing
Hears my plaint, and, as he passes,
Quietly lets these words fall:
    "Why, there; just over there...."

  O Race, though melancholy, strong,
Persistent in solicitude,
Who ne'er hast known what is fatigue,
Nor the torment of what lies beyond,
"Just over there..." thou ever find'st
Whate'er thou dost desire to find;
And thus, with this sublime disdain
With which to distances thou giv'st
A knowing irony, one feels
An emotion of eternity....

  From thee I learn—and learn with ease,
For I hold ancestral title here—
To make of each far-distant scene
Familiar ground, horizon known;
And, henceforth, when I start in quest

un remotísimo Ideal,
cuando persiga un loco ensueño,
cuando prepare un vuelo audaz,
si adónde voy se me pregunta,
ya sé que debo contestar,
sin medir tiempos ni distancias:
   — Ahí, no más....

Of some Ideal far removed,
When some wild dream I would pursue,
Or seek to make some daring flight,
If one should ask me whither I go,
My answer I already know,
No measure made of time or space:
    "Why, there; just over there...."

TUÉRCELE EL CUELLO AL CISNE

Tuércele el cuello al cisne de engañoso plumaje
que da su nota blanca al azul de la fuente;
él pasea su gracia no más, pero no siente
el alma de las cosas ni la voz del paisaje.

Huye de toda forma y de todo lenguaje
que no vayan acordes con el ritmo latente
de la vida profunda... y adora intensamente
la vida, y que la vida comprenda tu homenaje.

Mira el sapiente buho cómo tiende las alas
desde el Olimpo, deja el regazo de Palas
y posa en aquel árbol el vuelo taciturno....

El no tiene la gracia del cisne, mas su inquieta
pupila que se clava en la sombra, interpreta
el misterioso libro del silencio nocturno.

Y PIENSO QUE LA VIDA...

Y pienso que la vida se me va con huída
inevitable y rápida, y me conturbo, y pienso
en mis horas lejanas, y me asalta un inmenso
afán de ser el de antes y desandar la vida.

¡Oh, los pasos sin rumbo por la senda perdida,
los anhelos inútiles, el batallar intenso!
¡Cómo flotáis ahora, blancas nubes de incienso
quemado en los altares de una deidad mentida!

Páginas tersas, páginas de los libros, lecturas
de espejismos enfermos, de cuestiones oscuras...
¡Ay, lo que yo he leído! ¡Ay, lo que yo he soñado....

Tristes noches de estéril meditación, quimera
que ofuscaste mi espíritu sin dejarme siquiera
mirar que iba la vida sonriendo a mi lado....

(¡Ay, lo que yo he leído! ¡Ay, lo que yo he soñado!...)

WRING THE NECK OF THE SWAN

Wring the neck of the swan with plumage deceiving,
The note of white upon the lake of blue;
He parades his beauty merely, but has no clue
To the soul of things, no voice in the scene perceiving.

Flee all forms, all language, their harmonies weaving,
That fail to accord with the rhythm deep and true
Of life profound.... Give adoration due
To life, beyond all risk of misconceiving.

Behold the sapient owl, how he spreads his wings;
From Pallas' lap on Olympus high he springs,
And on yon tree rests from his silent flight....

No beauty of the swan has he; but his restless eye,
Which pierces through the darkness, can descry
Deep meanings in the silence of the night.

LIFE ESCAPES ME

And I think that life escapes me with a flight
Inevitable and swift; and, pained, reflect
On distant hours, and fain would resurrect
The man I was, retread old ways aright.

Alas, those aimless steps, no path in sight,
Those useless sighs, the hard fight! Now, in effect,
Ye float like incense lying gods expect
To rise from their altar-fires in clouds of white.

Smooth pages, pages out of books, and reading
Of feeble fictions, questions nowhere leading...
Ah, me! the things I've read, the things I've dreamed!....

Sad nights of fruitless musing, phantoms vain,
Ye did not even permit my clouded brain
To see that life beside me smiling beamed....

(Ah, me! the things I've read, the things I've dreamed!)

MAÑANA LOS POETAS...

Mañana los poetas cantarán en divino
verso que no logramos entonar los de hoy;
nuevas constelaciones darán otro destino
a sus almas inquietas con un nuevo temblor.

Mañana los poetas seguirán su camino
absortos en ignota y extraña floración,
y al oír nuestro canto, con desdén repentino
echarán a los vientos nuestra vieja ilusión.

Y todo será inútil, y todo será en vano;
será el afán de siempre y el idéntico arcano
y la misma tiniebla dentro del corazón.

Y ante la eterna sombra que surge y se retira,
recogerán del polvo la abandonada lira
y cantarán con ella nuestra misma canción.

LA PIEDAD QUE PASA

Cayó sobre la arena un pétalo de rosa....
Para que no lo estrujen los pies del peregrino,
mi mano suavemente lo apartó del camino
y le cavó en el musgo la tumba silenciosa.

Bajo rosal materno, el pétalo reposa...
Sobre el rincón que guarda su sueño y su destino,
de la cercana fuente el chorro cristalino
hará crecer la hierba y ocultará la fosa.

Los pájaros del huerto han detenido el ala...
La vesperal penumbra en el jardín instala
su indecisión de tintes cual funeraria ofrenda....

Cuando caigan los velos de la noche oportuna,
la Piedad revestida con ropaje de luna
y un dedo sobre el labio, cruzará por la senda.

TOMORROW POETS WILL SING

Tomorrow poets will sing in strains divine
To which we poets of today can not attain;
New stars on their unquiet souls will shine,
And novel tremors will for them ordain.

Tomorrow poets their own way will follow;
Their minds some strange, new flourish will engross;
Hearing our song, our old illusion hollow
They'll throw to the winds with quick disdainful toss.

And all will be in vain, and useless toil;
Always the same, the urge, the secret coil;
The same, the mists within the heart that throng.

And, 'mid the gloom that rises and retires,
They will snatch up again the abandoned lyres
And with them sing once more the same old song.

PITY THAT PASSES

There fell to earth the petal of a rose....
Lest passing pilgrims' feet its form should crush,
I gently took it from the wayside brush
And for its silent tomb the moss I chose.

Beneath the mother bush it finds repose;
The crystal streams that from the fountain gush
Shall hide the grave with verdure growing lush
In the nook that guards its dream, its fate that knows.

The birds in the garden cease to flap their wings;
Like funeral gift eve to the garden brings
Her tints obscure and in them all things dips;

And when the veils of night fall opportune,
Pity, in vesture silvered by the moon,
Will cross the path, a finger on her lips.

ESTA TARDE HE SALIDO AL CAMPO

Esta tarde he salido al campo jovialmente....
Voy a sorber aromas, a mirar al poniente
lleno de lumbres nuevas y de nuevos matices;
a ver cómo circulan bandadas de perdices
que sospechan mi falta de instintos cinegéticos;
a contemplar la ciénaga, y los aires proféticos
de una garza que encuentro siempre (no sé por qué)
inmóvil, pensativa y parada en un pie....

Llevo en la mano un libro, un libro que no leo,
cogido en mis estantes al azar.... Un deseo
vago me hace hojearlo distraido. ¿Quién es
el autor?... Por encima del título en francés,
hay este nombre exótico: Francis Jammes.... Y digo:
Oh, divino poeta, ¿quién te trajo conmigo?...
Hojeo y rememoro.... Hace tiempo que nada
me ha conturbado tanto como esa desmañada
poesía de verso rugoso, sin aliños,
como el rudimentario balbucir de los niños;
ese sentir ingenuo de formas y paisajes,
esa desnudez única, los olores salvajes
de la naturaleza, y las cosas secretas,
¡oh, vida, que has contado a tan pocos poetas!...

«Francis Jammes, tu casa a tu faz se parece;
la recubre la hiedra y un pino la ensombrece»...
Así voy mascullando de memoria la cita
de Guerín (duerme en paz, alma noble y bendita,
alma suave, alma triste a quien duro destino
y prematura muerte cerraron el camino)...
Un pin l'ombrage ... Suena el habla primitiva
y el desnudo concepto, la voz alerta y viva
tan fresca, tan ingenua, tan sencilla, tan pura,
sin inflexiones sabias, pero de gran hondura;

AFTERNOON IN THE COUNTRY

Today in happy mood I sought the country....
There I'll inhale the perfumes, watch the sunset
Filled with flames and shades of colors new;
I'll see the wheeling partridges in coveys
That must suspect I lack the hunter's instinct;
And gaze upon the marsh, and the airs prophetic
Of a heron I always meet (why, I know not)
Immobile, pensive, perched upon one foot....

I carry in my hand, but do not read, a book
Taken at random from my shelves.... A vague
Desire impels me idly to turn the pages.
Who is the author? Over the title in French
Is the exotic name of Francis Jammes.*
O poet divine, I say, who brought you here?
I scan the pages and remember.... For some time
Nothing has so perplexed me as this verse,
Awkward and rugged, void of ornament,
Like the rudimentary babble of a child;
That feeling fair and frank for forms and landscapes,
That nakedness unique, the scents of nature
In the wild, and the secret things that thou, O Life,
Hast given to poets all too few to know.

"Thy dwelling, Francis Jammes, is like thy face;
The ivy covers, and a pine tree shades it"...
Thus mumble I from memory the lines
About Guérin (he sleeps in peace, a noble
And blessed soul, gentle and sad, for whom
Stern fate and early death have closed the way) ...
Un pin l'ombrage ... The speech sounds primitive,
The idea is bare, the voice alert and living,
So fresh, so frank, so simple and so pure,
With no display of learning, but great depth;

* A number of poems by Francis Jammes, a recent French poet, have been translated by González Martínez.

la que cantó los mansos burros «cuyas orejas
se sacuden los palos, las moscas, las abejas,»
y el perro por quien pide en sublime piedad
la gloria de los buenos por una eternidad....
¡Oh, la sincera plática, las voces misteriosas
de quien conoce el alma de seres y de cosas!...
«Oh, hijo de Virgilio»... va diciendo el pasaje
final del ya citado y divino homenaje
del poeta difunto....
               El toque de oración
comenta aquel apóstrofe de un noble corazón,
y siento en esa hora el alma suspendida
como un jirón de bruma entre el libro y la vida....

The voice that sang the patient ass "whose ears
Shake off the cudgels, and the flies and bees,"
And the dog for whom with piety sublime
He prays for the glory good men know for ever....
"O Son of Virgil"... runs the closing passage
I've quoted from the lofty tribute paid
To the poet dead....
                    The bell for prayer comments
On that apostrophe to a noble heart,
And in this hour I feel my soul suspended
Like a wisp of cloud between the book and life....

LOS PÁJAROS ERRANTES

Era en las cenicientas postrimerías del otoño, en los solitarios archipélagos del sur.

Yo estaba con los silenciosos pescadores que en el breve crepúsculo elevan las velas remendadas y transparentes.

Trabajábamos callados, porque la tarde entraba en nosotros y en el agua entumecida.

Nubes de púrpura pasaban, como grandes peces, bajo la quilla de nuestro barco.

Nubes de púrpura volaban por encima de nuestras cabezas.

Y las velas turgentes de la balandra eran como las alas de un ave grande y tranquila que cruzara, sin ruido, el rojo crepúsculo.

Yo estaba con los taciturnos pescadores que vagan en la noche, y velan el sueño de los mares.

En el lejano horizonte del sur, lila y brumoso, alguien distinguió una banda de pájaros.

Nosotros íbamos hacia ellos y ellos venían hacia nosotros.

Cuando comenzaron a cruzar sobre nuestros mástiles, oímos sus voces y vimos sus ojos brillantes que de paso nos echaban una breve mirada.

Rítmicamente volaban y volaban unos tras los otros, huyendo del invierno, hacia los mares y las tierras del norte.

La peregrinación interminable, lanzando sus breves y rudos cantos, cruzaba, en un arco sonoro, de uno a otro horizonte.

Insensiblemente, la noche que llegaba iba haciendo una sola cosa del mar y del cielo, de la balandra y de nosotros mismos.

Perdidos en la sombra, escuchábamos el canto de los invisibles pájaros errantes.

Ninguno de ellos veía ya a su compañero, ninguno de ellos distinguía cosa alguna en el aire negro y sin fondo.

Hojas a merced del viento, la noche los dispersaría.

Mas nó; la noche que hace de todas las cosas una informe obscuridad, nada podía sobre ellos.

Los pájaros incansables volaban cantando, y si el vuelo los llevaba lejos, el canto los mantenía unidos.

THE BIRDS OF PASSAGE

It was in the last ashen-gray days of autumn, in the solitary archipelagoes of the south.

I was with the silent fishermen, who in the brief twilight raise their patched and transparent sails.

We worked in silence, for the evening was descending upon us and upon the surging waters.

Clouds of purple, like great fishes, passed under the keel of our vessel.

Clouds of purple flew over our heads.

And the swelling sails of the bark were like the wings of a great and tranquil bird that crossed noiselessly the red twilight.

I was with the taciturn fishermen, who voyage in the night and keep watch over the dreams of the sea.

On the distant southern horizon, hazy and lilac-colored, someone descried a flock of birds.

We were moving toward them and they were coming toward us.

When they began to cross over our masts, we heard their cries, and saw their brilliant eyes which in passing cast a hurried glance on us.

Rhythmically they flew and flew, one behind the other, fleeing from the winter, toward the seas and lands of the north.

In their interminable flight, giving forth their short, harsh cries, they stretched in a sonorous arc from one horizon to the other.

Insensibly the coming night was making as one the sea, the sky, the ship, and ourselves.

Lost in the darkness, we heard the cry of the invisible wandering birds.

No longer did any one of them see its companion; none of them could distinguish anything in the black and fathomless air.

Leaves at the mercy of the wind, the night would disperse them.

But no; the night, which brings all things to a formless blackness, had no power over them.

The unwearied birds flew on, singing; and, if their flight carried them far, their song kept them united.

Durante toda la fría y larga noche del otoño pasó la banda inagotable de las aves del mar.

En tanto, en la balandra, como pájaros extraviados, los corazones de los pescadores aleteaban de inquietud y de deseo.

Inconsciente, tembloroso, llevado por la fiebre y seguro de mi deber para con mis taciturnos compañeros, de pié sobre la borda, uní mi voz al coro de los pájaros errantes.

LAS MANOS

Manos de la amada dignas de una reina
¡si una reina digna de ellas fuera!

Manecitas breves
con florecillas de azul entre la nieve
y con menudos dedos
que en sonrosadas uñas se florecen.

Manos compasivas, cariñosas,
con cuánta bondad siempre se posan
sobre mi frente; manos blancas,
cuando ayudáis a bien sufrir,
sois unas santas.

En el tiempo bueno, magas divinas
palmoteando aumentasteis la alegría,
locas manos de niña.

Y siempre os extendéis prestando ayuda
nobles manos menudas.

Previsoras sin que os rinda la fatiga
sois las hormiguitas de la vida.

Manos blancas de azuladas venas,
haced que mi vida sea buena.

Manecitas mías,
otorgadme mi parte de alegría
y si hada sois, llenad de flores
nuestro común jardín de los amores.

During the whole of the cold, long, autumn night, passed this endless flock of sea birds.

Meanwhile, on board the ship, like birds astray, the hearts of the fishermen fluttered within them with inquietude and longing.

Trembling unconsciously, agitated by fever, and knowing my duty toward my taciturn companions, I stood on deck and joined my voice to the choir of the wayfaring birds.

THE HANDS OF MY BELOVED

The hands of my beloved would grace a queen
If any queen were worthy of them!

Short little hands
With little flowers of blue among the snow
And tiny fingers
On which the nails like roses blow.

Hands, loving and compassionate,
With how much kindness they are ever placed
Upon my brow; white hands,
When by your aid to suffer well I'm braced,
'Tis very saints you are.

Divine magicians, you, when days are bright,
Augment my joy, clapping your child-like hands
With mad delight.

And ever, noble hands though slender,
You are extended needed aid to render.

And prudent, letting not fatigue o'erpower you,
You're like the little ants of life.

White hands with bluish veins,
Make my life good.

Dear little hands of mine,
Grant me my share of joy,
And, if you fairies are, fill full with flowers
The garden that our mutual love embowers.

Cuando muera,
haced que mis párpados se cierren,
pero haced que se cierren lentamente,
¡así mis ojos turbios vuestra imagen lleven
más allá de la muerte!

LÁZARO

—¿Quién me llama?—y Lázaro, saliendo de la tumba,
miró a Jesús y lo comprendió todo.
—¿Eres tú ¡oh sol! el que alumbras?
¿Eres tú, o todo es un sueño? ¡María,
mi hermana! ¡Marta, hermana mía!—...
Hablaba lenta y vagamente, como un canto
que brotara de las aguas.
Sus miradas sin hielo iban errantes
por el ardiente paisaje de Judea.
Su voz estaba impregnada del opaco
silencio de la muerte.
Y su faz, serena y pálida, comenzaba a rizarse
como un lago dormido a la llegada del céfiro.
Una frágil apariencia revestía su cuerpo.
Trasparentaba su carne los truncos,
futuros designios,
adivinábase un empeño interrumpido
de trasformarse en lirios,
en miel de los higos,
en agua y en aire alado.

Marta y María contemplaban atónitas
el curso revelado de un misterio.
Un tenor ardiente y una alegría enloquecedora
corrían como fuego por sus venas.
Allí el hermano, y el devenir del hermano;
allí Lázaro vivo y el anuncio de sus lirios.
Tan sólo la muerte no estaba en parte alguna.

And when I die,
Close you my eyelids,
But let them slowly close,
That so my darkened eyes may bear your image
Beyond death's bourne!

LAZARUS

"Who calls me?" and Lazarus, issuing from the tomb,
Regarded Jesus and understood it all.
"Is it thou, O Sun, who shed'st this light?
And is it thou, or is this all a dream,
Mary, my sister, and Martha, sister mine?"

Slowly he spoke and vaguely, like a song
Arising from the waters.
His glances, not unmoved, went wandering
Over the burning landscape of Judea.
His voice was veiled and hollow
With the silence of death;
And his face, serene and pale, wrinkled to smile,
Like a sleeping lake when the zephyr breathes upon it.
A fragile-seeming form reclothed his body;
And through his flesh there showed
Designs for future days suspended,
One perceived a task frustrated
Of turning into lilies,
Into fig-tree honey,
Into water, and wingèd air.

Martha and Mary beheld astonished
A mystery revealed before their eyes.
A burning passion and a maddening joy
Coursed through their veins like fire.
The brother there, and the brother as he would be;
Lazarus alive, and the tokens of his immortality.
Only of death was nowhere any sign.

La muerte es un instante fugaz,
el vuelo de un segundo, el cambio de un estado.

—¡Lázaro, anda!—exclamó Cristo.
Lázaro pareció no oir, e inmóvil
en la puerta del sepulcro, dijo al Nazareno:
—Como tú me llamaste, me llamaban
las raices de las vides y de los olivos,
para resucitar en aceite y vino,
con igual imperio que el tuyo,
el agua me inducía a disgregarme
y a huir con ella.
Empecé a comprender con el morir
el sentido de la voz de las cosas,
y todas ellas no cesaron de llamar,
innúmeras vocecillas llenan los sepulcros;
—¡Lázaro, ven! ¡Lázaro, canta! ¡Lázaro,
sube por nosotras y en nuestro perfume vuela!—
exclamaban las silvestres flores de mi tierra.
¡Oh, poder de las voces veladas de la tumba!
Yo, solícito, en mitad de todas ellas,
como arena insegura que entre los dedos pasa,
me sentía escurrir. Era
un caer sin fondo,
blando como el sueño de un niño.

—¡Qué de secretos descubiertos
en el comienzo de mi transfiguración:
El dolor de mi sangre
camino de ser roca!
¡El triste revolar de los cabellos
alentando sobre mi frente como las hojas secas,
cuando el viento campesino se colaba
por las rendijas de la losa!
Las hormigas trepaban sobre mis piernas
como yo, de muchacho, por las suaves
colinas de Bethania; y mordían mi carne
como pican los mineros

Death is a fleeting instant,
A moment's flight, mere change of one's estate.

"Lazarus, come forth!" exclaimed the Christ.
But Lazarus seemed not to hear, and, motionless
At the gate of the tomb, addressed the Nazarene:
"As Thou hast called me, so also have called
The roots of the vines, and of the olive trees,
To live again in oil and wine;
And, with command imperious as Thine own,
The water urged me to dissolve
And flee with her.
And then with death I began to understand
The feeling in the voice of things;
And none of these have ceased to call;
Unnumbered little voices fill the tombs;
'Come, Lazarus; Lazarus, sing; Lazarus,
Arise with us, and through our perfume fly!'
Exclaimed the wild flowers of my native soil.
How powerful are those veiled sepulchral voices!
And, among them all, solicitous, I felt,
Like grains of sand that through the fingers slip,
My being ebb away. It was
A fathomless descent,
Soft as the sleep of a child.

"What secrets I discovered
As the great change began!
What anguish in my blood
On the way to becoming rock!
How sad the blowing of my hair
About my forehead, like the dry leaves,
When the wind from the fields blew in
Through the chinks of the sepulcher!
The ants crawled over my legs,
As I when a boy had climbed the gentle slopes
Of Bethany; and bit my flesh,
As the miners chip and pick

a las montañas de oro.
Cuando vivimos, es un dolor el dar;
cuando muertos, una gran alegría.
Es el único camino que nuevamente
conduce a la vida.
¡Mi carne se entregaba gozosa
a la santa labor de las hormigas!

—Jesús, tú que todo lo das,
y con placer, en vida;
tú que juntas con el vivir la única
alegría de la muerte ¿mueres o vives?
¿o quedas más allá de la muerte y de la vida?—

Y Lázaro lloró y dijo:—Yo lo sabía;
sí, yo lo sabía cuando durmiendo estaba;
pero toda mi conciencia de la tumba
rueda a lo más hondo del olvido.
¡Ay! para siempre he perdido
el saber que alcanzara en mi agonía.
Por eso lloro—...

Y como llorara
los ojos opacos de Lázaro adquirieron brillo;
quedamos con la luminosa y húmeda
mirada de los vivos.
Y Lázaro exclamó en medio de sus lágrimas:
—Si por la muerte gimo
como por un bien perdido,
por la vida que retorna, río.—

Y volvía la sangre a sus mejillas y a sus labios,
y el fuego del amor a su corazón.
Cayendo de hinojos bajo el plateado
follaje de los olivos, dijo
con una voz que parecía arañar los corazones:
—He pasado y pasamos por la vida
y por la existencia que se sigue a la muerte.

At the mountains of gold.
While still alive, we find it pain to give;
When dead, it is a joy supreme;
The only way that leads
To life again.
My flesh surrendered gladly then
To the sacred labor of the ants!

   "O Jesus, Thou who, living, giv'st,
And givest all, with joy;
Thou who with living dost combine
The happiness unique that death affords,
Liv'st Thou, or art Thou dead?
Or art Thou now past death and life alike?"

   And Lazarus wept and said: "I knew it;
Yes, I knew it as I lay asleep;
But all my knowledge of the tomb
Rolls back into oblivion's deepest night.
Alas! forever have I lost
The knowledge in my agony I gained.
For this I weep...."

         And, as he wept,
A gleam shot into his lackluster eyes,
And we could feel the moist and luminous look
Of a living man.
And Lazarus, looking through his tears, exclaimed:
"If for death I moan,
As for a boon I've lost,
For life returned I laugh."

   And to his cheeks and lips the blood returned,
And the fire of love to his heart.
Then, falling on his knees
Beneath the silvery olive-leaves, he said,
With a voice that seemed to wring our souls:
"We pass, as I have passed, through life,
And that existence which comes after death.

Y cuando rige el imperio de una de ellas,
se borra de la otra la memoria.
¡Gracias, muro inconmensurable del olvido,
atalaya de ambos mundos que en la muerte te elevas!
¡Oh recia muralla impenetrable
que nadie escala, si no renuncia
a su saber antiguo!
gracias, porque quien no recuerda
el embeleso de la muerte,
puede abrazar a la vida con placer.
¿Qué muerto no estuvo entre los vivos?
¿Qué vivo no fué entre los muertos?
Y así como nadie guarda memoria
de su estadía en el materno vientre,
nadie alcanzará jamás a recordar
cuando muerto, a la vida;
cuando vivo, a la muerte.

—Para mí se evapora la ciencia del no ser
como el rocío que cae por la noche
y que el sol bebe con avidez.
Ya ignoro los goces del sepulcro;
ya las cerradas colinas y las rojas
amapolas, y los ojos de María
me ciegan de amor.
Llueve a torrentes el olvido
sobre mi ser.

—Vuelvo como viajero que retorna
de islas remotas, cien veces más bellas
que los paternos lares.
Y porque regreso, vengo
sumido en un goce que mece más suave
que las ondas azules.
Vuelvo a mis duros terrones
con amor prodigioso que todo lo enaltece,
y veo que ellos se alzan más deseables
que las islas maravillosas del otro lado del mar.

When one of these holds sway,
The memory of the other is wiped out.
Thanks, wall immeasurable of forgetfulness,
Watchtower of both worlds that in death thou raisest!
Rampart impregnable,
Which none may scale, and still retain
His former knowledge!
Thanks; for only he who can no more recall
The ecstasy of death,
With pleasure can embrace this life.
What dead soul has not been among the living?
What living soul was not among the dead?
For, as no man the memory retains
Of life within his mother's womb,
So none will ever call to mind,
When dead, what thing was life;
Or, living, what was death.

"For me, the knowledge of the world of nonexistence
Fades as the dew that falls by night
And greedily is sucked up by the sun.
No more I know the raptures of the tomb;
Already the enclosing hills,
The poppies red, and Mary's eyes
Blind me with love.
Oblivion sweeps over me
Like torrential rain.

"I come like a voyager who returns
From distant isles, a hundred times more fair
Than the paternal home.
And, having so returned, I feel
Sunk in a joy more lulling to the sense
Than the azure waves.
I return to my hard-baked fields
With love o'erflowing, which exalts them all,
And see them more to be desired
Than wondrous islands far beyond the sea.

—¡Cuánto a la vida vivifica el olvido!
Envuelto en su manto clemente,
siento que todo es posible para mí.
¡Brota otra vez límpida y hermosa
una esperanza interminable!—

Entre las yerbas, Marta y María yacían agotadas;
estremecidos los Apóstoles, veían llorar a los judíos,
pero sólo el Nazareno comprendía
la voz de Lázaro....

—¡Muerte dulce, vida intensa, esposas mías!
Por vosotras dos se ha estremecido mi corazón;
pero al volver a tu lado,
¡Oh vida en juventud perenne,
arribo como llegaría el viudo
a quien le fuese dable gozar otra vez
de las ardientes caricias
de su primer amor desvanecido!—

"How much oblivion revives my life!
With its mild mantle clad,
I feel all things are possible for me.
Again there springs up pure and beautiful
A hope that ne'er shall end."

    Exhausted, on the grass, Martha and Mary lay;
The apostles, trembling, saw the Jews in tears;
But only the Nazarene could comprehend
The words of Lazarus....

"O Life intense, sweet death—both, consorts mine!
For both my heart has quivered with desire;
But, returning to thy side, O Life,
In youth perennial,
I come as might the widower
To whom 'twas granted to enjoy once more
The warm embrace
Of his first love departed!"

NADA

Era un pobre diablo que siempre venía
cerca de un gran pueblo donde yo vivía;
joven, rubio y flaco, sucio y mal vestido,
siempre cabizbajo.... ¡Tal vez un perdido!
Un día de invierno lo encontraron muerto
dentro de un arroyo próximo a mi huerto,
varios cazadores que con sus lebreles
cantando marchaban.... Entre sus papeles
no encontraron nada.... Los jueces de turno
hicieron preguntas al guardián nocturno:
éste no sabía nada del extinto;
ni el vecino Pérez, ni el vecino Pinto.
Una chica dijo que sería un loco
o algún vagabundo que comía poco,
y un chusco que oía las conversaciones
se tentó de risa.... ¡Vaya unos simplones!
Una paletada le echó el panteonero;
luego lió un cigarro, se caló el sombrero
y emprendió la vuelta.... ¡Tras la paletada,
nadie dijo nada, nadie dijo nada! ...

NOTHING

He was a luckless devil who used to come
Around the big town where I had my home;
Young, reddish, weakly, dirty and ill clad,
Forever shamefaced.... Another gone to the bad!
One winter day some hunters found him dead
In a little creek that near my garden led,
As, singing, with their hounds they tramped along....
The papers that he had they searched among,
But nothing found.... The local judges made
Inquiry of the night watchman, but he said
That he knew not a thing of the deceased;
And Pérez and Pinto, neighbors, not the least.
A young girl said he might have been insane,
Some wandering wastrel seeking food in vain;
A man who heard their chatter saw a joke
And tried to laugh.... Well, they were simple folk!
Over the dead man's corpse the sexton let
A few clods fall; then rolled a cigarette,
Pulled down his broad-brimmed hat, and went his way....
After the clods, no one had aught to say!...

TARDE EN EL HOSPITAL

    Sobre el campo el agua mustia
cae fina, grácil, leve;
con el agua cae angustia;
        llueve....

    Y pues solo en amplia pieza,
yazgo en cama, yazgo enfermo,
para espantar la tristeza,
        duermo.

    Pero el agua ha lloriqueado
junto a mí, cansada, leve;
despierto sobresaltado;
        llueve....

    Entonces, muerto de angustia,
ante el panorama inmenso,
mientras cae el agua mustia,
        pienso.

AFTERNOON IN THE HOSPITAL

A light and drizzling rain descends
And softly falls upon the plains;
And with it comes the pang that rends;
    It rains....

And, since alone in the spacious room
Sick and in bed I vigil keep,
To daunt the fears that round me loom
    I sleep.

But near me still the steady shower
Its light but weary drip maintains;
I waken up; for fright I cower;
    It rains....

Then, dead with terror that appals,
Before the vast expanse I shrink,
And, while the weary water falls,
    I think.

BALADA DEL VIOLÍN

Aquel mozo enfermo y flaco
tocaba el violín al sol
por un sorbo de alcohol
o un puñado de tabaco.

¡Y buen dar! cuando tocaba
algún rondel español
o alguna sonata eslava....

Aquel mozo enfermo y flaco
salía a buscar el sol
y a llenar su viejo saco,
por un sorbo de alcohol
o un puñado de tabaco.

Salía a matar su esplín
cuando tocaba el violín,
cuando como un caracol
salía a buscar el sol.

Aquel mozo enfermo y flaco
murió tocando el violín,
¿Qué queréis? Halló su fin
en un sorbo de alcohol
y un puñado de tabaco.

Le hallaron tendido al sol
y abrazado a su violín....

THE VIOLIN

That fellow, weak and dropping for lack o'
A meal, played his old violin
In the sun for a taste of gin
    Or a fill of tobacco.

And well for him when he played
    Some Spanish roundel
    Or Slav sonata....

That fellow, ailing and slack,
Would go out and bask in the sun
And fill his time-worn sack,
For the gin he never could shun
    Or a fill of tobacco.

When he played his violin,
'Twas to ease his deep chagrin,
When like a snail he won
His chance to bask in the sun.

That fellow, weak for lack o'
A meal, died playing his violin.
What would you have? Did he not win
His end in a taste of gin
    And a fill of tobacco?

Stretched out in the sun they found him,
    Embracing his violin....

BALBUCEO

Triste está la casa nuestra,
triste, desde que te has ido.
Todavía queda un poco
de tu calor en el nido.

Yo también estoy un poco
triste desde que te has ido;
pero sé que alguna tarde
llegarás de nuevo al nido.

¡Si supieras cuánto, cuánto
la casa y yo te queremos!
Algún día cuando vuelvas
verás cuánto te queremos.

Nunca podría decirte
todo lo que te queremos:
es como un montón de estrellas
todo lo que te queremos.

Si tú no volvieras nunca,
más vale que yo me muera...;
pero siento que no quieres,
no quieres que yo me muera.

Bien querida que te fuiste,
¿no es cierto que volverás?
para que no estemos tristes
¿no es cierto que volverás?

FALTERING UTTERANCE

Sad, sad this home of ours
Since thou hast gone away.
Yet in the nest some warmth
Of thine still seems to stay.

I too am somewhat sad
Since thou hast gone away;
Yet to the nest, I know,
Thou wilt return some day.

Could'st thou but know how much
This home and I do love thee!
Some day when thou return'st
Thou'lt know how much we love thee.

I ne'er can hope to tell
All our love for thee:
Like stars all heaped on stars,
Our sum of love for thee.

If thou should'st ne'er return,
'Twere better I should die...;
But yet I feel thou would'st not,
Thou would'st not I should die.

My well-beloved, departed,
Wilt thou indeed return?
Lest we should dwell in sadness,
Wilt thou not sure return?

LA ESTATUA

I

¡Oh, mujer de los brazos extendidos
y los de mármol ojos tan serenos,
he arrimado mis sienes a tus senos
como una rama en flor sobre dos nidos!

¡Oh, el sentimiento grave que me llena
al no escuchar latir tu carne fría
y saber que la piedra te condena
a no tener latido en ningún día!

¡Oh, diamante arrancado a la cantera,
tu forma llena está de Primavera,
y no tienes olor, ni luz, ni trino!

Tú que nunca podrás cerrar la mano,
tienes, en gesto de cariño humano,
la única mano abierta en mi camino.

II

No te enciende el pudor rosas rosadas,
ni el suceder del Tiempo te da injuria,
ni levanta tus vestes consagradas
a la mano temblante de lujuria.

A tus pies se dan muerte las pasiones,
las euménides doman sus cabellos
y se asustan malsines y felones
al gesto inmóvil de tus brazos bellos.

Luz del día no cierra tus pupilas,
viento no mueve el haz de tus guedejas,
ruido no queda preso en tus oídos.

Pues eres, ¡oh, mujer de aras tranquilas!,
un vetusto ideal de edades viejas
transmitido a los tiempos no venidos.

THE STATUE

I

O woman with those arms so wide extended,
And with those eyes of marble so serene,
My forehead when upon thy breasts I lean
Is a bough in bloom over two nests suspended!

How troubled is the thought that fills my mind
To hear no heartbeat in thy flesh so cold,
And know that thou art, being stone, destined
No throb of life at any time to hold.

Thou art a diamond from the quarry brought,
And with the Spring thy form is fully fraught;
Thou hast no perfume, light, or bird-like lay.

Thou never wilt have power to close thy hand,
But hast, in sign of humankindness bland,
The only open hand that greets my way.

II

No shame shall blush in crimson on thy cheek,
Nor lapse of time have power to do thee hurt,
Or let a hand with lust atremble seek
To raise the sacred garment round thee girt.

The passions at thy feet yield them for dead,
The furies quell their snaky locks' alarms,
Felons and scandalmongers see with dread
The unmoving gesture of thy beauteous arms.

No light of day can make thee close thine eyes,
Nor wind e'er move the tresses of thy hair,
Nor sound, a prisoner in thine ear succumb;

For thou who dost o'er quiet altars rise
Art from past ages an ideal fair
Transmitted to the ages still to come.

III

Mujer, que eres mujer porque eres bella
y porque me haces ir el pensamiento
por senda muda de recogimiento
al símbolo, a la estrofa y a la estrella,

nunca mujer serás: tu carne vana
jamás palpitará de amor herida,
nunca sonreirás una mañana
ni serás una tarde entristecida.

Y sin embargo soy de ti cegado,
y sin embargo soy de ti turbado,
y al propio tiempo bueno y serenado,

y quisiera partir mi pan contigo
y pasear de tu mano en huerto amigo
en busca de esa paz que no consigo....

IV

Arrimadas mis sienes a tus senos
siento que me penetra alevemente
frío de nieve y humedad de cienos...
¡Siempre materia y siempre indiferente!

Quién tuviera, ¡oh mujer que no suspira!
esa inmovilidad ante la suerte,
esa serenidad para la ira,
en la vida, esa mano de la Muerte.

Mi espíritu jamás podrá animarte,
ni turbar un instante solamente
el gesto grande que te ha dado el arte.

¡Quién pudiera esperar la muerte tarda,
sereno cual la piedra indiferente,
callado como el Ángel de la Guarda!...

III

Woman, for so thou art, since thou art fair,
And mak'st my meditations range afar
In silent pathways of retirement, there
To find the symbol deep, the verse, the star;

Woman thou ne'er shalt be; for thy vain flesh
Shall never quiver wounded by love's dart,
Nor shalt thou smile upon the morning fresh,
Nor meet the evening with a saddened heart.

And yet, when in thy presence, I am blind,
And yet by thee I am disturbed in mind,
And, when time fits, serene at heart and kind;

And I with thee my bread would gladly share,
And, holding thy hand, through friendly garden fare,
Seeking that peace I yearn for in despair....

IV

When on thy breast I let my temples lean,
I feel snow's chill, and ashy dampness sent
Right through my members like to traitors mean...
Dead matter ever, and indifferent!

O woman who ne'er sighest, would that I
Might have such unconcern to meet my fate,
In face of danger such serenity,
This hand of Death, while life still holds her state!

My spirit ne'er to thee can life impart,
Nor for a moment even disturb the calm
And noble gesture given to thee by art.

Would that death's slow approach I might regard
Serene as is this stone without a qualm,
And silent as the Guardian Angel's ward!

ESPÍRITU GENTIL...

Espíritu gentil que de Valclusa
las selvas de laurel paseaste tanto,
razonando de amores con la musa
que alargaba el honor de tu quebranto:

como a ti me ha dejado una confusa
esperanza materia para el llanto,
mas no me dió el ingenio asaz excusa
para hacerla materia de mi canto.

Maestro soy en el amar doliente,
aunque no en la elegancia del estilo
ni en la ilustre nobleza del dictado;

pero viendo el laurel que honra tu frente,
pienso, grave y tranquilo,
que un sentimiento igual nos ha acercado.

THOU GENTLE SPIRIT...*

    Thou gentle spirit, who so oft didst stray
Among the laurel thickets of Vaucluse,
Holding in amorous colloquy the muse
That found thee honor in thy heart's dismay;

    For me, as even for thee, a false display
Of hope has left matter for tears profuse,
But has not given my mind valid excuse
To make of it the subject of my lay.

    In anguished love I am a master now,
Though not, like thee, in elegance of style,
Nor in thy verse with lofty grandeur wrought;

    But when I see thy laurel-crownèd brow,
In grave tranquillity I think the while
By kindred feelings we are closer brought.

---

* Petrarch.

CUATRO CAMINOS

Cuatro caminos frente a mi ventana.
Me llamaron de todos los caminos,
y al llamado en la noche soberana
acudieron mis sueños peregrinos.

Por ir a todas partes a ninguna
pudo llegar mi corazón vencido,
eterno enamorado de la luna
de lo que ha muerto o de lo que se ha ido.

Cuatro caminos para la quimera,
bajo las flores y bajo los trinos...
¡Oh, si mi pobre corazón pudiera
ser un aroma en todos los caminos!

LEJANA

I

Noche de lluvia. Perfume
triste de tierra mojada.
Mi corazón pensativo
se envolvía en tu fragancia.
  Bajo la sombra la inmensa
comprensión de tu mirada
que en mis ensueños caía
como una música mansa.
  Noche de lluvia. Tu voz
se unía a la voz del agua:
canción de cuna amorosa
para mi antigua nostalgia.
—Buenas noches.—¡Que piadosa
ternura desconsolada
me dieron al despedirme
tus manecitas heladas!

THE FOUR ROADS

Before my window four roads meet.
They called from east, west, south, and north,
And into the royal night to greet
The call my vagrant dreams rushed forth.

Yearning by every path to move,
My baffled heart could follow none,
Forever with the moon in love,
With what is dead or what is gone.

Four tempting roads for phantasy,
Beneath the flowers and warbled odes...
Oh, would that my poor heart might be
Perfume diffused o'er all those roads!

DISTANT

I

A night of rain. A perfume sad
Exhales from the moistened ground.
My pensive heart, with fragrance come
From thee, was wrapped around.
   Beneath the shade, thy glance so full
Of understanding deep,
That used to fall like music soft
Upon my dreams in sleep.
   A rainy night. With the voice of the rain
Thy voice conjoined would come,
A loving cradle-song to soothe
Old yearnings for my home.
   "Good night." What tenderness, so full
Of pity and of grief untold,
Thy hands gave me, as we took leave,
Thy little hands, ice-cold!

II

En el sueño de la tarde
muere el cantar melancólico.
Tus manos en el teclado
despiertan un sueño de oro.
   Yo pienso:—Tus labios nunca
serán míos,—y en el fondo
sereno de mi tristeza
pasa un vuelo de abandono.
   El viento oscuro dispersa
las hojas. Vierte el Otoño
sobre los campos dormidos
su silencio milagroso.

III

   Tarde en el campo. Una voz
se aleja por los caminos.
Sale de los pozos muertos
un silencio pensativo.
   Junto a nosotros el agua
dice un secreto. Es un hilo
de agua que lleva en el fondo
reflejado el infinito
   Los sapos cantan. Prolonga
sus letanías un grillo.
¡Quién te besara las manos
que, moviendo el oro tibio
de los ramajes, despiertan
los vuelos enloquecidos!

II

Amid the dreaminess of even
The doleful song expires.
Thy touch upon the ivory keys
A dream of gold inspires.
 I ponder: "Thy lips never shall
Be mine," and o'er the deeps
Serene of sadness in my soul
Careless abandon sweeps.
 The wind obscure scatters the leaves,
And over the sleeping fields
Autumn sheds its silence deep
That spell of wonder wields.

III

An evening countryside. A voice
On the highway fades away.
From lifeless pools a silence deep
And pensive seems to stray.
 Near where we stand, the water tells
A secret. 'Tis a thread,
A river, with the infinite
Reflected in its bed.
 The toads sing, and a cricket still
His litany prolongs.
If only one could kiss thy hands
That, moving the warm, red gold
Of the branches, waken up the flights
Of the wild birds they hold!

IV

Jazmines del Cabo. Noche
de meditaciones grises.
Fragancia pura y doliente
de jazmines imposibles.
Tus pensamientos de nieve
perfuman todo lo triste.
Jazmines del Cabo. Noche
de meditaciones grises.
Me está diciendo el aroma
lo que nunca me dijiste.

V

Oh! si alguna vez hubiera
confesado mi ternura,
hacia tus senos de nieve
y hacia tus manos de luna...
Quería mi corazón
ser como la fuente oscura,
que adelgaza los rumores
cuando sabe que la escuchas.
Y era su felicidad
mirar de cerca la tuya,
envolverte en sus palabras
como la vertiente obscura
y adormecer tus quimeras
en un cabezal de música.

IV

    Cape jasmines. Night is all suffused
With meditations gray.
About me, pure and sad the scents
Of impossible jasmines play.
    Thy snow-white thoughts, like perfume, charm
My sadness all away.
Cape jasmines. And the night is filled
With meditations gray.
The perfume still is telling me
What thou didst never say.

V

    If now and then I could have told
My love, and let thee know
How I adored thy moon-white hands,
Thy bosom like the snow...
    But still my heart desired to be
Like the fountain deep in shade,
Which, when it knew that thou didst hear,
Its murmur softer made.
    And its supreme felicity
Was but to look on thine,
As with a dark cascade of words
Thy spirit to entwine,
And on a tuneful pillow let
Thy phantasies recline.

VI

Alta mar. Viento bravío
que extiende sus resonancias
y sus voces de tragedia
sobre las olas opacas.
　Viajeros desconocidos,
desconocidas palabras;
luces ambiguas. Canciones
de leyendas ignoradas,
canciones jamás oídas
y que no me acompañaban.
　En mi recuerdo perfuman
tus manos. A la distancia
navegan mudas y lentas
embarcaciones fantasmas.

VII

　Pueblos románticos. Sitios
que no miraron mis juegos
de niño. Callejas donde
jamás florece un recuerdo.
　Teatros exóticos. Danzas
de dioses y de mancebos
orientales. Pecadora
música de encantamiento.
Barrios sombríos. Escalas
misteriosas. Fumaderos
de opio que alargan su aroma
de pesadumbre y de ensueño.
　Labios fríos que me daban
los besos que no me dieron
tus labios. Entristecidos
y nostálgicos paseos
a las orillas del mar
o en el mudo cementerio.

VI

    Far out at sea. A blustering wind,
That far resounding raves,
And sends its voice of tragedy
Over the dull, black waves.
    My fellow-passengers unknown,
Their language strange to me;
Deceptive lights. Strange legends sung
To uncouth melody,
Songs I had never heard before,
For me no company.
    The perfume of thy hands still haunts
My memory. Over the tips
Of the waves afar, glide silently
And slowly, phantom ships.

VII

    Cities romantic. Spots that never
My childhood's games beheld,
And little lanes where memory
To flowering never swelled.
    Exotic theaters, and dances
Of Eastern gods and boys.
Voluptuous music that enchants
The ear with unholy joys.
Districts of gloom. Mysterious
Dark stairways. Dismal rooms
Where opium breathes out 'mid dreams
And pain its drowsy fumes.
    Cold lips that gave to me the kiss
That your lips never gave;
And saddened walks, with heart homesick,
Where by the shore the waves
Come dashing in, or in the cemetery
Beside the silent graves.

¡Como he pensado en la muerte!
Morir lejos, morir lejos
de los campos que reciban
la limosna de tus huesos....

VIII

El barco navega cerca
de la costa. Un rumoroso
viento mueve los ramajes
meditabundos y torvos.
Es en la tarde. Una vaga
tarde que enciende fastuosos
rumores en la infinita
calma de los mares solos.
Un cuervo. Un cuervo. En el mástil
se ha detenido. El medroso
vuelo de la noche avanza.
Un cuervo va con nosotros....

IX

Hiere una barca el silencio
melancólico del río.
Quién ha dejado en mis manos
la lumbre de estos anillos?
Ópalos brujos y azules
fantásticos y malignos,
que desde su broche de oro
me están mirando lo mismo
que dos pupilas hieráticas.
Muere la tarde en el río....
En la lejanía inmensa
se prolongan los caminos
por donde nunca anduvieron
mis esperanzas de niño....

How I have pondered over death!
To die—and dying leave
Far, far away, the fields that may
The alms of thy bones receive....

VIII

The vessel now is sailing near
The coast. A murmuring wind
Is stirring in the cordage stern
Its meditative mind.
  'Tis evening, and in the evening vague
Rich murmuring sounds are born,
That kindle in the infinite
Calm of the seas forlorn.
  A crow. A crow. Upon the mast
It has stayed its flight. And low
The night with dreadful wing descends.
And with us goes a crow....

IX

A vessel breaks upon the somber
Silence of the stream.
  These rings? Who is it that has left
In my hands their magic gleam?
  Opals they seem, bewitched and blue,
Fantastic and malign,
Which like two eyes hieratic gaze,
From their setting of gold, on mine.
Now evening in the river dies....
  Far off, long roads extend,
On which my wildest hopes in days
Of boyhood ne'er did wend....

X

Una muchacha me dice
palabras de amor y celos.
Me ha conmovido su clara
ternura para mis sueños.
Su risa me ha recordado
tu fresca risa y he vuelto
a sufrir lo que sufría....
Ella se queda en silencio.
Se entristece al comprender
que vive mi sufrimiento
a pesar de su ternura
y a pesar de su consuelo.

XI

¿Me esperan tus manos blancas
en la paz de tus jardines?
Mujer de ensueño y de luna,
tristemente me sonríes
en el recuerdo. Te alejas
y mis dolores te siguen.
—Ha muerto.—La lluvia lenta
y el invierno me lo dicen.
Llega una voz en las noches,
lejana, débil y triste,
y mi espíritu se aroma
de ternura y de imposible
y me envuelve la profunda
fragancia de tus jazmines....

X

   A simple maiden speaks to me
Words of love and devotion.
Her bright-eyed sympathy with my dreams
Stirs in me deep emotion.
   Her laughter has brought back to me
Thy cheerful laugh, and the pains
I used to suffer, hurt again....
In silence she remains.
   And she turns sad when she perceives
That still my anguish lives,
Despite her tenderness and all
The comfort that she gives.

XI

   Do thy white hands, amid the peace
Of thy gardens, wait for me?
   O woman of my moonlight dreams,
In memory I see
Thee sadly smile. Thou vanishest,
And my griefs follow thee.
The rain, slow-falling, and the winter
Say to me, "Dead is she."
   By night a voice comes, distant, weak,
And sad; and my soul with old,
Impossible things is as with fragrance filled;
And the perfumes of thy jessamines
My weary heart enfold....

LA MAESTRA RURAL

La Maestra era pura.—Los suaves hortelanos
—decía—de este predio, que es predio de Jesús,
han de conservar puros los ojos y las manos,
guardar claros sus óleos, para dar clara luz.—

La Maestra era pobre. Su reino no es humano
(Así en el doloroso sembrador de Israel).
Vestía sayas pardas, no enjoyaba su mano
¡y era todo su espíritu un inmenso joyel!

La Maestra era alegre. ¡Pobre mujer herida!
Su sonrisa fué un modo de llorar con bondad.
Por sobre la sandalia rota y enrojecida,
tal sonrisa, la insigne flor de su santidad.

¡Dulce ser! En su río de mieles, caudaloso,
largamente abrevaba sus tigres el dolor!
Los hierros que le abrieron el pecho generoso
¡más anchas le dejaron las cuencas del amor!

¡Oh, labriego, cuyo hijo de su labio aprendía
el himno y la plegaria, nunca viste el fulgor
del lucero cautivo que en sus carnes ardía:
pasaste sin besar su corazón en flor!

Campesina, ¿recuerdas que alguna vez prendiste
su nombre a un comentario brutal o baladí?
Cien veces la miraste, ninguna vez la viste
¡y en el solar de tu hijo, de ella hay más que de ti!

Pasó por él su fina, su delicada esteva,
abriendo surcos donde alojar perfección.
La albada de virtudes de que lento se nieva
es suya. Campesina, ¿no le pides perdón?

(*Lucila Godoy Alcayaga)

THE RURAL TEACHER

The Teacher was pure. "The kindly gardeners," she said,
"Who till this soil, the garden of our Lord,
Must have pure eyes, unstainèd hands, and ever
Keep clear their oil, a clear light to afford."

The Teacher was poor; her kingdom not of men
(As His, who sadly sowed o'er Israel's field).
Her garments dull in hue, her hands unjeweled;
But her soul one great and glowing gem revealed.

The Teacher was glad of heart. Poor wounded woman!
Her smile was token of a grief benign.
Over the sandal torn and bloodstained shone
That smile, of saintliness the blossom fine.

Sweet soul! In her abounding honeyed current
Grief long was wont to quench its tiger's thirst.
The sword that pierced her generous breast but left
More wide the gates through which affection burst.

O laborer, you, whose son from her lips learned
Both hymn and prayer, you never saw the gleam
Of the captive star that in her body burned;
You passed, nor worth a kiss her heart did deem!

And, peasant woman, you recall how oft
From her name some coarse or brutal jest you drew;
You've seen her a hundred times, yet never known her:
In your son's face there's more of her than of you!

O'er him her delicate, fine plowshare passed,
Opening a furrow where seed of truth might rest;
The snow-white dawn of virtue slowly rising
Is hers. From her pardon to beg were best!

Daba sombra por una selva su encina hendida
el día en que la muerte la convidó a partir.
Pensando en que su madre la esperaba dormida,
a La de Ojos Profundos se dió sin resistir.

Y en su Dios se ha dormido, como en cojín de luna;
almohada de sus sienes, una constelación;
canta el Padre para ella sus canciones de cuna
¡y la paz llueve largo sobre su corazón!

Como un henchido vaso, traía el alma hecha
para volcar aljófares sobre la humanidad;
y era su vida humana la dilatada brecha
que suele abrirse el Padre para echar claridad.

Por eso aún el polvo de sus huesos sustenta
púrpura de rosales de violento llamear,
¡Y el cuidador de tumbas, cómo aroma, me cuenta,
las plantas del que huella sus huesos, al pasar!

ÍNTIMA

Tú no oprimas mis manos.
Llegará el duradero
tiempo de reposar con mucho polvo
y sombra en los entretejidos dedos.

Y dirías:—No puedo
amarla, porque ya se desgranaron,
como mieses, sus dedos.—

Tú no beses mi boca.
Vendrá el instante lleno
de luz menguada, en que estaré sin labios
sobre un mojado suelo.

Her crannied oak gave shadow like a forest
That day when death constrained her to depart;
Thinking her mother waited while she slept,
To the Deep-eyed Virgin she resigned her heart.

In God she sleeps, light of the moon her pillow,
A constellation, cushion for her brow;
The Father sings His cradle songs for her;
As copious rain, peace falls on her heart now.

Her soul was made as an o'erflowing vase
To scatter pearls before our human sight;
And her life on earth was but the widened breach
That the Father makes to shed His own clear light.

Hence even the dust to which her frame has come
Sustains red roses of a violent flame,
And the sexton tells how the feet of those, who passing
Tread on her bones, are perfumed with the same.

INTIMATE

Press not my hands.
For there will come a time
Of lasting rest, of darkness
And of dust, upon these fingers
Intertwined.

And thou might'st say: "No longer
Can I love her, for like grains
From the ripened ear her fingers
Fall apart."

Kiss not my mouth.
A moment needs must come,
With feeble light suffused,
When I on the dank earth
Lifeless shall lie.

Y dirías:—La amé, pero no puedo
amarla más, ahora que no aspira
el olor de retamas de mi beso.—

Y me angustiara oyendote,
y hablaras loco y ciego,
que mi mano sobre tu frente
cuando rompan mis dedos,
y bajará sobre tu cara llena
de ansia mi aliento.

No me toques, por tanto. Mentiría
al decir que te entrego
mi amor en estos brazos extendidos,
en mi boca, en mi cuello,
y tú, al creer que lo bebiste todo
te engañarías como un niño ciego.

Porque mi amor no es sólo esta gavilla
reacia y fatigada de mi cuerpo,
que tiembla entera al roce del cilicio
y que se me rezaga en todo vuelo.

Es lo que está en el beso, y no es el labio;
lo que rompe la voz, y no es el pecho;
¡es un viento de Dios, que pasa hendiéndome
el gajo de las carnes, volandero!

And thou might'st say: "I loved her,
But love her more I cannot,
Now that she breathes no more
My kiss broom-scented."

And, hearing thee, I'd suffer pain;
And madly, blindly thou would'st talk,
For on thy brow my hand shall rest
When my fingers loose their bonds,
And on thy anguished face
My breath shall fall.

And therefore, touch me not,
For I should lie were I to say
I yield my love in these extended arms,
This mouth and neck,
And thou, believing thou hadst all,
Would'st still deceive thyself
Like a child that's blind.

Because my love is not alone this body,
This corn-sheaf, stiff and wearied out,
Which shudders as the cilice chafes
And lags behind whenever I would soar.

'Tis not the lips, yet it is in the kiss;
And not the breast, yet trembles in the voice;
It is a wind from God, which passing cleaves
The tissues of my flesh.

BALADA

Él pasó con otra;
yo lo ví pasar.
Siempre dulce el viento
y el camino en paz.
¡Y estos ojos míseros
le vieron pasar!

Él va amando a otra
por la tierra en flor.
Ha abierto el espino;
pasa una canción.
¡Y él va amando a otra
por la tierra en flor!

Él besó a la otra
a orillas del mar;
resbaló en las olas
la luna de azahar.
¡Y no untó mi sangre
la extensión del mar!

Él irá con otra
por la eternidad.
Habrá cielos dulces.
(Dios quiere callar)
¡Y él irá con otra
por la eternidad!

SONG

He passed with another;
I saw him go by.
Sweet as ever the wind,
The path lies in peace.
And these eyes of mine, wretched,
They saw him go by!

He goes loving another
O'er the country in bloom.
The hawthorn is flowering,
A song fills the air.
And he goes loving another
O'er the country in bloom!

He has kissed this other
By the shores of the sea;
With the bloom of the orange
The moon tips the waves...
And no salve for my wound
In the width of the sea!

He will go with another
For ever and ever.
Sweet skies will shine again.
(God wills to be silent)
And he will go with another
For ever and ever!

EL RUEGO

Señor, tú sabes cómo, con encendido brío,
por los seres extraños mi palabra te invoca.
Vengo ahora a pedirte por uno que era mío,
mi vaso de frescura, el panal de mi boca,

cal de mis huesos, dulce, razón de la jornada,
gorjeo de mi oído, ceñidor de mi veste.
Me cuido hasta de aquellos en que no puse nada;
¡no tengas ojo torvo si te pido por éste!

Te digo que era bueno, te digo que tenía
el corazón entero a flor de pecho, que era
suave de índole, franco como la luz del día,
henchido de milagro como la primavera.

Me replicas, severo, que es de plegaria indigno
el que no untó de preces sus dos labios febriles,
y se fué aquella tarde sin esperar tu signo,
trizándose las sienes como vasos sutiles.

Pero yo, mi Señor, te arguyo que he tocado,
de la misma manera que el nardo de su frente,
todo su corazón dulce y tormentado
¡y tenía la seda del capullo naciente!

¿Qué fué cruel? Olvidas, Señor, que le quería,
y que él sabía suya la entraña que llagaba.
¿Qué enturbió para siempre mis linfas de alegría?
¡No importa! Tú comprende: ¡yo le amaba, le amaba!

Y amar (bien sabes de eso) es amargo ejercicio;
un mantener los párpados de lágrimas mojados,
un refrescar de besos las trenzas del cilicio
conservando, bajo ellas, los ojos extasiados.

THE PRAYER

Thou knowest, Lord, how with impassioned zeal
I lift my voice to Thee for souls unknown.
I pray Thee now for one who was mine own,
My cup of refreshing, honey for my mouth,
Strength of my bones, sweet end of each day's toil,
A warbling in mine ear, a girdle for my cloak.
I cherish even those who are naught to me;
Let not Thine eye look cold if I pray for him!

I tell Thee he was good, tell Thee he had
A heart o'erflowing, that by nature he
Was kindly, frank as the light of day, and like
The flower of spring, a miracle full blown.
Dost Thou, austere, reply: "Unworthy he
Of prayers, whose fever'd lips no prayer graced,
And who, without Thy call, that night rushed off,
His temples like frail vases shattering?"
But Lord, I do protest that just as I
Have touched the spikenard of his brow, so too
All his sweet, tortured heart I've felt, and found
It soft and silken as the opening bud.

Cruel, Thou say'st? But, Lord, Thou dost forget
That I loved him, that well he knew 'twas his
The heart that gave the wound. What was it, then,
That made the fountains of my joy forever
Turbid? It matters not! Thou understand'st:
For I loved him; yes, loved him; and to love,
(Thou know'st this well) is bitter exercise:
To have the eyelids ever moist with tears,
To kiss fresh life into the hair shirt's web,
Maintaining still the eyes of ecstasy.

El hierro que taladra tiene un gustoso frío,
cuando abre, cual gavillas, las carnes amorosas.
Y la cruz (Tú te acuerdas ¡oh Rey de los judíos!)
se lleva con blandura, como un gajo de rosas.

Aquí me estoy, Señor, con la cara caída
sobre el polvo, parlándote un crepúsculo entero,
o todos los crepúsculos a que alcance la vida,
si tardas en decirme la palabra que espero.

Fatigaré tu oído de preces y sollozos,
lamiendo, lebrel tímido, los bordes de tu manto,
y ni pueden huírme tus ojos amorosos
ni esquivar tu pie el riego caliente de mi llanto.

¡Dí el perdón, dilo al fin! Va a esparcir en el viento
la palabra el perfume de cien pomos de olores
al vaciarse; toda agua será deslumbramiento;
el yermo echará flor y el guijarro esplendores.

Se mojarán los ojos oscuros de las fieras,
y, comprendiendo, el monte que de piedra forjaste
llorará por los párpados blancos de sus neveras:
¡toda la tierra tuya sabrá que perdonaste!

There's pleasure ev'n in the chill of piercing steel,
That tears apart like sheaves the loving flesh;
And (Thou rememb'rest, O Thou King of the Jews!)
The cross may be, like roses, sweetly borne.

   And here am I, O Lord, with head bowed down
In the dust, pleading with Thee as falls the night,
Licking, like timid hound, Thy mantle's fringe,
Nor can Thy loving eyes put me to flight,
Nor Thy feet avoid my scalding flood of tears.

   Speak pardon, Lord, at length, and the world shall waft
On the wind the scent of a hundred fragrant jars
New emptied; every stream shall dazzling run,
The waste show flowers, the rocks be bright with gems;
Pity shall dim the eyes of savage beasts,
And, understanding, the mount Thou mad'st of stone
Shall melt in tears from eyelids white with snow:
That Thou hast pardoned, all Thy world shall know!

CAMPANITA NOCTURNA

Campanita nocturna
de mis pesares,
ya se ha llevado el viento
los azahares.

No cantes, campanita,
tu melodía,
que el corazón se muere
de lejanía.
¡Las flores del naranjo
bajo la nieve!
Sus senos pequeñitos,
flores de muerte.

No toques, campanita,
tu melodía,
que ya se la ha tragado
la tierra fría.

CUANDO ME MUERA...

Cuando me muera
plantad sobre mi cuerpo
un laurel o una higuera.
Por el laurel
sabré dar a los hombres
sombra, trinos y miel.
Por la higuera,
frutos dulces
para cualesquiera.
No queméis mi cuerpo,
dejadlo alegremente
en claro huerto.
No me habéis de remachar

BELLS BY NIGHT

O little bell that toll'st by night
My weary hours,
The wind has swept away
The orange flowers.

Sing not, O little bell,
Thy melody,
For, far from her, my heart
Must surely die.
The orange blossoms lie
The snow beneath;
Her tiny little breasts
Are flowers of death.

Ring not, O little bell,
Thy melody,
Now that cold earth has taken
My love from me.

WHEN I AM DEAD...

When I am dead,
A laurel or a fig tree plant
Over my head.
For with the laurel then
Cool shade, and songs, and honey
I shall provide for men;
And with the tall fig tree
Delicious fruits
For all, whoe'er they be.
My body do not burn,
But joyfully, in a garden fair,
My dust to earth return.
Nor must you seek to keep me fast

bajo hierro y piedra:
yo quiero dar, dar, dar.
Dadme al placer
de ser gajo húmedo
al amanecer.
Daré a mis amigos
frescor, trinos e higos.

VERSOS DE PROFECÍA

Señor Jesucristo, por mi siglo veinte,
por bueno y por malo, por toda la gente,
déjame decirte la súplica ardiente.
Porque el tigre rompa carnicero diente,
porque un cataclismo corra de repente
sobre el mundo malo de oriente a poniente.
Señor Jesucristo, que resucitaste
al tercero día que el mundo dejaste,
mira que mi siglo tu amor no malgaste.
Mira que desnudas y desmelenadas
como una manada de yeguas caldeadas
andan las pasiones ya desatentadas.
Te niegan los chulos y los comerciantes,
ya no se protegen de ti los amantes,
por negras faunalias los negros turbantes
de tus cardenales modernos y bravos
van pasando en manos de inmundos esclavos
de pueblos latinos y pueblos eslavos.
Señor Jesucristo, tu aliento de cumbre,
tu palabra lenta, tus ojos de lumbre,
derritan la costra de esta podredumbre.
El loco germano que quiso perderte
—su lengua era bronce, su cerebro fuerte—
nos dió sus venenos y sales de muerte.
Por él los nacidos de matriz humana,
el gesto batracio, la idea pagana,

With iron bars or stone:
I wish to give, give, give to the last.
Grant me the joy, I pray,
To be a cluster moist with dew
At break of day.
The shade and songs the laurel lends
I'll offer with my figs to friends.

PROPHETIC VERSES

For this, the twentieth century, O Lord,
For evil men and good, for all the people,
Let me present to Thee my fervent prayer,
That the tiger may break forth with savage tooth,
That of a sudden a cataclysm may sweep
Over this wicked world from east to west.
Lord Jesus Christ, Thou who did'st rise again
The third day after passing from the world,
See that this age of mine waste not Thy love.
Mark how the passions, naked and dishevelled,
Like to some herd of wild, hot-blooded mares,
Range heedless of restraint. Merchants, no less
Than knavish youths, deny Thee. Lovers now
No longer seek protection at Thy hands.
Through black faunalias, the hands of slaves
Impure, of Latin race or Slav, bear up
Thy modern, sumptuous cardinals' black turbans.
Lord Jesus Christ, may Thy breath from the heights,
Thy words, slow-spoken, and Thine eyes of flame,
Melt quite away the crust of this corruption.
The German who insane would have destroyed Thee,
—His brain was powerful, and his tongue of bronze,—
On us his poison poured and salt of death.
Through him, we who are shaped in human mould,
With frog-like gestures and ideas pagan,

hacemos letrina de mitra romana.
Te adoró en España todo caballero,
el germano rubio te negó primero,
el blasfemo Nietzsche y el diablo Lutero.
Pero ya se anuncian las grandes pavuras;
llameará la tierra por sus aberturas,
se alzarán los muertos de las sepulturas.
Los dinamiteros romperán sus grillos,
saldrán las espadas, los largos cuchillos
de los hombres negros y los amarillos.
Señor Jesucristo de las suavidades,
en estos fragores y estas tempestades
que azotan campiñas e incendian ciudades,
mi alma es una barca que no tiene oriente,
doncella desnuda sobre la corriente
de zumos viciados de mi siglo veinte.
Para Compostela, profundo romero,
con mi don Quijote me fuí, caballero
de mirada pura, de gesto ceñero.
Pero en el camino, bajo las estrellas,
hubo ronda alegre de blancas doncellas,
vino de manzanas, manjar de grosellas.
Siguiendo mi ruta por otro camino,
me ví frente a frente con Tomás de Aquino
comí de su carne, bebí de su vino.
Pero, sin embargo, Señor Jesucristo,
mis ojos tan grandes terrores han visto
que a toda palabra de amor me resisto.
Y en esta tragedia yo te ando buscando
para que me digas el cómo y el cuándo,
porque yo recuerdo, Maestro, que estando
Lázaro, el mendigo, la tarde nefanda,
sumido en el sueño de una muerte blanda,
le dijiste:—Lázaro, levántate y anda.—
Y hoy que estamos muertos hombres y mujeres,
y se inicia el reino de los mercaderes,
necesita el mundo tus amaneceres.

Have made of the Roman miter a vile latrine.
In Spain of yore each noble knight adored Thee;
Blond Germans were the first who Thee denied,
The blasphemous Nietzsche and the devil Luther.
But greater terrors now announce their coming;
Through fissures in the earth the flames will rise,
And dead men from their tombs will issue forth.
The dynamiters now will break their chains,
Swords will leap out, and yellow men and black,
In anger their long knives will brandish high.
O Jesus Christ, Lord of all gentleness,
My soul, midst all this clamor and these tempests,
That lash the fertile plains, and fire the towns,
Is like a vessel with no guiding star,
A naked virgin borne along by the stream
Of this twentieth century's contamination.
To Compostela, as a pilgrim, I
Devout in heart with my Don Quixote went,
A knight, pure-eyed, and lofty in his mien.
But, by the way, as 'neath the stars I passed,
There was a happy crowd of maidens white,
And apple-wine to drink and fruit for food.
Continuing on, but by another road,
With Thomas Aquinas I came face to face;
From him had flesh to eat and wine to drink.
Yet notwithstanding, O my Lord Jesus Christ,
My eyes have looked upon such frightful terrors
That I stand obdurate to every word of love.
And, in this tragic case, I seek Thee still,
That Thou may'st tell to me the How and Why;
For I remember, Master, how Thou said'st
To the beggar, Lazarus, that mournful afternoon,
When he was lying lapped in death's soft slumber,
"Lazarus, I say to thee, arise and walk."
Today, since we are dead, both men and women,
And the reign of sordid traffickers begins,
'Tis needful for the world Thy dawn should break.

Ven con tu tridente; metiendo tu espada
en torre vetusta, en ciudad poblada,
en casa de mármol, y en tierra sembrada.
Ven con mano airada, con semblante adusto,
y que en tu presencia se muera de susto
el malvado, el necio y el sabio y el justo.
Ven con pestilencias, con grandes temblores;
corran sobre el mundo siniestros horrores,
visiones de muerte, locos estertores.
Los galgos celestes en el paroxismo
arrastren los huesos de abismo en abismo
y dance la tierra bajo el cataclismo.
Caigan las estrellas como desgajadas
por vientos agudos y despedazadas
rompan catedrales y torres alzadas.
Se cuele tu furia por las mil rendijas
de la tierra rota, ruede por las guijas
la sangre mezclada de madres y de hijas.
Señor Jesucristo, por mi siglo veinte
pasaron los bárbaros de oriente y poniente
metiendo su espada, clavando su diente.
Cebaron sus potros en tus catedrales,
en piscina santa de aguas bautismales
lavaron su lepra con blancos pañales.
Y porque se cumpla la frase divina,
te pido, mi Cristo, vestido de sayos,
que en tierra sajona y en tierra latina
desates la furia de todos tus rayos.

Come with Thy trident; lay Thy avenging sword
On ancient tower and populated city,
On marble halls and cultivated fields.
Come Thou with wrathful hand, with features stern,
And let the rogue, the fool, the wise, the just,
Expire with mortal terror in Thy presence.
Come Thou with pestilence, with great earth-tremblings;
May frightfulness range grimly o'er the world,
Visions of death, mad gurglings of the dying.
And at the crisis may the hounds of heaven
Drag forth the bones from one abyss to another,
And the earth itself dance in the cataclysm.
May the stars fall like severed branches, torn
By sharp and biting winds, and, split in pieces,
Crash through cathedrals and through lofty towers.
Let Thy fierce anger well from the ruptured earth
By a thousand fissures, and let the mingled blood
Of mothers and of daughters drench the stones.
O Christ, in this twentieth century of mine,
Barbarous hosts from east and west have passed,
Drawing their swords to fight, gnashing their teeth;
In Thy cathedrals have they fed their horses,
And washed their leprous sores with snowy linen
In the holy waters of the font baptismal.
And, that Thy word divine may be fulfilled,
I pray Thee, Christ, in simple raiment dressed,
That on the Saxon, as on the Latin world,
Thou loose the fury of all Thy thunderbolts.

AUSENCIA

Ausencia de catorce años,
silencio, mar y distancia,
tienes dormidos los ojos
en lejanías de nácar,
azucenas de tus pies
asomando en hojarasca,
mástil roto be bajeles
en la arena de la playa.

¡Qué dulces ojos me pones,
qué suaves manos, oh, patria!

Marinero de ilusiones,
capitán en una barca
teñida de plata y rosa,
teñida de rosa y plata,
pescador que tiró redes
de sirenas de Montmartre,
y en desiertos que no son
guió locas caravanas.

¡Qué dulces ojos me pones,
qué suaves manos, oh, patria!

No quiero ver mi destierro,
ausencia que te haces grata,
pluma sobre mi sombrero,
bajo mi nariz fragancia;
deslumbramiento en los ojos,
en mis orejas campana,
hormigas que se alimentan
de la inquietud de mis plantas.

¡Qué dulces ojos me pones,
qué suaves manos, oh, patria!

ABSENCE

Absence for fourteen years,
Silence, distance, the sea;
In pearly haze thine eyes
Seem closed in sleep to me;
Among the withered leaves
Thy feet like lilies show;
On the wrinkled sand of the beach
A wrecked ship's mast lies low.

How sweet the eyes thou turn'st on me,
Thy hands, how soft, my native land!

The captain of my bark,
Illusion's sailor I,—
The sails of rose and silver,
Of rose and silver dye,—
For sirens of Montmartre
A fisher who cast the net,
And for caravans mad in the deserts
Of mirage their courses set.

How sweet the eyes thou turn'st on me,
Thy hands, how soft, my native land!

I care not to view my exile,
For absence, thou hast lent
To my hat the grace of a feather,
To my nostrils a fragrant scent,
To my eyes a dazzling brightness,
To my ears the sound of a bell,
Ants that on restless yearnings
Feed wherever I dwell.

How sweet the eyes thou turn'st on me,
Thy hands, how soft, my native land!

Ahora vuelvo y no soy;
se me fatigaba el alma,
ceniza de muchos fuegos
me da color de mortaja,
sombras de muchas pasiones
las tengo ya sepultadas,
no sabré decir si puedo
volver a gozar tus aguas.

¡Qué dulces ojos me pones,
qué suaves manos, oh, patria!

Porque te quise de lejos,
me apretaron las entrañas
acontecimientos que
tu nitidez empañaban,
y mis frases en tu cuerpo
agudos filos de espada,
y en tu corazón desnudo
la flor azul de mis ansias.

¡Qué dulces ojos me pones,
qué suaves manos, oh, patria!

Por el costado sangriento
se asoman lenguas moradas,
ogros y carabineros
te tenían secuestrada,
volaban bajo tu cielo
gavilanes de uñas largas,
las palomas del recuerdo
llegaban aliquebradas. . . .

¡Qué dulces ojos me pones,
qué suaves manos, oh, patria!

Pueden enjugar mis manos
las resinas de tus llagas,
en mis colmenares traigo
mieles para tus desgracias,

Now I return, yet not I:
My heart with toil is bowed,
Much fire's dead ashes give me
The color of a shroud;
The shades of many passions
Long since interred remain;
I wonder, can I enjoy
Thy waters once again?

How sweet the eyes thou turn'st on me,
Thy hands, how soft, my native land!

Because from far I loved thee,
My inmost soul has been
By incidents sore vexed
That dimmed thine honor's sheen.
And the blue flower of my longing
Must have been, like my words,
In thy heart and flesh all naked
Like the keen edge of swords.

How sweet the eyes thou turn'st on me,
Thy hands, how soft, my native land!

Along thy bleeding side
Deep crimson tongues appear,
And carbineers and ogres
Held thee in bondage drear;
Under thy sky were flying
Hawks, long-clawed, cruel things;
The peaceful doves of memory
Reached me with broken wings.

How sweet the eyes thou turn'st on me,
Thy hands, how soft, my native land!

My hands can stanch the blood
That oozes from thy wounds,
And in my beehives, honey
For all thy ills abounds;

la abeja que me las hizo
no era abeja sino infanta
por artes de una hechicera
catorce años encantada....

¡Qué dulces ojos me pones,
qué suaves manos, oh, patria!

Se me deshace la ausencia
entre el ayer y el mañana,
designios de mi futuro
en las patas de una araña,
que teje telas azules,
que teje flores delgadas,
para abrigarte los pechos,
y el jazmín de las espaldas....

¡Qué dulces ojos me pones,
qué suaves manos, oh, patria!

Recíbeme en tus sonrisas,
arco iris de tus albas,
recógeme en tus ensueños,
limpideces de tus aguas,
que quiero volver a ser
cabrero de tus montañas,
sobre tus senos dormirme
con el candor de una guagua.*

¡Qué dulces ojos me pones,
qué suaves manos, oh, patria!

Ausencia de catorce años,
marinero en tierra extraña,
por acordarme de ti
tengo las sienes de plata,
si quieres guardarme el vuelo
acaríciame las alas,
¡Qué dulces ojos me pones,
qué suaves manos, oh, patria!

* *guagua,* Chilean, a baby.

No bee it was that made it,
But a child by visions haunted
And by some witch or fairy
For fourteen years enchanted.

How sweet the eyes thou turn'st on me,
Thy hands, how soft, my native land!

    Between what's past and the morrow
Absence dissolves away,
The patterns for my future
As the feet of a spider stray,
Which is weaving a rich blue fabric
And weaving flowers fine
To wrap about thy bosom
And those jasmine shoulders of thine.

How sweet the eyes thou turn'st on me,
Thy hands, how soft, my native land!

    Receive me then with thy smiles,
Rainbows at dawn of day,
Hold me fast in thy dreams,
Clear as thy waters' play,
For a goatherd on thy mountains
I fain would be again,
And like a baby, trustful,
Asleep on thy breast remain.

How sweet the eyes thou turn'st on me,
Thy hands, how soft, my native land!

    Absent for fourteen years,
A sailor on foreign strand,
With thinking still on thee
My brow with silver spanned;
If thou would'st guard my flight,
By thee my wings be fanned.
How sweet the eyes thou turn'st on me,
Thy hands, how soft, my native land!

CARTA LÍRICA A OTRA MUJER

Vuestro nombre no sé, ni vuestro rostro
Conozco yo, y os imagino blanca,
Débil como las brotes iniciales,
Pequeña, dulce...Ya ni sé...Divina.
En vuestros ojos placidez de lago
Que se abandona al sol y dulcemente
Le absorbe su oro mientras todo calla.
Y vuestras manos finas, como aqueste
Dolor, el mío, que se alarga, alarga,
Y luego se me muere y se concluye
Así, como lo véis, en algún verso.
Ah ¿sois así? Decidme si en la boca
Tenéis un rumoroso colmenero,
Si las orejas vuestras son a modo
De pétalos de rosas ahuecados....
Decidme si lloráis, humildemente,
Mirando las estrellas tan lejanas,
Y si en las manos tibias se os aduermen
Palomas blancas y canarios de oro.
Porque todo eso y más, vos sois, sin duda;
Vos, que tenéis el hombre que adoraba
Entre las manos dulces, vos la bella
Que habéis matado, sin saberlo acaso,
Toda esperanza en mí....Vos, su criatura.
Porque él es todo vuestro: cuerpo y alma
Estáis gustando del amor secreto
Que guardé silencioso...Dios lo sabe
Por qué, que yo no alcanzo a penetrarlo.
Os lo confieso que una vez estuvo
Tan cerca de mi brazo, que a extenderlo
Acaso mía aquella dicha vuestra
Me fuera ahora...¡sí! acaso mía...
Mas ved, estaba el alma tan gastada
Que el brazo mío no alcanzó a extenderse:

A LYRIC LETTER TO ANOTHER WOMAN

    I do not know your name; I have not seen
Your face; and yet I think you fair,
Delicate as the early-opening buds,
Little, and sweet . . . I do not know . . . divine.
Within your eyes, the stillness of the lake
That to the sun lies open and absorbs
Its golden glow while all things silent rest.
Those hands of yours, too, fine as is this grief
Of mine, which lengthens, ever lengthens out,
And, after, dies away, reaching its end
In this way, as you see, in some mere verse.
Ah! are you so? Tell me if in your mouth
You have the music of the murmurous bees,
If that your ears are fashioned in the mould
Of rosy petals with their edges curled. . . .
Tell me if in humility you weep
When you behold the stars so far away,
And if in your warm hands white doves
And gold canaries lull themselves to sleep.
Because all this, and more, you doubtless are;
You who now hold within those soft, sweet hands
The man whom I adored, you beauteous one
Who, without knowing it perhaps, have killed
All hope in me. . . . You are his all, alone.
Because he is all yours, body and soul,
Yours is the enjoyment of that secret love
That I kept silent . . . God alone knows why:
The reason I have failed to penetrate.
I will confess that once he was so near
That if I had but opened wide my arms,
Perhaps that happiness you now enjoy
Would have been mine today . . . Yes, mine, perhaps! . . .
But see, my spirit had become so weak,
To stretch my arms out was beyond my power:

La sed divina, contenida entonces,
Me pulió el alma.... Y él ha sido vuestro!
¿Comprendéis bien? Ahora, en vuestros brazos
El se adormece y le decís palabras
Pequeñas y menudas que semejan
Pétalos volanderos y muy blancos.
Acaso un niño rubio vendrá luego
A copiar en los ojos inocentes
Los ojos vuestros y los de él
Unidos en un espejo azul y cristalino....
¡Oh, ceñidle la frente! ¡Era tan amplia!
¡Arrancaban tan firmes los cabellos
A grandes ondas, que a tenerla cerca
No hiciera yo otra cosa que ceñirla!
Luego dejad que en vuestras manos vaguen
Los labios suyos; él me dijo un día
Que nada era tan dulce al alma suya
como besar las femeninas manos...
Y acaso, alguna vez, yo, la que anduve
Vagando por afuera de la vida,
—Como aquellos filósofos mendigos
Que van a las ventanas señoriales
A mirar sin envidia toda fiesta—
Me allegue humildemente a vuestro lado
Y con palabras quedas, susurrantes,
Os pida vuestras manos un momento,
Para besarlas, yo, como él las besa...
Y al recubrirlas, lenta, lentamente,
Vaya pensando: Aquí se aposentaron
¿Cuánto tiempo, sus labios, cuánto tiempo
En las divinas manos que son suyas?
Oh, qué amargo deleite, este deleite
De buscar huellas suyas y seguirlas
Sobre las manos vuestras tan sedosas,
Tan finas, con sus venas tan azules!
Oh, que nada podría, ni ser suya,
Ni dominarle el alma, ni tenerlo

The thirst divine, held in restraint just then,
Refined my spirit.... And he has been yours!
You understand me well? Now in your arms
He falls asleep, and in his ear you speak
Those little, insignificant words that seem
Like white and fluttering petals in the air.
Perhaps a fair-haired* child will come one day
To show a copy in his innocent eyes
Of your eyes and of his
United in a crystal mirror blue....
Oh, bind his brow about! So ample 'twas!
His flowing locks, so strong, in massive waves
Broke over it, and having it so near
No other thing I'd do but wreathe it round.
Permit then that those lips of his may stray
Over your hands; one day he said to me
That there was nothing to his soul more sweet
Than to place kisses on a woman's hands...
And sometime, I perhaps, I who have gone
Wandering on the outer fringe of life—
Just like those philosophic mendicants
Who come to the windows of baronial halls
And gaze, unenvying, at every feast—
May, modestly approaching, reach your side,
And, whispering, with quiet accents, beg
Your hands to kiss one moment, as he does...
And as you draw them slowly, very slowly back,
I shall be thinking: Oh, how long, how long
Have his lips lodged on those hands divine, now his?
And oh! what bitter joy 'twill be, this joy
Of seeking out his traces, following them
Over those hands of yours, that are so fine,
So silky, with their veins so blue!
For neither to be his, nor dominate
His soul, nor yet to hold him here as one
Surrendered at my feet—nothing to me

---

* "fair-haired"—as opposed to the swarthy complexion of the majority of Latin Americans; therefore, in a certain sense, aristocratic.

Rendido aquí a mis pies, recompensarme
Este horrible deleite de hacer mío
Un inefable, apasionado rastro.
Y allí en vos misma, sí, pues sois barrera,
Barrera ardiente, viva, que al tocarla
Ya me remueve este cansancio amargo,
Este silencio de alma en que me escudo,
Este dolor mortal en que me abismo,
Esta inmovilidad del sentimiento
Que sólo salta, bruscamente, cuando
Nada es posible!

Would compensate for this delight so grim,
Of making mine some vestige passionate,
Beyond the power of language to describe.
And there, in you yourself I find it, yes,
For you a barrier prove, aflame, alive,
Which when I touch, my bitter weariness
Has gone, and gone this silence of the soul
That is my shield, this mortal grief in which
I sink, this immobility of feeling
Which only leaps up roughly into life
When nothing can be done!

MAESTRANZAS DE NOCHE

Fierro negro que duerme, fierro negro que gime
por cada poro un grito de desconsolación.
Las cenizas ardidas sobre la tierra triste....
Los caldos* en que el bronce derritió su dolor....

Cada máquina tiene una pupila abierta
para mirarme a mí.

Y el grito se me crispa como un nervio enroscado
o como la cuerda rota de un violín....

En las paredes cuelgan las interrogaciones,
florece en las bigornias el alma de los bronces†,
y hay un temblor de pasos en los cuartos desiertos.

Y entre la noche negra, desesperadas, corren
y sollozan las almas de los obreros muertos....

POEMAS DE AMOR

> Escribiré los poemas de mi cuerpo y
> de lo mortal porque así tendré los
> poemas de mi Alma, y lo Inmortal.
> —Whitman

I

¡Déjame sueltas las manos,
y el corazón, déjame libre!
Deja que mis dedos corran
por los caminos de tu cuerpo.
La pasión—sangre, fuego, besos—
me incendia a llamaradas trémulas....
¡Ay! tú no sabes lo que es esto!

---

* *caldos*, literally, broths; also, commercially, wines, oils, etc.; here the huge tanks of rape oil into which the forgings after being turned and bored are plunged for hardening.
† *bronces*, bronzes; but also, as here, the big guns.

ARSENAL BY NIGHT

Black iron sleeping, iron black that groans
through every pore with moans disconsolate.
The red-hot ashes on the dismal earth....
The cauldrons where the bronze has fused its pain....

And each machine has opened wide an eye
to stare at me.

And the moaning makes my flesh to creep, like a nerve
that's jarred, or a violin's broken string....

Upon the walls interrogations hang,
on the anvils flowers the spirit of the guns,
in the deserted workshops footsteps tremble.

And through the black night, despairingly, there run
sobbing, the souls of workmen dead and gone....

POEMS OF LOVE

> And I will make the poems of my body
> and of mortality,
> For I think I shall then supply myself with
> the poems of my soul and of immortality.
> —Whitman.

I

Let loose my hands and my heart
and leave me free!
Permit my hands to wander
over thy body's highways.
Passion—blood, fire, kisses—
kindles tremulous flames within me....
Alas! thou know'st not what this means!

Es la tempestad de mis sentidos
doblegando la selva sensible de mis nervios.
¡Es la carne que grita con sus ardientes lenguas!
¡Es el incendio!
¡Y estás aquí, mujer, como un madero intacto
ahora que vuela toda mi vida hecha cenizas
hacia tu cuerpo lleno, como la noche, de astros!

¡Déjame libres las manos
y el corazón, déjame libre!

¡Y sólo te deseo, yo sólo te deseo!
¡No es amor, es deseo que se agosta y se extingue,
es precipitación de furias,
acercamiento de lo imposible,
pero estás tú,
estás para dármelo todo,
y a darme lo que tienes a la tierra viniste,
como yo para contenerte,
y desearte,
y recibirte!

II

¡Es cierto, amada mía, hermana mía, es cierto!
¡Como las bestias grises que en los potreros pastan,
y en los potreros se aman, como las bestias grises!

¡Como las castas ebrias que poblaron la tierra
matándose y amándose, como las castas ebrias!

¡Como el latido de las corolas abiertas
dividiendo la joya futura de la siembra,
como el latido de las corolas abiertas!

¡Empujado por los designios de la tierra
como una ola en el mar hacia ti va mi cuerpo!

¡Y tú, en tu carne, encierras
las pupilas sedientas con que miraré cuando
estos ojos que tengo se me llenen de tierra!

It is the whirlwind of my senses
bending the sensitive forest of my nerves.
It is the flesh that cries out with its burning tongues!
It is fire!
And thou, woman, art here, like a beam untouched
while all my life, turned to ashes, flies
toward thy body filled, like night, with stars!

Let loose my hands and my heart
and set me free!

I desire thee only, I desire thee only!
It is not love, it is desire that consumes and destroys itself,
a precipitation of furies,
a striving after the impossible,
but thou art there,
thou art there to give me all,
and to give me what thou hast, art thou come to earth,
as I am come to hold thee
and desire thee
and receive thee!

II

It is true, my beloved, my sister, it is true!
Like the gray cattle that pasture on the prairies,
and on the prairies love each other, like the gray cattle!

Like the inebriate tribes that peopled the earth,
killing and loving each other, like the inebriate tribes!

Like the throb of the open corolla
separating from the seed the jewel of the future,
like the throb of the open corolla!

Urged on by the designs of the earth
like a wave of the sea my body makes toward thee!

And thou in thy flesh enclosest
the thirsting eyes with which I shall look forth
when those eyes I have are filled with earth!

III

¡Canción del macho y de la hembra!
¡La fruta de los siglos
exprimiendo su jugo
en nuestras venas!

¡Mi alma derramándose en tu carne extendida
para salir de ti más buena,
el corazón desparramándose,
estirándose como una pantera,
y mi vida, hecha astillas, anudándose
a ti como la luz a las estrellas!

Me recibes
como al viento la vela.

Te recibo
como el surco a la siembra.

¡Duérmete sobre mis dolores
si mis dolores no te queman,

amárrate a mis alas
acaso mis alas te llevan,

endereza mis deseos
acaso te lastima su pelea! ...

¡Tú eres lo único que tengo
desde que perdí mi tristeza!

¡Desgárrame como una espada
o táctame como una antena!

¡Bésame,
muérdeme,
incéndiame,
que yo vengo a la tierra
solo por el naufragio de mis ojos de macho
en el agua infinita de tus ojos de hembra!

III

Song of the male and of the female!
The fruit of the ages
pressing out its essence
in our veins!

My soul pouring itself over thy extended flesh
to issue from thee more good,
my heart squandering itself,
rearing itself like a panther,
and my life, all shattered, cleaving
to thee like light to the stars!

Thou receivest me as the sail does the wind.

I receive thee
as the furrow the seed.

Fall asleep over my sorrows,
if my sorrows burn thee not;

lash thyself to my wings,
perhaps my wings will bear thee;

set straight my desires,
perhaps their conflict irks thee....

Thou art the only one I have
since I have lost my sadness!

Rend me like a sword
or touch me gently like an antenna!

Kiss me,
bite me,
inflame me,
for I come to earth
solely for the shipwreck of my eyes of a man
in the infinite waters of thine eyes of a woman!

IV

Es como una marea, cuando ella clava en mí
sus ojos enlutados,
cuando siento su cuerpo de greda blanca y móvil
estirarse y latir junto al mío,
es como una marea, cuando ella está a mi lado.

He visto tendido frente a los mares del Sur,
arrollarse las aguas y extenderse
inconteniblemente,
fatalmente,
en las mañanas y al atardecer.

Agua de las resacas sobre las viejas huellas,
sobre los viejos rastros, sobre las viejas cosas,
agua de las resacas que desde las estrellas
se abre como una inmensa rosa,
agua que va avanzando sobre las playas como
una mano atrevida debajo de una ropa,
agua internándose en los acantilados,
agua estrellándose en las rocas,
agua implacable como los vengadores
y como los asesinos silenciosa,
agua de las noches siniestras
debajo de los muelles como una vena rota,
o como el corazón del mar
en una irradiación temblorosa y monstruosa.

Es algo que me lleva desde adentro y me crece
inmensamente próximo, cuando ella está a mi lado,
es como una marea rompiéndose en sus ojos
y besando su boca, sus senos y sus manos.

Ternura de dolor, y dolor de imposible,
ala de los terribles deseos,
¡que se mueve en la noche de mi carne y la suya
con una aguda fuerza de flechas en el cielo!

IV

It is like a tide when she fixes on me
her darkened eyes,
when I feel her mobile, chalk-like body
tighten and throb close to mine,
it is like a tide when she is beside me.

Stretched out facing the Southern seas, I've seen
the water rolling and extending
boundlessly,
fatally,
in the mornings and evenings.

Water surging over the old footprints,
over ancient trails and over ancient things,
surging water which from the stars
opens up like an immense rose,
water which creeps upward over the beaches
like a daring hand under a garment,
water piercing into the bold headlands,
water dashing upon the rocks,
water implacable as avengers
and, like assassins, silent,
water in the sinister nights
under the wharves like a broken vein,
or like the heart of the sea
in a tremendous and monstrous irradiation.

It is something from within that bears me on and grows
very near to me, when she is at my side,
it is like a high tide breaking on her eyes
and kissing her mouth, her breasts, her hands.

Sensitiveness to pain, a yearning for the impossible,
a wing of terrible desires,
which in the night arises from my flesh and hers
with the piercing violence of arrows in the sky!

Algo de inmensa huida,
que no se va, que araña adentro,
algo que en las palabras cava tremendos pozos,
¡algo que, contra todo, se estrella, contra todo,
como los prisioneros contra los calabozos!

¡Ella, tallada en el corazón de la noche,
por la inquietud de mis ojos alucinados;
ella, grabada en los maderos del bosque
por los cuchillos de mis manos,
ella—su goce junto al mío,
ella—sus ojos enlutados,
ella—su corazón, mariposa sangrienta
que con sus dos antenas de instinto me ha tocado!

¡No cabe en esta estrecha meseta de mi vida!
¡Es como un viento desatado!

¡Si mis palabras clavan apenas como agujas
debieran desgarrar como espadas o arados!

¡Es como una marea que me arrastra y me dobla,
es como una marea, cuando ella está a mi lado!

Something of an immense fleeing
which does not go away, but burrows inward,
something which opens yawning chasms in my speech,
something that dashes itself against everything—everything,
like prisoners against the walls of their dungeons!

She, carved in the heart of the night
by the disquiet of my deluded eyes;
she, graved on the trunks of the trees
by the knives of my hands,
she—her joys together with mine,
she—her dark-veiled eyes,
she—her heart, a blood-red butterfly
that with her antennae of instinct has touched me!

On the restricted plateau of my life it finds no room!
It is like a wind let loose!

If my words hardly pierce like needles,
they ought to tear like arrows or plows!

It is like a tide that drags me along and subdues me,
It is like a tide when she is beside me!

ADIÓS

París
Una estrella desnuda
Se alumbra sobre el llano
      Esa estrella la llevara en mi mano
En Notre Dame
    los ángeles se quejan
Al batir las alas nacen albas
Mas mis ojos se alejan
Todas las mañanas
Baja el sol a tu hostia que se eleva
Y en Montmartre los molinos
    la atmósfera renuevan
París
En medio de las albas que se quiebran
Yo he florecido tu Obelisco
Y allí canté sobre una estrella nueva

ADIÓS

Llevo sobre el pecho
Un collar de tus calles luminosas
Todas tus calles
    me llamaban al irme
Y en todas las banderas
Palpitaban adioses
Tus banderas de los nobles ardores
Al pasar
    arrojo al Sena
        un ramo de flores
Y entre los balandros que se alejan
Tus balandros que pacen en las tardes
Dejar quisiera el más bello poema
El Sena
    bajo sus puentes se desliza
Y en mi garganta un pájaro agoniza.

ADIEU

   Paris
A naked star
Shows its light over the plain
     This star I would bear in my hand
In Notre-Dame
    the angels complain
At the beating of their wings dawns are born
But my eyes range afar
Every morning
Bows the sun to thy Host which is elevated
And in Montmartre the windmills
     renew the atmosphere
Paris
In the midst of the dawns that are breaking
I have adorned with flowers thine Obelisk
And there I have sung over a new star

ADIEU

I carry on my bosom
A necklace of thy luminous streets
All thy streets
    called to me as I departed
And in all the banners
Fluttered adieux
Thy banners of noble ardors
In passing
   I throw into the Seine
     a bunch of flowers
And among the ships that are leaving
Thy ships that find pasture in the light of sunset
I would leave the most beautiful poem
The Seine
   glides under its bridges
And in my throat a bird is agonizing.

HORIZONTE

Pasar el horizonte envejecido
Y mirar en el fondo de los sueños
La estrella que palpita

Eras tan hermosa
        que no pudiste hablar
Yo me alejé
        Pero llevo en la mano
Aquel cielo nativo
Con un sol gastado
    Esta tarde
        en un café
            he bebido
              Un licor tembloroso
              Como un pescado rojo
Y otra vez en el vaso escondido
Ese sueño filial
Eras tan hermosa
        que no pudiste hablar.
En tu pecho algo agonizaba
Eran verdes tus ojos
        pero yo me alejaba
Eras tan hermosa
        que aprendí a cantar.

HIJO

Las ventanas cerradas
        y algunas decoraciones deshojadas
    La noche viene de los ojos ajenos
Al fondo de los años
Un ruiseñor cantaba en vano.

La luna viva
Blanca de la nieve que caía
Y sobre los recuerdos
        Una luz que agoniza entre los dedos.

HORIZON

To pass beyond the agèd horizon
And to behold in the depth of the dreams
The star that trembles

Thou wast so beautiful
      that thou could'st not speak
I went away
      But I bear in my hand
That native sky
With an exhausted sun
    This afternoon
        in a café
          I have drunk
          A liquor tremulous
          As a red fish
And another time hidden in the glass
That filial dream
Thou wast so beautiful
      that thou could'st not speak.
In thy breast something was agonizing
Thine eyes were green
      But I went away
Thou wast so beautiful
      that I have learned to sing.

SON

The closed windows
      and some dilapidated decorations
    The night comes from the eyes of strangers
In the depths of the years
A nightingale was singing in vain.

The living moon
White as the snow that was falling
And over the recollections
      A light that agonizes among the fingers.

MAÑANA PRIMAVERA

Silencio familiar
           Bajo las bujías florecidas
Una canción
           asciende sobre el humo
Y tú
    Hijo
           hermoso como un dios desnudo
Los arroyos que van lejos
Todo lo han visto los arroyos huérfanos
           Un día tendrás recuerdos.

LA SENDA ERA TAN LARGA

Este viento venía de unas alas
Y los días pasan aullando al horizonte
           Como un balandro joven
           Crucé muchas tormentas
           Entre canciones marineras
Todas las gaviotas
           dejaron plumas en mis manos
Tras la última montaña
           los meses descendían
Un póstumo cantar nos cerró la salida.

SPRING MORNING

Silence familiar
        Under the flowering candles
A song
    ascends over the smoke
And thou
    my son
        beautiful as a naked god
The streams that go afar
The orphan streams have seen it all
One day thou wilt have recollections.

THE PATH WAS SO LONG

This wind was coming with wings
And the days pass howling to the horizon
        Like a young fishing-smack
        I passed through many storms
        Among songs of mariners
All the sea gulls
    left feathers in my hands
Behind the farthest mountain
    the months were descending
A posthumous song closed to us the outlet.

CAMPANARIO

A cada son de la campana
      Un pájaro volaba
Pájaros de ala inversa
      Que mueren entre las tejas
Donde ha caído la primera canción
Al fondo de la tarde
      Las llamas vegetales
En cada hoja tiembla el corazón
Y una estrella se enciende a cada paso
         Los ojos guardan algo
         Que palpita en la voz
Sobre la lejanía
      Un reloj se vacía.

BELL TOWER

At every peal of the bell
    A bird would fly
Birds with inverted wings
    that die among the roof tops
Where the first song has fallen
In the depths of the evening
    The flames of vegetation
Its heart trembles in each leaf
A star takes fire at every step
    The eyes retain something
    That quivers in the voice
Over the distance
    A clock was giving up its message.

CALLE DESCONOCIDA

Penumbra de la paloma
llamaron los judíos a la iniciación de la tarde
cuando la sombra aún no entorpece los pasos
y la venida de la noche se advierte
antes como advenimiento de música esperada
que como enorme símbolo de nuestra primordial nadería.
En esa hora de fina luz arenosa
mis andanzas dieron con una calle ignorada,
abierta en noble anchura de terraza
mostrando en las cornisas y en las paredes
colores blandos como el mismo cielo
que conmovía el fondo.
Todo—honesta medianía de las casas austeras,
travesuras de columnitas y aldabas,
tal vez una esperanza de niña en los balcones—
se me adentró en el corazón anhelante
con limpidez de lágrima.
Quizá esa hora única
aventajaba con prestigio la calle
dándole privilegios de ternura
haciéndola real como una leyenda o un verso;
lo cierto es que la sentí lejanamente cercana
como recuerdo que si parece llegar cansado de lejos
es porque viene de la propia hondura del alma.
Íntimo y entrañable
era el milagro de la calle clara
y solo después
entendí que aquel lugar era extraño,
que es toda casa un candelabro
donde arden con aislada llama las vidas,
que todo inmeditado paso nuestro
camina sobre Gólgotas ajenos.

AN UNKNOWN STREET

Penumbra of the dove
The Hebrews called the coming in of evening
When still the darkness deadens not our steps
And the approach of night is noticed
Rather as the arrival of expected music
Than as the vast symbol of our primordial nothingness.
Just at this hour of fine and sand-hued light
My wanderings chanced upon an unknown street
Opening upon a noble breadth of terrace
And showing on the cornices and walls
Colors as soft as in the sky itself
Moved in the background.
All this—the austere houses with their honest mediocrity,
The fanciful, small pillars and door-knockers,
Perhaps some girlish hope on a balcony—
All penetrated to my panting heart
With a tear's limpidity.
Perhaps this hour unique
Enhanced the fascination of the street
Giving it special gifts of tenderness
Making it splendid as a legend or a poem;
Certain it is, I felt it in a distant fashion near
Like memories which if they seem to come fatigued from far
Seem so as coming from the very depths of the soul.
Intimate and affectionate
Was the miracle of that clear-lit street
And only afterward
I understood that place was strange to me,
That every house is like a candelabrum
Where lives burn out their days, each flame apart,
And that each step of ours too near
Treads on another's Golgotha.

LA GUITARRA

He mirado la Pampa
de una patiecito de la calle Sarandí en Buenos Aires.
Cuando entré no la ví.
Estaba acurrucada
en lo profundo de una brusca guitarra.
Sólo se desmelenó
al entreverar la diestra las cuerdas.
No sé lo que azuzaban;
a lo mejor fué un triste del Norte
pero yo ví la Pampa.
Ví muchas brazadas de cielo
sobre un manojito de pasto.
Ví una loma que arrinconan
quietas distancias
mientras leguas y leguas
caen desde lo alto.
Ví el campo donde cabe
Dios sin haber de inclinarse,
ví el único lugar de la tierra
donde puede caminar Dios a sus anchas.
Ví la Pampa cansada
que antes horrorizaron los malones
y hoy apaciguan en quietud maciza las parvas.
De un tirón ví todo eso
mientras se desesperaban las cuerdas
en un compás tan zarandeado como éste.
(La ví también a ella
cuyo recuerdo aguarda en toda música.)
Hasta que en brusco cataclismo
se allanó la guitarra encabritada
y estrujóme el silencio
y hurañamente volvió el vivir a estancarse.

THE GUITAR

I have looked upon the Pampa
From a little patio in Sarandí Street in Buenos Aires.
When I entered I did not see her.
She was crouching
In the depths of a rude guitar.
Only her hair fell loose
As her right hand swept the strings.
I know not what it was they sang;
At the best some northern Gaucho tune,
But I saw the Pampa.
I saw great armfuls of sky
Over a tiny handful of pasture.
I saw a hillock, which the great distances
Thrust into a corner
While leagues and leagues
Drop down from above.
I saw the land where God finds room
And need not bend his head;
I saw the only place on earth
Where God can walk with freedom.
I saw the toil-worn plain
Where Indian raids of old spread terror,
And now in solid quiet the ripened corn sheds peace.
All this I saw at a glance
While the strings gave voice to their despair
To a lilting rhythmic movement such as this.
(Her also did I see
Of whom memories await me in all music.)
Until with one wild outburst
Like a rearing horse the rude guitar was still
And the silence crushed me
As life shyly returned to its placid pool.

Part Three
COMMENTARY

JOSÉ ASUNCIÓN SILVA

José Asunción Silva was born in Bogotá, Colombia, in 1865, and died there in 1896. He is properly regarded as one of the precursors of the Modernist movement, and is so grouped along with Julián del Casal, Manuel Gutiérrez Nájera, and José Martí by Arturo Torres-Ríoseco in his volume, *Precursores del modernismo* (Madrid, 1925). Blanco Fombona has asserted that Rubén Darío drew some of his inspiration from Asunción Silva;[1] but this is unlikely. The poems of Silva did not appear in book form till 1908, twelve years after the author's death. During his lifetime they circulated among his friends or appeared in local periodicals, but the likelihood that any of these local Colombian papers reached Buenos Aires, where Darío was then living, is remote. Moreover, there is no trace of the influence of Silva in Darío's *Prosas profanas* (1896), where, if anywhere, we might expect to find it. The further fact that Darío denied that Silva's work had influenced him in any way, should be conclusive. It is equally unlikely that Silva was influenced by Darío, for, although Darío's first important work, *Azul,* was published in 1888, it was little known till Juan Valera's appreciation (published by *La Nación,* Buenos Aires) gave it a wide publicity. By this time, however, all that part of Silva's work which is now extant had already been written. *Nocturno III* probably belongs to the year 1892 or 1893. Of Silva's last works nothing is known, the manuscript having been lost in the wreck of the "America" (1895).

The important fact is that the enthusiastic study of the more recent French writers was going on over the whole Spanish-speaking area from Chile and the Argentine Republic to Colombia and Mexico; and Darío came to be recognized as the leader of the movement because he arrived at the opportune moment to concentrate and condense, and to express with power and precision, the thoughts and feelings of a whole generation.

The complete edition of the *Poesías* of José Asunción Silva (Barcelona, 1908) is a comparatively small volume. The earlier poems, dealing with memories of childhood, are simple, natural, and sympathetic; but even in these there is an occasional touch of melancholy:

> La abuela se sonríe con maternal cariño,
> mas cruza por su espíritu como un temor extraño
> por lo que en lo futuro de angustia y desengaño
> los días ignorados del nieto guardarán.

---

[1] Blanco Fombona maintains this opinion; see *El modernismo y los poetas modernistas* (Madrid, 1929), p. 172.

This same way of looking at things is noticeable in his patriotic poem, *Al pie de la estatua*. His admiration and love for Bolívar are deep and sincere, yet it is not of Bolívar's great deeds as Liberator that the poet sings, but of the pettiness, selfishness, and ingratitude of his own generation. Even the children playing innocently in the garden around the statue give him a feeling of foreboding which he is unable to dispel with Gray's reflection in a similar situation:

> Yet, ah! why should they know their fate
> Since sorrow never comes too late,
> And happiness too swiftly flies?
> Thought would destroy their paradise.
> No more;—where ignorance is bliss,
> 'Tis folly to be wise.

This note of bitterness is seldom absent from Silva's work. In his *Día de difuntos* (in which we catch echoes of *The Bells* of Edgar Allan Poe) it is not the mournful notes of the great bells that move the poet with their

> acentos dejativos
> y tristísimos y inciertos...
> que les hablan a los vivos
> de los muertos,

but the ironic clang of the bell that tells the hours, and notes how easily the weeping widower finds another mate.

> Ella [the bell] ha marcado la hora en que el viudo
> habló del suicidio y pidió el arsénico,
> cuando aún en la alcoba recién perfumada
> flotaba el aroma del ácido fénico;
> y ha marcado luego la hora en que mudo
> por las emociones con que el gozo agobia,
> para que lo uniera con el sagrado nudo
> a la misma iglesia fué con otra novia.

The somber coloring of these poems is the reflection of the tragedy of the poet's life, and this may be best understood in the light of his aspirations as he reveals them in his prose work, *De sobremesa:*

> You know very well what it is: just as poetry attracts me, so everything draws and fascinates me irresistibly: all the arts, all the sciences, politics, speculation, luxury, pleasure, mysticism, love, war, all forms of human activity, all forms of life... all those sensations which through the urgency of my senses I require to have from day to day more intense and more delicate.[2]

---

[2] José Asunción Silva, *De sobremesa* (Bogotá, 1926), pp. 15–16.

And again:

> Ah! to live one's life! that is what I desire; to feel all that can be felt; to know all that can be known, to be able to accomplish all that can be accomplished!

This hunger of the spirit is one of the preëminent marks of the Modernist. For Silva, all hopes and efforts ended in frustration. The death of his father left him burdened with debt. Being a poet and a dreamer, he was never able to raise his head above business worries. His sensibility was wounded by the sordidness of his surroundings and the lack of sympathy with his ideals. His reading of pessimistic philosophy left him without faith of any kind; while the death of his beloved sister, Elvira, together with the loss of the manuscript of his last and presumably best work, and the fear of insanity, brought him to despair and finally to suicide.

His third *Nocturno,* in which he gives expression to his grief over the loss of his sister, is one of the most deeply moving poems in Spanish-American literature. Its gloom and utter desolation are unrelieved by any ray of hope; yet there is a haunting beauty in the lines to which translation can hardly do justice. The feeling of strangeness and mystery is heightened by the musical reiteration of certain vowel sounds,

> una noche toda llena de murmullos, de perfumes y de música de alas,

by an occasional assonance, and by the frequent repetition of phrases—all characteristic of the newer school of poetry. These repeated phrases provoked laughter among the critics; and, read casually, they may seem pointless; but recited by a master reader they might be made very telling. On this point Solar has an interesting note:

> Bertha Singerman has recited the *Nocturno,* interpreting it admirably. Her rich, warm voice, on reaching these lines,
>
> > ¡Y eran una sola sombra larga!
> > ¡Y eran una sola sombra larga!
> > ¡Y eran una sola sombra larga!
>
> sank softly, becoming each time thinner and more tremulous—as a phantom might grow, waver, and vanish away;—the syllables lengthened out with light inflections, and the accent became less and less marked until it expired in an imperceptible whisper. No one smiled. The hearers, less schooled but more intuitive than certain critics, had understood that each line, though identical in words with the preceding, had a different signification, evoked a new aspect of the quivering, changing shade, and all remained absorbed, as if the black wings of mystery had touched their spirits.[3]

[3] Eduardo Solar Correa, *Poetas de Hispano-América* (Santiago de Chile, 1926), p. 261.

Metrically, this poem was regarded as a daring innovation, for not only are the lines of irregular length, but also the meter is built up on a foot of four syllables with the accent on the third syllable (adopted later by José Gabriel y Galán, José Santos Chocano, and Ricardo Jaimes Freyre). The regular recurrence of the accent—more regular than is usual in the best Spanish poetry—serves only to enhance the feeling of melancholy and depression that pervades the whole poem.

In Silva's later poems the bitterness of his spirit finds vent in satire against the religious life, in *Don Juan de Covadonga;* against the love of women, in *Luz de luna;* against the futility of all human endeavor, in *Filosofías;* for

> cuando llegues en postrera hora
> a la última morada
> sentirás una angustia matadora
> de no haber hecho nada;

against the grossness of the materialistic philosophy of the time, in *Futura,* in which he sees the race gathered, in the twenty-fourth century, around the statue of its patron saint,

> Sancho Panza,
> ventripotente y bonachón;

and against the Philistine density of the critics, in *Un poema.* For into one great work of art the poet had poured all the power and beauty of his soul;

> Complacido en mis versos, con orgullo de artista,
> les dí olor de heliotropos y color de amatista . . .
> Le mostré mi poema a un crítico estupendo . . .
> Lo leyó cuatro veces, y me dijo . . . ¡No entiendo!

It is in this satirical sense that we must interpret the last poem in the volume, *Egalité.* In his book of table-talk, *De sobremesa,* Silva resents the imputation that he is a mere *asqueroso pornógrafo,* a charge which this poem might be held to justify; but the intention is obviously ironic. Silva was a man of rare culture and sensitive spirit. For him, the mandarin represents the flower of an age-old culture. But take that away and what remains? Nothing but the mere animal; and then

> Juan Lanas, el mozo de esquina,
> es absolutamente igual
> al Emperador de la China:
> los dos son un mismo animal.

RUBÉN DARÍO[4]

Yo soy aquel

THIS POEM, which appears, without title, at the beginning of the volume, *Cantos de vida y esperanza* (1905), is placed first in this selection from the works of Rubén Darío because it is largely autobiographical and furnishes perhaps better than any other the key to his poetry.

In Stanza 4 he speaks with some degree of self-pity of the sufferings of his childhood. In his *Autobiography* also he tells how he was oppressed by terrible dreams and was afraid of the dark; but there is nothing to show that he suffered from more than a highly nervous temperament. To a disinterested observer it would appear that as a youth he was more than usually fortunate, and that this reference,

> Yo supe de dolor desde mi infancia,
> mi juventud . . . ¿fué juventud la mía?

---

[4] Born, 18th January, 1867, at Matapa, Nicaragua. Baptismal name: Félix Rubén García Sarmiento. His parents separated when he was an infant, and he was adopted by an aunt from whom he took the name of Darío.

Was successively librarian, journalist, government representative, minister plenipotentiary, and throughout his life a Bohemian.

Spent the most productive years of his life in Buenos Aires, Paris, and Madrid, but also resided for longer or shorter periods in Chile, Salvador, Guatemala, Costa Rica, Cuba, Colombia, New York (in passing), and Italy, being everywhere hailed as the prophet of Modernism.

Died, 6th February, 1916, at León, Nicaragua.

WORKS—

VERSE	PROSE
Primeras notas. Managua, 1885	*A de Gilbert*. San Salvador, 1889
Abrojos. Valparaiso, 1887	*Los raros*. Buenos Aires, 1893
Azul. Valparaiso, 1888	*Castelar*. Madrid, 1899
Prosas profanas. Buenos Aires, 1896	*Peregrinaciones*. Paris, 1901
	España contemporanea. Paris, 1901
	La caravana pasa. Paris, 1903
Cantos de vida y esperanza. Madrid, 1905	*Tierras solares*. Madrid, 1904
Oda a Mitre. Paris, 1906	*Opiniones*. Madrid, 1906
El canto errante. Madrid, 1907	*Parisiana*. Madrid, 1907
	El viaje a Nicaragua. Madrid, 1909
Poema de otoño y otros poemas. Madrid, 1910	*Letras*. Paris, 1911
	Todo al vuelo. Madrid, 1912
Canto a la Argentina. Buenos Aires, 1910	*Historia de mis libros*. Buenos Aires, 1912
	Autobiografía. Barcelona, 1916 (Appeared in *Caras y caretas*, Buenos Aires, 1912)
	Cabezas. Buenos Aires, 1916
POSTHUMOUS VERSE	
Sol de domingo. Madrid, 1917	POSTHUMOUS PROSE
	El oro de Mallorca. Madrid, 1917

Obras completas. Madrid, 1917–1919. Twenty-two volumes

is an echo from Baudelaire, one of his favorite authors:

> Ma jeunesse ne fut qu'un ténébreux orage,
> traversé çà et là par de brillants soleils.

The poem further reflects the mood of despondency that clouded his later years, and probably belongs to the same period as the *Canción de otoño en primavera* in which the same feeling is apparent.

Yo soy aquel may be regarded as the poet's confession of faith so far as poetry is concerned. In it he reiterates the declaration of his *Palabras liminares,* the Preface to *Prosas profanas:*

> Is there in my veins a drop of the blood of Africa or of the aboriginal Indian? There may be; but here you see in my verses princesses, kings, things imperial, visions of countries distant or impossible. What would you have? I detest the life and the time into which I have been born; and I cannot bring myself to greet the president of a republic in the same language in which I sing to thee, O Heliogabalus, whose court—gold, silk, marble—comes to me in dreams.

In this poem, therefore, he gives a full and detailed picture of the dreamland which alone offers him a retreat from rude contacts with the world of reality, and which in its essential features is an idealization of the gardens of Versailles in the times of Louis XV. In his struggle against the world, the flesh, and the devil, he has become embittered and his art offers the only means of escape from the sordidness of the actual. The "selva sagrada" (another metaphor for his "jardín de sueño") symbolizes the home of the ideal. What suggested the figure was probably the picture by Puvis de Chavannes, *Bois sacré, cher aux muses et aux arts,* painted for the museum at Lyons. This sacred grove is a pagan paradise, where sensual instinct ranges unashamed. But the soul entering therein in pure and native simplicity, though stung by the reproaches of the prude or the puritan, will suffer no stain; rather, the inner flame will glow the brighter, and he will behold Life, Light, and Truth. The scoffer will see in all this nothing but sensuality; so much so that Darío's panegyrist, González Blanco, feels called upon to defend it.

> Pero sepan, vuesas mercedes [he writes], que la sensualidad es la fuerza impelente de las sociedades; que por la sensualidad se han acometido todas las vastas empresas,[5]

an amazing generalization in face of the multitude of instances that could be adduced to prove the contrary. Darío makes no such plea. Life has been

---

[5] Andrés González Blanco, *Estudio preliminar* (Madrid, 1910), p. 162.

unkind to him; his early works, *Azul* and *Prosas profanas,* have excited much criticism, some of it ill-natured; he is on his defense; but his conscience is clear, and calumny has no terrors for him.

> Pasó una piedra que lanzó una honda;
> pasó una flecha que aguzó un violento;

but with Brutus he can exclaim:

> I am armed so strong in honesty
> That they pass by me as the idle wind
> Which I respect not.

"La Galatea gongorina"..."la marquesa verleniana"... These references to Luis de Góngora (1561–1627) and Paul Verlaine (1844–1896) are significant and important. Darío had read widely in the older Spanish classics. Moreover, he had read them with the insight of a poet, and had in consequence been able to penetrate beneath the surface, to see through the eccentricity of Góngora, which had become almost a byword among critics, to the truth and poetic power underlying. That his study of Góngora influenced his style is highly probable; indeed, on account of the extravagant imagery in some of his early poems, Darío was called the "new Góngora," which was more of a compliment than his detractors intended.

Of his indebtedness to Verlaine, Darío makes no secret. He makes many references to him in his poems; for example, in his magnificent *Responso*. In his prose writings he speaks affectionately of "pauvre Lélian," and one of the most touching passages in his autobiography is his account of his one and only meeting with him in Paris shortly before Verlaine's death.

It is curious to find Darío in the poem before us describing the true poet as one,

> sin falsía,
> y sin comedia y *sin literatura;*

and, a little later, writing,

> Tal fué mi intento, hacer del alma pura
> mía una estrella, una fuente sonora,
> con el horror de la literatura....

Commenting on this apparent sneer at literature, Professor Coester remarks, "Apparently the poet who exercises restraint is guilty of 'literatura.'" I think, however, there can be no doubt that Darío is here echoing the concluding stanza of Verlaine's *Art poétique:*

> Que ton vers soit la bonne aventure
> Eparse au vent crispé du matin
> Qui va fleurant la menthe et le thym . . .
> Et tout le reste est littérature.

The sarcasm of the last line is obviously directed at those rhetorical and declamatory writers, whose writing, as Hamlet might have said, was merely "words, words, words"; writers like those whom Darío, in *Salutación al águila,* stigmatized as "retores latinos."

His claim to "una sensual hiperestesia"—a sensitiveness to sensuous impressions that was beyond the power of ordinary mortals—is very characteristic of the decadent school to which Darío belongs. He was no democrat: "Yo no soy un poeta para muchedumbres." He wrote for an audience of the *élite;* in short, he definitely ranges himself with Góngora and the other practitioners of the *culteranismo* of the seventeenth century.

El cisne (from *Prosas profanas*)

The influence of Wagner on the musical development of the nineteenth century is acknowledged on all hands; but his influence on the sister art of poetry, though not so great, is by no means negligible. *Lohengrin* was completed in 1850, but it was not till 1887, four years after the composer's death, that it was performed in Paris and became widely known. Darío made his first acquaintance with the opera in 1893 in Buenos Aires, where, as he tells us, he was initiated into the Wagnerian secrets by a Belgian musician and writer, M. Charles de Gouffre, and was inspired by *Lohengrin* to write this sonnet, *El cisne.* He here renders homage to the swan and its importance in classical and Scandinavian mythology, but regards the swan of modern times as something more significant. The swan that brings Lohengrin to the rescue of Elsa is a new inspiration and introduces the poet to a new world of the imagination:

> fué en medio de una aurora, fué para revivir. . . .

This is the sentiment uttered by Wordsworth a hundred years earlier; but it was no less the spirit that animated the younger poets of Spanish America at the time Darío was writing, for to them also

> Bliss was it in that dawn to be alive,
> But to be young was very heaven.

The swan was their symbol, and the symbolism of the swan is authoritatively expounded in this poem.

Like the Romantic poets, Byron, Espronceda, and Zorrilla, Darío cherished his "lost illusions." The world around him was a vain thing; there was nothing in life to inspire lofty thoughts or noble actions. Hence he addresses the swans:

> ¿Qué haremos los poetas sino buscar tus lagos? ...
> —que habéis sido los fieles en la desilusión.
> —*Los cisnes.*

The swans, at least, cannot serve any base utilitarian ends. They live apart, "like chiseled, wandering icebergs," thus symbolizing their cold aloofness from the ordinary things of life. Theirs is a pride Olympian—"de orgullo olímpico sois el resumen." They represent the absolute Beauty, existing for the sake of Beauty and for that alone. In this poem the swan, "eucharistic" in its purity, becomes for the new poetry the symbol of the ideal, the pure, the eternal.

"La espada de Argantir" ... is probably a reminiscence of the poet's reading of Leconte de Lisle. (See *Poèmes barbares,* 1862.)

In this as in other poems, for example, *Blasón, Los cisnes, Leda,* we note the poet's preoccupation with the story of Leda and the Swan, with which we may compare Milton's early fondness for the story of Orpheus and Eurydice; the difference in the stories pointing to a characteristic difference in the mind and temperament of the two poets.

In form *El cisne* is a sonnet written in lines of fourteen syllables (the Spanish Alexandrine). Darío asserted that this form was his invention, the first example being his sonnet, *Caupolicán* (published in *Azul,* 1888); and, though critics dispute the assertion, for one or two examples by earlier writers have been found, it is certain that this use of the Spanish Alexandrine by Darío gave it an immense popularity. It has become so popular, indeed, that it is safe to say that the majority of sonnets produced since *El cisne* have been written in this form. The longer line gives greater freedom to the writer; but to my mind it gives a feeling of diffuseness that is not always pleasant. In translating, I have adopted a line of approximately the same rhythmic effect, and in English I think the feeling of diffuseness is still more apparent.

Blasón (from *Prosas profanas,* 1896)

Blasón, dedicated to the Countess of Peralta, a French lady kindly disposed to poets, "propicia a los poetas," was written, as Darío informs us, during his stay in Madrid in connection with the Columbus centenary celebrations.

The lady's coat-of-arms shows a swan on a field azure; hence it gave the poet an opportunity for paying a pretty compliment to his friend and for singing at the same time the praises of the swan, the symbol of his art and aspirations. Discussing this poem, the distinguished Uruguayan critic, José Enrique Rodó, says:

> If one were to ask oneself for a living thing which might symbolize the genius of his [Darío's] poetry it would be necessary to mention not the lion or the eagle which obsessed the imagination of Victor Hugo, nor even the nightingale beloved of Heine, but the swan that rises at each moment over the waving foam of his verses, called up by insistent evocation, and whose image, when the nobility of the poets is emblazoned, might be engraved on one of the quarters of his shield, as one might engrave on the poetic escutcheon of Poe the ominous raven, or on that of Baudelaire the pensive and hieratic cat.[6]

In this poem, as in *El cisne,* Darío brings together all the pleasing myths that in his mind were associated with the swan; first, the myth of Leda and the Swan, and, by association, Leonardo da Vinci, who painted a great picture on this subject, of which, however, only a sketch has been preserved. A nineteenth-century engraving by Le Roux helped to give a fresh popularity to this story. A further classical reference is contained in "la fuente Castalia"; for, according to one version of the story, Cygnus, pursuing the nymph Castalia, found her, when she took refuge on the slopes of Parnassus, changed into a spring (thereafter sacred to the Muses), and was himself transformed by the pitying gods into a swan so that he might ever after be near his beloved.

The reference to the Danube has puzzled the commentators; it is separated from the Lohengrin story by the reference to Leonardo, and seems to have nothing to do with the operatic legend. It may point to the widespread fame of the swan, because the Danube in ancient times was the limit of civilization; but perhaps a simpler explanation is nearer the truth. It is probably connected with the Lohengrin legend, for, although the incidents of that story are supposed to have occurred on the lower Rhine, any other German river would have done as well, and "Danubio" happened to offer a novel and interesting rhyme for the later epithet, "rubio."

The mention of Lohengrin suggests Wagner, and that leads to the introduction of Louis II, King of Bavaria from 1864 to 1886. Louis, a young man of an impressionable and highly romantic temperament, early conceived a great affection for Wagner, invited him to Munich, supported the produc-

---

[6] José Enrique Rodó, *Cinco ensayos* (Madrid, 1915).

tion of his operas, gave him a handsome pension, and enthusiastically supported the idea of building a special opera-house for Wagnerian opera at Bayreuth. He thus became the idol of the poets of the day, and was the subject of eulogistic poems, notably by Verlaine and Amado Nervo. Near the end of his reign he staged a great performance of the opera, *Lohengrin,* beside the Starnsee near his castle of Berg, he himself appearing as Lohengrin, clad in shining armor, in a barge drawn by a mechanical swan, while an orchestra on shore played the appropriate music. Hence the "lago sonoro." Of the king's death by drowning in the lake shortly afterward, the actual circumstances have never been ascertained, as his only companion, his physician, was drowned at the same time. This death is the "novia de Luis de Baviera" for whom the gondola of gold is waiting.

<blockquote>El alado aristócrata . . .</blockquote>

The swan is the aristocrat among birds, as Darío felt himself to be an aristocrat of the spirit in the midst of a sordid democracy. He speaks of himself as "abominando la democracia, funesta a los poetas, así sean sus adoradores como Walt Whitman." Hence, his mind turns naturally to courtly scenes. In imagination he sees the blue expanse of the lake crossed by the glittering white swans, and this reminds him of the fleurs-de-lis, the emblem of the kings of France. This again carries him back to the court of Louis XV, to the lake at Versailles, and to the king's favorite, Madame de Pompadour, lavishing her favors on the swans.

Metrically, this is another of Darío's experiments in versification, the line consisting of three anapaests with the hypermetrical syllable; or, technically described, it is anapaestic trimeter, hypercatalectic.

Sinfonía en gris mayor (from *Prosas profanas*)

This poem, as Darío observes, naturally recalls the *Symphonie en blanc majeur* of Théophile Gautier (written about 1852), and it seems fair to assume that here Darío deliberately offers a challenge to the French poet.

Gautier in his *Symphonie,* seeking symbols whereby he may convey to his reader the dazzling whiteness of one of the fabled "femmes-cygnes" that swim singing in the Rhine, paints a picture of extraordinary brilliance. Whence comes it, he asks,

<blockquote>
De quel mica de neige vierge,
De quelle moelle de roseau,
De quelle hostie et de quel cierge
A-t-on fait le blanc de sa peau?
</blockquote>

And the remainder of the poem is a bringing together of all the white and rare and beautiful things in nature as possible sources of this splendor: le marbre blanc, la laiteuse opale, l'ivoire, des papillons blancs, l'hermine vierge de souillure, les blanches dentelles des vasques, fleurs de l'ondine en l'air figés, etc. The images are beautiful, and the smoothness and beauty of the language intensify the effect. But the effect is almost overpowering: there is no escape from this "implacable blancheur"; there is no background or relief. The poem lacks, to make it truly symphonic, as the title suggests that it should be, the contrast of tone and movement that every good symphony possesses.

The *Sinfonía en gris mayor* is an equally graphic presentation of its subject. Darío notes that this poem was "drawn from nature," and adds:

> I have seen these stagnant waters, those blazing coasts, the old sea-wolves who loaded the dye-wood on their sloops and brigantines, and departed with sails set for Europe. Drinking, morose, or smiling, they sat on the poop in the evenings, singing songs of Normandy or Brittany, and accompanying themselves on their accordeons, while the woods and estuaries near by, overgrown with mangrove, sent forth puffs of hot wind and night-dew from the marshes.[7]

Such is the picture Darío paints in prose, a picture little less brilliant than that in the poem. In the latter, however, the power of suggestion is greater. "A common grayness silvers everything," and is almost palpable. We feel the tang of salt in the air, and hear the insects' monotonous buzz that gives a feeling of reality to the tropical afternoon. The artistic instinct of Darío, it seems to me, shows itself truer than that of Gautier, for in the Nicaraguan's poem the grayness is not unrelieved: the burnished face and the red nose of the old mariner give the variety necessary in a poem that proclaims itself a symphony.

In metrical structure this poem is dodecasyllabic, the syllables being distributed into four amphibrachs, catalectic in the second and fourth lines in each stanza. As in most modern Spanish-American verse, the recurrence of the accent is more regular than is customary in earlier Spanish verse.

Friso (from *Prosas profanas*)

Darío's interest in classical mythology and his method of adapting it to his own purposes find illustration in *Friso*. This may be regarded as another effort on the part of the poet to escape from the dullness and materialism of

---

[7] Darío, *Historia de mis libros*, p. 194.

his immediate surroundings and to find in the myths of ancient Greece the beauty that forever eluded him. There is evidence that he was not a profound classical scholar; but no more was Keats. Like Keats, however, he had so steeped himself in the ancient myths that their spirit lived again in him; their world became more intensely real than the actual world about him. Like Keats, too, he had the power to put life into the dry bones of the Dictionary of Classical Mythology. Compare, for instance, the note he found in *Le Petit Larousse* with the paraphrase he makes of the traditional list of the nine Muses:

> Clio présidait à l'histoire, Euterpe à la musique, Thalie à la comédie, Melpomène à la tragédie, Terpsichore à la danse, Erato à l'élégie, Polymnie à la poésie lyrique, Uranie à l'astronomie, enfin Calliope à l'éloquence et à la poésie héroïque.

> > Clio está en frente hecha de aurora,
> > Euterpe canta en esta lengua fina,
> > Talía ríe en la boca divina,
> > Melpómene es ese gesto que implora;
> > en estos pies Terpsícore se adora;
> > Polymnia intenta a Caliope proceso
> > por esos ojos en que Amor se quema.
> > Urania rige todo ese sistema;
> > ¡La mejor musa es la de carne y hueso!
> > —*Balada en honor de las musas de carne y hueso.*

Thus the poet supplies the same touch of life as Shakespeare gives to turn the narrative of Plutarch into the drama of *Julius Caesar*.

In *Friso* he essays a picture of Greek life in the Golden Age. He has seen, or imagined, the frieze of some Grecian temple; the figures take life before him, and the whole procession passes the lover and his beloved. Almost inevitably this poem suggests a comparison with Keats's *Ode on a Grecian Urn*. Both are Greek; but the latter preserves the restraint and severity of tone that we associate with the art of Athens, while the former is warm, pulsing with life, luxuriously sensuous—Corinthian, in fact, as is suggested by the reference to the Corinth vine under which the action develops. It is a picture of life looked at with the eyes of the Italian Renaissance, or of France under the *ancien régime*. As Darío himself said:

> > Amo más que la Grecia de los griegos
> > la Grecia de la Francia, porque en Francia
> > al eco de las risas y los juegos
> > su más dulce licor Venus escancia.

There is a difference, also, in the point of view: Keats looks on from the outside, detached from the emotions animating the figures before him; Darío identifies himself with the speaker, puts himself into the heart of the scene, and is the central figure presented in the frieze, fixed by the sculptor at the supreme moment in the life of the lover.

> What if Heaven be that fair and strong,
> At life's best, with our eyes upturned,
> Whither life's flower is first discerned,
> We, fixed so, ever should abide?

The speaker is at this point of attainment, and in tune with his mood the procession appears.

Darío, it is evident, has definitely aimed at producing the effect of a sculptured frieze, that is to say, of a thin line of figures in movement, the action never being allowed to cease entirely, each group leading on the group that follows, and eventually bringing the reader back to the point from which he started,

> cabe la fresca viña de Corinto.

This continuous, processional movement is reflected in the verse-form, just as Milton, desiring to describe the intricate interweaving of parts in the Elizabethan madrigal, does so

> In notes with many a winding bout
> Of linkèd sweetness long drawn out;
> With wanton heed and giddy cunning,
> The melting voice through mazes running;
> Untwisting all the chains that tie
> The hidden soul of harmony.

We may note here in passing Darío's use of the words "efebo" and "canéfora."[8] "Efebo" he borrows from the French, as the French borrowed it from the Greek "ephebos," meaning a young man between the ages of fifteen and twenty. Although found in French as early as 1611, it was rarely used until popularized by the Decadent poets of the latter part of the nineteenth century. "Canéfora" is taken directly from the Greek. In ancient Greece it

---

[8] It is interesting and significant to find both words in a stanza by Gutiérrez Nájera:
> Nosotros los efebos sonrientes
> llevaremos cantando a tus altares
> los junios mirtos y las rosas sueltas,
> como iban las canéforas esbeltas
> a los templos olímpicos de Ares.
> —*Canto a Hidalgo.*

was applied to maidens selected to bear on their heads wicker baskets containing the sacred utensils and offerings. In this poem it is particularly appropriate. Darío uses it again in *Responso,* his elegy on the death of Verlaine:

>Que púberes canéforas te ofrenden el acanto ...

It was on the suggestion of this line that those who organized the funeral of Darío were acting when, as the local newspapers inform us, "las más bellas vírgines de León, vestidas de canéforas, regaban flores," a touching and beautiful symbol.

Friso is written in blank verse in ordinary hendecasyllabic lines. Darío, however, allows himself much more freedom in the use of the *enjambement* than did his more immediate predecessors, for example, José María Heredia, and produces a more varied rhythm by varying the position of the caesura, in this respect going back for his model to the works of Garcilaso de la Vega (1503–1536).

Canción de otoño en primavera (from *Cantos de vida y esperanza*)

In the *Historia de mis libros* Darío writes:

>En *la Canción de Otoño en primavera* digo adiós a los años floridos, en una melancólica sonata, que, si se insiste en paragonar, tendría algo como un sentimental eco mussetiana. Es de todas mis poesías la que más suaves y fraternos corazones ha conquistado.[9]

This *Canción* has been described as the most beautiful lyric poem produced in the Spanish language since the sixteenth century. For it the poet has chosen the somewhat intractable enneasyllabic meter, but by his consummate skill has made it the vehicle of the deepest emotion. The poem throughout is suffused with a tender melancholy, which, in the refrain,

>Cuando quiero llorar, no lloro,
>y a veces lloro sin querer ...

almost breaks through into a sob.

"Herodías y Salomé" ... The "dulce niña" was fascinating, domineering, cruel, like Herodias, but her grace and beauty exercised over the poet the irresistible power of seduction that legend attributes to Salome.

"Me acerco a las rosales del jardín" ... Under this figure Darío symbolizes the perennial attraction of love.

---

[9] P. 211.

"¡Mas es mía Alba de Oro!" Glory and immortality are the reward of the poet; these will never grow old.

In *Cabezas,* speaking of Amado Nervo and of the years they spent together in Paris, Darío writes:

> ¡Todo pasa, en verdad, y la juventud más pronto que todo! De aquellos años quedaron para el poeta los versos imperecederos y un amor perecedero [Nervo's sweetheart had died in Paris]. El poeta ha clamado trenos y elegías. *¡Mas es suya el Alba de Oro!*

Mía

In *Mía* we have a passionate love-poem, filled with intense feeling made more forcible by extreme compression.

The metaphor "Tu sexo fundiste"... leaves something to be desired; for two metals fused in the crucible will produce one alloy, not two. What is probably intended is that the weakness of the woman will be counteracted by the strength of the man, which in turn will be humanized in presence of the fragility of the woman.

The poem is interesting as an example of Darío's experiments in versification. He retains the rhyming scheme of the sonnet; but, instead of the ordinary hendecasyllable, he employs a short line of six syllables with entire success.

Para una cubana

This poem presents another of Darío's experiments in sonnet-form variations, this time in lines of eight syllables; but it is more remarkable for the exotic rhymes upon which it is built. Indeed, it looks as if the poet had played first with the rhymes and eventually found a subject to which they could be fitted. Triple rhymes (proparoxytones) are not common in earlier Spanish verse; but certain of Darío's followers make great play with them.[10]

The adjective "eucarística" is one of Darío's favorite epithets. He applies it in *Blasón* to the swan's wing—"el ala eucarística y breve." It reminds the poet of the whiteness of the sacramental Host; and further suggests purity, holiness, mystery.

Margarita

Margarita is the record of a vivid personal experience. Marguerite Gautier is the heroine of the novel, *La Dame aux camélias,* by Alexandre Dumas *fils*. Darío in his *Historia de mis libros* notes, however, that it was not death

---

[10] See Leopoldo Lugones, *El lunario sentimental.*

that separated the lovers; they merely drifted apart. In his autobiography he relates how on a later occasion they actually met again, but as little more than strangers to each other. In this sonnet the poet uses the line of fourteen syllables, one of his most successful innovations.[11]

Los tres reyes magos

In *Los tres reyes magos* the poet attempts to recapture the spirit of the earliest known Spanish poems, such for example as the *Auto de los reyes magos,* extant in a manuscript attributed by Menéndez y Pelayo to the twelfth century. It illustrates his interest in the older literature of Spain. The months he spent in the National Library at Managua were devoted to reading the Spanish classics; and traces of this study are to be found in his poems, *Dezires, leyes y canciones,* which were based on material found in a *Cancionero castellano del siglo XV.*

A comparison of Darío's poem with the earlier treatment of the same subject shows that he has succeeded in retaining some of the simplicity and directness of the ancient writer. Each of his kings makes the simple announcement of his gift and does not attempt to explain its significance. On the other hand, the sentiment of the lines,

> La blanca flor tiene sus pies en lodo;
> y en el placer hay la melancolía...

is not medieval; rather it is characteristic of the Decadent school to which Darío belonged. The same applies to the metaphor in the third stanza:

> el lucero puro
> que brilla en la diadema de la Muerte.

The meaning here is obscure; indeed, the last line seems to have been suggested by the necessity for finding a rhyme for "fuerte."

La dulzura del ángelus

Commenting on this poem, González Blanco holds that it may be regarded as a proof of Darío's deeply religious nature and his ardent Catholicism.[12] Such a view, however, seems exaggerated and about as ridiculous as his panegyric on the poet's *sensualismo*. What we have here is nothing more than the reaction of a sensitive mind to the aesthetic charm of a quiet countryside as the bells ring out their message; and one need no more be an

---

[11] Cf. *El cisne.*   [12] Andrés González Blanco, *Estudio preliminar* (Madrid, 1910), p. 146.

ardent Catholic to appreciate its beauty than one need be a Catholic to feel the charm of Millet's picture, the *Angelus*. Reproductions of that picture were very popular at the time Darío was writing, and may have suggested the subject to his mind. More important as characteristic of Darío and his school is the almost morbid preoccupation with the thought of death, the prospect of which seems to fill him with a strange fear. He returns to this subject in other poems, notably in *Lo fatal,* in which his fears, doubts, and questionings are more fully though not more beautifully expressed.

> Ser y no saber nada, y ser sin rumbo cierto,
> y el temor de haber sido y de un futuro terror...
> . . . .
> y no saber adónde vamos,
> ni de dónde venimos!...

In spite of all, however, he gets no farther than Omar Khayyám:

> "I came like water, and like wind I go."
> Into this Universe, and why not knowing,
> Nor whence, like water willy-nilly flowing;
>   And out of it, as wind along the waste,
> I know not whither, willy-nilly blowing.

Here we may note the curious and beautifully poetic figure,

> El áureo ovillo vespertino
> que la tarde devana tras opacos cristales
> por tejer la inconsútil tela de nuestros malos,
> todos hechos de carne y aromados de vino,

an example of the kind of imagery that earned for Darío the title of the "new Góngora." Though somewhat obscure, it seems possible to trace its evolution. Mention of the "rudo destino" has recalled to the mind of the poet the classical legend of the three fates spinning the thread of man's destiny. But to Darío man's life seems more than a single thread; it is a complicated web of many strands, of good and evil, inextricably interwoven; and though for the moment the skies seem bright, fate holds behind them and hidden from our eyes ("tras opacos cristales") the yarn all spun and ready for its weaving.

It seems plain from the line,

> todos hechos de carne y aromados de vino...

that Darío was conscious that much of the suffering he endured was the fruit of his own intemperance; but the pathos and delicacy of this line might win him pardon!

Salutación del optimista

It is a proof of the versatility of Darío that on occasion he was able to leave his "ivory tower" and concern himself with the life of ordinary men around him. Hence, we have a number of poetical pieces which display certain important characteristics of his mind and art, and which at the same time illustrate the movement of thought and feeling that was going on in Spanish-American countries about the time he wrote.

Of these poems the *Salutación del optimista* is important as pointing to a change of attitude in Spanish-American writers toward the mother country, Spain. It is a far cry from Darío to Dr. Fernández Madrid, a native of Colombia, who wrote about 1830:

> Sangre española corre por mis venas;
> Mío es su hablar, su religión mía;
> Todo menos su horrible tiranía.

This writer actually looked forward (in his poems, at least) to the restoration of the throne of the Incas.

> Cesó la ignominia del yugo español;
> Ya estamos vengados,
> Y reinan de nuevo, con leyes más justas
> Más dignos del padre, los hijos del Sol.

Similar expressions of hate for Spain are to be found in the work of Olmeda (Ecuador), Sarmiento (Argentina), José Victorino de Lastarria (Bolivia), and Bernardo de Vera, author of the Chilean national anthem:

> El cadalso o la antiqua cadena
> Os presenta el soberbio español ...
> Arrancad el puñal al tirano,
> Quebrantad ese cuello feroz.

This spirit prevailed over the whole of Spanish America; but the old order was not without its defenders. In Peru, for example, Fernando Velarde violently espoused the cause of Spain; but his violence and his ill temper made Peru politically too hot for him. The same fate followed him to Ecuador, Bolivia, and Guatemala. He died in London in 1881.

An early anticipation of the attitude of Darío, and later of Chocano, is found in Ventura de la Vega (1807-1865). Though born in Buenos Aires, he lived principally in Madrid, and could therefore speak with safety. Writing in 1857, he says:

> La madre España en su seno
> Me dió acogida amorosa;
> Suyo fuí; mas siempre yo
> Recuerdo con noble orgullo
> Que allá mi cuna al arrullo
> De las auras se meció.
> Mientras rencor fratricida
> Ardió en uno y otro bando
> Mis lágrimas devorando,
> Calló mi musa afligida.
> Hoy que a coyunda tirana
> Suceden fraternos lazos,
> Y España tiende los brazos
> A la América, su hermana;
> Bañado en júbilo santo,
> Yo americano-español
> A la clara luz del Sol
> La unión venturosa canto.[13]

The reaction which this quotation presents was no doubt due to a softening of feeling as the Spanish oppression of the colonies passed into the distance; but it was also due in some measure to the fact that the various revolutions that resulted in independence from Spain did not at once bring in the millennium. On the contrary, they brought the various states under the control of a series of more or less irresponsible dictators, like Porfirio Díaz in Mexico, or Juan Manuel Ortiz de Rosas in Argentina. What, however, contributed more than anything else to the revulsion of feeling of which this poem of Rubén Darío is evidence, was the war between the United States and Spain (1898). By this time, the original bitterness toward Spain had abated. Experience of the rigors of the dictatorships had allowed the growth of a kindlier feeling toward the mother country, and throughout Spanish America the attitude of the United States was bitterly resented.

The great celebrations that had taken place in 1892 on the occasion of the fourth centenary of the discovery of America had also their effect in bringing closer together the scattered members of the Spanish race.

In the line where the poet speaks of the fall of the colossi and the sundering of the two-headed eagles, some critics have thought they detected a prophecy of the disasters of the World War. Darío, however, was not a prophet. What he had in mind was more probably the defeat of Russia in

---

[13] Quoted by Menéndez y Pelayo, *Historia de la poesía hispanomericana*, 2:430.

the Russo-Japanese War, or the approaching dissolution of the Austro-Hungarian Empire. The latter had been a commonplace of political prophecy for half a century, but was not accomplished in Darío's lifetime.

A Roosevelt

Darío concludes his preface to *Cantos de vida y esperanza,* in which the ode to Roosevelt appeared, with these words:

> Si en estos cantos hay política, es porque aparece universal. Y si encontráis versos a un presidente, es porque son un clamor continental. Mañana podremos ser yanquis (y es lo más probable); de todas maneras, mi protesta queda escrita sobre las alas de los inmaculados cisnes, tan ilustres como Júpiter.

In this ode we find the Spanish-American feeling toward the United States given full expression. Personally, Darío had no animosity for Roosevelt; indeed, in *Todo al vuelo* he speaks of him as "a marvelous example of mankind, free and untamed." He adds later, however, that he is "the genuine incarnation of the spirit and of the tendencies of his colossal country.... He is the 'representative man' of the great and growing people who seem to have eaten the Wellsian food-of-the-gods, and whose pranks and megalomania cause a natural disquiet among their neighbors."[14] This is the point of view taken by Darío in this poem, the Latin-American view of the United States, the natural reaction to the later developments of the Monroe Doctrine. It was not the first expression of this feeling, but it is the first in which a really great writer gave it the weight of his personal prestige. The fear of American "imperialism" had recently received great impetus from the acquisition by the United States of the concession to build a canal through the Isthmus of Panama. The same fear continues and finds expression today in spite of the "peace missions" of Mr. Hoover, Colonel Lindbergh, and Will Rogers. Darío eulogizes, as he himself says, "the solidarity of the Spanish-American spirit in face of possible imperialistic movements of the men of the North."

In view of these facts it becomes obvious that the references in the first line to the Hebrew prophets and to Walt Whitman are ironical, referring to the alleged Pharisaism of the New England politicians and to the democracy lauded by Walt Whitman, which Darío disliked intensely.

---

[14] *Todo al vuelo,* p. 153.

Salutación al águila (from *El canto errante*, 1907)

This Greeting to the Eagle was written, as Darío informs us, on the occasion of his appointment as secretary of the Nicaraguan delegation to the Pan-American Conference at Río de Janeiro (1904). A comparison with the ode to Roosevelt reveals a difference of tone so remarkable as to be almost incredible. It must certainly have amazed and embarrassed the friends of the poet. It may be best explained, I think, as a diplomatic "gesture"—in the sense in which this word has recently become popular—intended to remove any irritation caused by the earlier poem among some members of the Pan-American group. Compared with the Roosevelt ode, it admirably illustrates the difference between the utterance of a man who has something to say and that of a man who "has to say something." Darío does not attempt to justify his change of attitude; he merely asserts that, as the eagle and the condor are closely related, therefore there ought to be amity between the peoples they symbolize. Only a poet, however, could see in a merely ornithological affinity a basis for international friendship.

His temporary conversion to the doctrine of the strenuous life,

> que los hijos nuestros dejen de ser los retores latinos,
> y aprendan de los yanquis la constancia, el vigor, el carácter ...

in view of what he had already written of its great apostle, seems strange; and no less strange in this, the most rhetorical of Darío's poems, is his sneer at the "retores latinos." He was apparently unconscious of the irony; but Pegasus, encumbered with the harness of politics, is an awkward steed to drive, and may easily carry its rider into unaccustomed places—and far enough from poetry.

Still, Darío was a poet, as this splendid stanza testifies:

> Es incidencia la Historia. Nuestro destino supremo
> está más allá del rumbo que marcan fugaces las épocas.
> Y Palenque y la Atlántida no son más que momentos soberbios
> con que puntúa Dios los versos de su augusto Poema.

There is almost a Miltonic suggestion in his use of the proper names, Palenque and Atlántida.[15] "Atlántida" has already been mentioned in the ode to Roosevelt,

> la Atlántida
> cuyo nombre nos llega resonando en Platón ...

---

[15] Cf. Where the great vision of the guarded mount
Looks towards Namancos, and Bayona's hold.

the reference being to the *Timaeus,* or to a passage in the *Critias,* where Plato makes it the site of his ideal republic.[16]

With "Palenque" the poet opens new vistas to the imagination, following a line he had already marked out in a passage inserted parenthetically in his remarks prefatory to his *Prosas profanas,* a passage on which José Santos Chocano based his New Americanism of the aborigine:

> Si hay poesía en nuestra América, ella está en las viejas cosas: en Palenque y Utatlán, en el indio legendario, y en el inca, sensual y fino, y en el gran Moctezuma de la silla de oro. Lo demás es tuyo, demócrata Walt Whitman.

Buried amidst vast forests in southern Mexico, in the state of Chiapas, are the ruins of Palenque, which must at one time have been a great city with temples, palaces, and other monuments. Deserted by its inhabitants at least three hundred years before the arrival of the Spaniards, it was not rediscovered till 1750; and even today, though archaeologists are agreed on attributing it to the Mayas, they can give no definite pronouncement as to the date of its construction.

> Unlike Copan, yet buried, too, 'mid trees,
> Upspringing there for sumless centuries,
> Behold a royal city, vast and lone,
> Lost to each race, to all the world unknown
> Like famed Pompeii 'neath her lava bed,
> Till chance unveiled the 'City of the Dead.'
> Palenque! seat of kings!
> —Southey, *Madoc.*

The reference to the Southern Cross "que Dante miró" is an interesting proof of Darío's wide reading. The passage, in *Purgatorio,* Canto I, is thus translated by Cary:

> To the right hand I turned, and fix'd my mind
> On the other pole attentive, where I saw
> Four stars ne'er seen before save by the ken
> Of our first parents. . . .
>
> (Io mi volsi a man destra e posi mente
> All' altro polo, e vidi quattro stelle
> Non viste mai fuor ch' alla prima gente. . . .)

Whether this mention of the Southern Cross was, as Darío believed, a prophetic intuition on Dante's part, for in Dante's day this constellation was not known in Europe, or whether it had come to his knowledge through Arab traders, is not clear; nor does it here concern us.

---

[16] See Plato, Jowett's translation (Oxford, 1892), vol. 3, *Timaeus,* p. 446; *Critias,* pp. 535-542.

DARÍO'S HEXAMETERS

In *Salutación del optimista* and *Salutación al águila* Darío puts into practice the theory that he had stated with some vigor in his preface to *Cantos de vida y esperanza:*

> In all cultured countries in Europe the absolutely classical hexameter has been used without causing either in the lettered majority or in the well-read minority any dismay with this manner of singing. In Italy, without going back to the ancients, it is long since Carducci authorized hexameters; in English, I should hardly dare—out of respect to the culture of my readers—to point out that the *Evangeline* of Longfellow is in the same meter as that in which Horace uttered his finest thoughts.

In his *Historia de mis libros* he returns to the same topic:

> I chose the hexameter as being of the Greco-Latin tradition. I believe, after having studied the matter, that in our language there are, despite the opinion of many professors, long and short syllables and that what has been lacking is a deeper and more musical analysis of our prosody.[17]

Ricardo Jaimes Freyre takes issue with him on this point:

> The ear equalizes the syllables, no matter what may be the number and position of their components. No one nowadays seeks the key to our versification in the prosody of Latium; but attempts continue to be made in the composition of Spanish hexameters and pentameters, with a tenacity the more deplorable as there is no possibility of deceiving oneself as to the fruit of these painful labors.[18]

He adds later,

> It has been experimentally proved that the accent, the intensity of the syllables varies, but not the duration.[19]

Unfortunately, he gives no account of the experiments that he held to have proved his statement. More recently, Navarro Tomás in his laboratory in Madrid has examined the matter, and by an ingenious mechanical device has measured in hundredths of seconds the exact duration of syllables in Spanish verse, taking as example the first twelve lines of Darío's poem, *La princesa era triste*. The results of this experiment are recorded in the *Revista de filología española.*[20] They prove conclusively that there are long and short syllables in Spanish verse, but that the same syllable may be at one time long and at another short; i.e., that in Spanish a vowel is not long by nature or by position, as in Latin verse; and that its length is determined by

---

[17] P. 205.
[18] *Leyes de la versificación castellana*, pp. 16–17.
[19] *Ibid.*, p. 18.
[20] Vol. 9, 1922.

its position with regard to the principal accents of the line and to the final pause. So far, therefore, Darío was right in his contention. Navarro Tomás further proved that in general the long syllables coincided with the accents. Had this been the whole of the matter, Darío's experiments in hexameters might have been successful. But one of the principal beauties of the Latin hexameter was its artful interweaving of dactyls and spondees; and in Spanish, even more than in English, a natural spondee is impossible, as each word having more than one syllable has but one principal accent, and never has two accented syllables together. Hence no imitation of the classical hexameter in English or in Spanish can give the effect of the spondee as found in Virgil or Horace. It would be impossible, for example, to reproduce in Spanish such an effect as Horace gets in the line:

In scen|am miss|us mag|no cum | pondere | versus.

Here, of course, Horace is poking fun at the author who overloads his line with spondees; but, writing seriously, he gives us:

Mox eti|am pec|tus prae|ceptis | format am|icis
Asperitatis et invidiae corrector et irae;

where, especially in the first line, the effect of the spondees is very striking and pleasing. Darío, to get spondees into his line, is forced to do violence to the language. Thus the line,

La di|vina | reina de | luz, la ce|leste Espe|ranza,

cannot be scanned as a hexameter unless the first two syllables are treated as a spondee, and the next two as another; and I do not think a cultured Spaniard would read the line in that way. As if to compensate for the weakness of the spondee in his verse, Darío takes a liberty that is fairly common in modern Spanish poetry. If his caesura is preceded by one or two unaccented syllables, he disregards them and introduces two more unaccented syllables before the next strong accent, as in the line

y en la | caja pan|dórica || de que | tantas des|gracias sur|gieron....

These added syllables are described by Jaimes Freyre as *sílabas agregadas,* and are held to be absorbed (*embebidas*) in the pause. Whether this is so or not, they certainly give a heaviness to the line that is neither Virgilian nor Horatian. In his best lines, as in the first line of *Salutación del optimista,*

Inclitas razas ubérrimas, sangre de Hispania fecunda ...

Darío makes as near an approximation to the Latin hexamater as Longfellow did in *Evangeline;* but neither attains the dignified movement of real Virgilian verse:

> Tantae molis erat Romanam condere gentem.

The closest parallel to the Darían hexameter is to be found in Carducci, and it was probably the rhythm of his verse that Darío had in mind when he wrote *Salutación del optimista*. The following lines, for example, from *Sogno d'estate,* show the same departures from the classical hexameter as Darío was in the habit of making—the anacrusis in lines (2) and (3), and the *sílabas agregadas* in lines (3) and (4).

> (1) E un' aura dolce movendo quei fiori e gli odori
> (2) *v*eniva giú dal mare; nel mar quattro candide vele
> (3) *an*davano and*avano cu*llandosi lente nel sole,
> (4) che mare e terra e *cielo s*fo*lg*orante circonfondeva.[21]

In many lines, however, Darío's verse follows no definite pattern: his dithyrambic utterance may be best regarded as an eloquent or grandiloquent kind of free verse.

◇ ◇ ◇

AMADO NERVO[22]

AMADO NERVO IS, next to Darío, the most widely read of Spanish-American poets. He was an intimate friend of Darío's, and, like him, spent the most productive years of his life in Paris and Madrid. From 1905 to 1918 he was secretary to the Mexican legation in the Spanish capital.

In his home as a child, he had been surrounded by an atmosphere of tranquil piety. He studied with the intention of entering the priesthood, and

---

[21] *Antologia Carducciana* (Bologna, 1929), p. 219.
[22] Born at Tepic, Mexico, 27th August, 1870. Died at Montevideo, Uruguay, 24th May, 1919.
WORKS—

VERSE	PROSE
Perlas negras. Mexico, 1898	*El bachiller.* Mexico, 1896
Poemas. Paris, 1901	*Otras vidas.* Barcelona, n.d.
El exodo. Mexico, 1902	*Almas que pasan.* Madrid, 1906
Las flores del camino. Mexico, 1902	*Juana de Asbaje (estudio sobre Sor Juana de*
Perlas negras, Místicas, Las voces. Paris, 1904	*la Cruz).* Madrid, 1910
Los jardines interiores. Mexico, 1905	*Ellos.* Paris, 1912
En voz baja. Madrid, 1909	*Mis filosofías.* Paris, 1912
Serenidad. Madrid, 1914	*El diablo desinteresado.* Madrid, 1916
Elevación. Madrid, 1916	*Plenitud.* Madrid, 1918
El estanque de los lotos. Madrid, 1918	
El arquero divino. Madrid, 1920 (posthumous)	

Los cien mejores poesías. Introduction by E. González Martínez. Mexico, 1919
Obras completas. Madrid, 1920–. Twenty-eight volumes

was just on the point of taking the final step before becoming a priest when he withdrew, preferring the secular life. The influence of his early surroundings and training is visible in the distinctly religious tone of most of his writings; and in his life in Paris, though he mingled freely with gay companions, he was known as *el monje de la poesía*. At times, indeed, the tone of the preacher predominates in his verse to the detriment of his poetry.

His long association with Darío was due to a deep sympathy with Darío's aims and ideals, a sympathy which finds expression in the poem, *Homenaje*, written on the occasion of Darío's death (1916). In this poem, the refrain

> Ha muerto Rubén Darío,
> ¡el de las piedras preciosas!

is significant, indicating the aspect of the master's work that most strongly appealed to the younger man. What Amado Nervo most admired was evidently the clear-cut imagery, the precision and delicacy of his workmanship, such that each poem

> twinkled with diamond sparks,
> Myriads of topaz-lights, and jacinth-work
> Of subtlest jewellery;

and this delicacy of workmanship he was eminently successful in reproducing in his own work.

Thus we find in Amado Nervo the same fondness for experimenting with new metrical effects as in Darío, the same sensitiveness to the musical quality of words and rhythms, the same felicity of phrase, and the touch of melancholy characteristic of the Modernist school—though he wears his rue with a difference.

Yet there are elements in the work of Amado Nervo that are hardly perceptible in that of Darío. For example, his early poems display a certain pantheistic sentiment, as in *La hermana agua* and *Viejo estribillo:*

> Oh, Señor, ¡la belleza sólo es, pues, espejismo;
> Nada más. Tú eres cierto, sé Tú mi último dueño.
> ¿Dónde hallarte, en el éter, en la tierra, en mí mismo?
> —Un poquito de ensueño te guiará en cada abismo,
> un poquito de ensueño. . . .

Later, in *El puente*—the fanciful title reminds one of *The Pulley,* by George Herbert, another mystic—he comes very close to the thought of Wordsworth.

Dime, ¿has estado en un éxtasis alguna vez? ¿Sentiste
uno de esos instantes en que el pensar no existe;
porque—lo dijo Wordsworth—"expiró en la alegría"?

en que mueren las dudas, en que se explica todo:
la excelencia del astro, la ignominia del lodo,
y el mundo es como un símbolo de sutil poesía?

Parenthetically we may note that this mention of Wordsworth is somewhat remarkable, as it would seem from the writings of other poets that almost the only poetical work in English known in Spanish America is that of Walt Whitman or of Edgar Allan Poe. It is also an evidence of the broad culture of Amado Nervo. What he has in mind is obviously the *Tintern Abbey* lines in which Wordsworth speaks of

> that serene and blessed mood
> In which the affections gently lead us on,
> Until, the breath of this corporeal frame
> And even the motion of our human blood
> Almost suspended, we are laid asleep
> In body, and become a living soul;
> While with an eye made quiet by the power
> Of harmony, and the deep power of joy,
> We see into the life of things.

Nervo, however, did not attain to this power of mystic absorption without struggle. Like Darío, like Verlaine, he experienced the seductions of the flesh and the torments of a stylite; but the combat between the soul and the body, the spiritual and the material, Christ and Pan, which in Darío ceased only with death, had in the Mexican poet an earlier and happier ending. In 1914, he wrote:

> Siento que estoy en las laderas
> de la montaña augusta de la Serenidad;

and, having attained this peace of mind, he was able at last to comprehend the meaning of things:

> Comprendo al fin el vasto sentido de las cosas...

which furnishes an interesting anticipation of the teaching of González Martínez (*q.v.*).

It is this struggle and its "quiet consummation" that are illustrated in the poems here translated. *Cobardía,* which appeared in the volume entitled *Serenidad* (1914), with its touch of irony probably belongs to an earlier period, as do one or two others, which are dated, in the same collection. In this poem Nervo uses the dodecasyllable arranged in four amphibrachs. This form was a favorite with him, and he celebrated it in a poem beginning:

> El metro de doce son cuatro donceles,
> donceles latinos de rítmica tropa....[23]

El día que me quieras appeared in a posthumous volume, *El arquero divino* (1920). It also seems to belong to an early period in the poet's career, probably between 1910 and 1914. It is, I think, unique in modern Spanish-American poetry, for if there is one thing more remarkable than another in the poetical work of this period, it is the note of melancholy, tending usually to become morbid. Here there is nothing of that kind. Instead, we have the spontaneous welling up of a spirit at peace within itself, and able to look out upon the world and find all things good. This is the happiest poem of the period under consideration.

This, however, is not the prevailing tone of Nervo's work. Dominating its transparency of form and its almost overpowering sweetness is the note of an ascetic melancholy. This is not the melancholy of Milton, austere and majestic,

> Whose saintly visage is too bright
> To hit the sense of human sight;

nor yet the melancholy of Darío and Burns, which found its source in a pained reflection over the past and an equally painful anticipation of the future:

> But och! I backward cast my e'e
> On prospects drear,
> An' forward, though I canna see,
> I guess an' fear;

nor even the whimsical melancholy of Jaques. Nervo's melancholy is a wistful and expectant longing for the great revelation that is to come:

> El ansia del misterio me agita y desespera...

but death will reveal all:

> La Muerte se aproxima; ¡de sus labios oirás el celeste secreto!

Closely allied to this melancholy is the sense of mystery in outward nature and in human life. Something of this power of suggesting the mysterious is found in the poem, «*Tel qu'en songe*», where the reiteration of the phrase,

---

[23] *Obras completas*, 7:63.

"en los sueños," has a very curious effect. So in nature he finds secret meanings which he attempts to interpret to men. In *La hermana agua,* for example, he reads the lesson which he condenses into: "Ser dócil, ser cristalino; ésta es la ley y los profetas." In this spirit he lived and wrote.

As has been already hinted, Nervo's life was not without its struggle. In *Delicta carnis* (1904) he portrays the conflict of the flesh and the spirit with a vividness and power of introspection in which, I think, he excels Darío. *La montaña* (1914) shows a marked difference of feeling. By force of will he has gained a serene outlook upon life.

>   Soy sereno porque soy fuerte:
>   la fuerza infunde serenidad.
>   ¿En qué radica mi fuerza?
>   En una
>   indiferente resignación
>   ante los vuelcos de la fortuna
>   y los embates de la aflicción. . . .
>   —*Temple.*

In this mood his insight into the heart of things is deepened; he finds God everywhere, in nature and in his fellow-men; and from this springs a well of sympathy for all mankind.

For some years before his death Nervo was attracted by the teachings of Buddhism, and some of his later poems show this influence very strongly. Thus, in *Al cruzar los caminos* (1915) he exclaims:

>   He matado al anhelo para siempre jamás. . . .

In complete renunciation of desire of every kind he has found Nirvana. Yet not quite:

>   Sólo pido una cosa:
>   ¡Que me libres, oh Arcano, del horror de pensar! . . .

but to this he becomes reconciled, on one condition:

>   Sea yo como el árbol, y la espiga, y la fuente
>   que se dan en silencio. . . . ¡sin saber que se dan!

It is in this frame of mind that he writes the final poem given in this selection, *En paz,* in which thought, feeling, and poetic expression are combined to produce the harmony that is a joy forever.

The whole struggle is figured forth allegorically in *La conquista* (in *El estanque de los lotos,* the last volume published in the poet's lifetime). In this poem, the hero, Miguel, whose love has been rejected by Helena, at first determines to win her, come what may; later, counseled by "una voz augusta, nunca jamás oída" (the voice of the "dios interior"), that fortifies him with a strange mixture of the philosophies of Buddha and Schopenhauer, he reaches the point where all desire is quenched, love's power over him ceases, and he finds his real happiness in the single life devoted to contemplation. One feels, however, that the scales were rather unfairly weighted against the lady, who was only eighteen while her lover was forty. Had Miguel been twenty years younger, one doubts whether either Buddha or Schopenhauer would have counted for more than two grains of sand in the balance.

◇ ◇ ◇

RICARDO JAIMES FREYRE

AND THE THEORY OF MODERNIST VERSIFICATION

AS WAS INEVITABLE in a scientific age, the emergence of a new poetic genius and of the imitators who more or less successfully followed him, led to an attempt to find the secret of the new beauty that had been revealed. It was evident that Darío had paid little heed to the rules of the older school, but in spite of that, or because of it, had attained effects of surprising beauty. It followed, therefore, that the older conceptions of what was desirable or permissible in verse were inadequate. To find a system or formula that should cover the newer developments and make possible the discovery of others was the object of the investigation undertaken by Ricardo Jaimes Freyre; and the results of his researches he has embodied in his book, *Leyes de la versificación castellana*.[24]

Jaimes Freyre dismisses very shortly the "Classical" theory with its postulates of syllables either long or short, for, he declares, Spanish verse is purely accentual.[25] He discards equally the "American" theory of Andrés Bello, Luis Quintín Vila, and Eduardo de la Barra, for, retaining only the five metrical feet, iambus, trochee, dactyl, anapaest, and amphibrach, with strong and weak accents in place of long and short syllables respectively, they leave no room for a measure like that introduced by José Asunción Silva, who successfully wrote in a measure composed of feet of four syllables ∪∪-∪

---

[24] Ed. 2, La Paz, 1919.   [25] See the discussion of this point, *supra*, "Darío's Hexameters."

(— representing an accented, and ⏑ an unaccented syllable), which one might describe as an "augmented anapaest":

| Ў̆ mĭ sōmbră |
pŏr lŏs rāyŏs | dĕ lă lūnă | prŏyēctădă. . . .

What he calls the "vulgar" or "commonly accepted" theory he finds equally unsatisfactory, for it attempts to assign a definite number of syllables to each line, and indicates certain fixed points at which the rhythmical accents must appear. This unduly limits the freedom of the poet; and in fact modern poets disregard any such regulation.

Setting aside these theories, Jaimes Freyre states his new law as follows: In Spanish verse the line consists of one or more *prosodic periods;* each prosodic period consists of one or more syllables up to the number of seven, the last syllable in each period bearing a strong accent, the *rhythmic accent,* although the period may contain other secondary accents.

These periods may be (1) *equal,* i.e., containing the same number of syllables; (2) *analogous,* i.e., containing different numbers of syllables, but either *all even* numbers, or *all odd* numbers; or (3) *different,* i.e., containing different numbers of syllables, but some even, some odd. The combination of *equal* or *analogous* periods gives verse; the combination of *different* periods gives prose.

If a period ends (1) with an oxytone (*aguda*), the period is *pure;* if it ends (2) with a paroxytone (*grave*), it is *compound;* and if it ends (3) with a proparoxytone (*esdrújula*), it is *compound.* In (2) and (3), before a metrical pause, the unaccented syllable or syllables (*sílabas agregadas*) are not counted as part of the following period, being absorbed (*embebidas*) in the metrical pause.

It is at this point that the theory, it seems to me, gets into difficulties; for it appears that, in spite of what has just been said, the added syllables (*agregadas*) *may* or *may not* be counted as part of the following period, at the discretion of the poet or critic. Thus,

        Volaba el Mercurio de Juan de Bolonia

(strong accents underlined) is cited as made up of two pentasyllabic periods; that is, the *-rio* (sixth syllable) is absorbed in the metrical pause; whereas

        No hallarás el órden del Universo . . .

and   Si no ves del cielo la clara luz . . .

are also treated as pairs of pentasyllabic periods, the *-en* and the *-lo* (sixth syllables) being counted as integral parts of the second period.
Similarly, in

A mis ojos mortales escondido (1)

and

Oh, dulces prendas por mi mal halladas (2)

in order to get analogous periods—in (1) of six and four syllables, and in (2) of four, four, and two syllables—the *-les* and the *-das* have to be counted as integral parts of the second period. In other words, for the sake of his theory, Jaimes Freyre is reduced to the predicament of Malvolio: "Yet to crush this a little, it would yield to me!" This, it seems to me, vitiates the whole theory, for in the longer lines the whole question as to whether the periods are analogous or not turns on the treatment of those added syllables.

Again, we read: "The mixture of periods, unequal in the number of their syllables, but always even, or always odd, always forms verse. According to the nature of the combination, this verse will be more or less agreeable and harmonious."[26] Let us consider the first line of Lope de Vega's sonnet, *Judith,* beginning:

Cuelga sangriento de la cama al suelo
el hombro diestro del feroz tirano....

Here we have two analogous periods, of four and six syllables (or three periods of four, four, and two syllables)—

Cuelga sangriento de la cama al suelo;

but if we change *cuelga* to *colgó* (a mere change of tense), though the analogous periods remain as before, the harmony of the line is gone. What has destroyed the harmony? In the first place, the balance of the vowel sounds has been altered. Cuelga sangriento ... suelo, forms a combination pleasing to the ear; whereas colgó sangriento ... suelo, results in a clashing that is distinctly disagreeable. In the second place, as concerns the distribution of accent, the balance of the line has been impaired. The principal rhythmic accents remain, but the secondary accent has been changed. The importance of the secondary accents is too great to be overlooked; and this is what Jaimes Freyre does. If a new theory of verse is to be evolved, it must take into account more carefully than has hitherto been done the value of these secondary accents. This applies, of course, not only to Spanish verse, but to

---

[26] *Leyes de la versificación castellana,* p. 64.

English verse as well. In one passage Jaimes Freyre touches on this matter, but he fails to follow it to its logical conclusion:

> There are other words in which the accent, without being lost, is reduced in intensity, and others in which it is diminished or increased according to its importance for the thought or its situation in the clause. These are real *phrase-accents*.[27]

But beyond observing that the rhythmic accent should coincide with this phrase-accent he does not go. Hitherto it has been customary to assume that the strong accent was always strong, and the weak accent always weak, and that a syllable must be either strong or weak. A sensitive ear, however, soon observes that this is not so. The strong accents are not all equally strong, nor are the weak accents all equally weak; there is, in fact, a subtle gradation of accent, and the skill of the poet consists in adjusting the weight of the line so that there is a perfect balance of parts.

In seeking to account for the beauty of modern poetry Jaimes Freyre seems to be so taken up with his theory of analogous periods that he overlooks certain other things that undoubtedly contribute to the general effect. Among these is the use of *enjambement*. Of this he disapproves, insisting on a metrical pause at the end of each line. But *enjambement,* with its related and complementary device, the variation in the placing of the caesura, or internal pause, is at least as important in securing poetic effectiveness as the analogous periods to which he attributes it. It is freely used by the classical writers, for example, Gaspar Melchor de Jovellanos (1744-1811), as in the following passage:

> Huye de aquí, profano; tú que llevas
> de ideas mundanales lleno el pecho,
> huye de esta morada, do se albergan
> con la virtud humilde y silenciosa
> sus escogidos: huye, y no profanes
> con tu planta sacrílega este asilo.
> —*Epístola de Fabio a Anfriso.*[28]

So also in these lines from Juan Ramón Jiménez (a Spanish follower of Rubén Darío):

> ¡Qué amena paz en este alejamiento
> de todo: oh prado bello, que deshojas
> tus flores; oh agua, fría ya, que mojas
> con tu cristal estremecido el viento!
> —*Otoño*

---

[27] *Leyes de la versificación castellana,* pp. 53-54.
[28] James Fitzmaurice-Kelly, *The Oxford Book of Spanish Verse* (Oxford, 1925), p. 263.

the charm lies not in the prosodic periods, but in the skill with which the rhythm is varied by placing the caesura after the fourth, second, third, and eighth syllables in the successive lines. One need hardly remark that this device is liable to abuse, as in the following:

> Yo no he querido nunca molestaros cantando—
> os.—Sí, este ramo blanco de rosas de ensueño
> puede hacer una música nueva y clásica . . . ;[29]

but used with care it may be very effective.

The last chapter of the *Leyes* is taken up with a discussion of free verse, which the author shows to be no novelty, but actually a return to the primitive, though set off by a poetic style that did not find its way into Spain till the fifteenth century. He believes that the rhythm of each line must contribute to the cadence of the whole strophe. He does not accept the theory held by writers of free verse in England and the United States that the length of the line is determined by the necessity for taking breath. Apparently Walt Whitman, to whom this form in English poetry must be traced, was a man of fine physique, with a deep chest, and lungs in proportion, so that it was possible for him to recite in one breath lines that leave his more puny successors gasping. English writers, however, still hold that the line should be what the reader can conveniently speak in one breath; and much modern English free verse seems to be constructed on this principle. Spanish writers follow a principle that seems more logical and more artistic; namely, that the rhythmic units must be created in accordance with the ideas, the figures, the images, the logic of the situation; that is, that each line should represent an imaginative or emotional moment in the development of the complete thought, each phase determining its own form, as a river carves out its own channel. Jaimes Freyre insists that the beauty of cadence desired can only be attained if the successive lines are formed of equal or analogous periods; but the practice of the best writers does not seem to confirm this view. The real poetic effect is obtained only where the poet has fed

> on thoughts, that voluntary move
> Harmonious numbers.

Jaimes Freyre's main contribution to the theory of verse is the recognition of the fact that the rhythmic unit may consist of groups of more syllables than the usually recognized two or three. Both Greek and Latin poets

---

[29] Juan Ramón Jiménez, *Elejías lamentables*.

used the tetrasyllabic foot they called the *choriambus* -◡◡-, which may be regarded as a combination of a trochee and an iambus; for example,

Quōd sī | mē lyrĭcīs | vātĭbŭs īn|sĕrīs,
Sūblī|mī fĕrĭām | sīdĕră vēr|tĭcĕ.

The tetrasyllabic foot used by Jaimes Freyre himself, and by Chocano, and apparently invented by José Asunción Silva, cannot be so resolved, but is an original rhythmic unit particularly suited to the genius of the Spanish language. With regard to the longer prosodic periods (of five, six, or seven syllables), it may safely be said that, as Jaimes Freyre admits the existence of secondary accents within them, they may be resolved into the feet hitherto recognized, with such variations as the poet guided by his instinct for harmony may be pleased to introduce.

◇ ◇ ◇

RICARDO JAIMES FREYRE[30]

JAIMES FREYRE, whose work on the theory of verse has just been discussed, is a poet of considerable merit, who has tried to put into practice in verse the principles he laid down in prose. It is possible, however, to read all his poems without becoming aware that such an attempt is being made, for their attraction lies not in the principles they exemplify, but in their own refinement and delicate beauty.

He was a close friend of Darío's during his stay in Buenos Aires, and collaborated with him in the production of a short-lived literary review, the *Revista de América,* by which they hoped to win over the more ardent spirits to the new gospel of Modernism. He was for many years Professor of Literature and Philosophy in the University of Tucumán, and in 1923 was appointed Bolivian Minister to the United States.

Like other Modernist poets, Jaimes Freyre seeks his inspiration in scenes remote from the world of the present and the actual, but not in the myth-

---

[30] Born in Bolivia, 1870(?).
WORKS—
    VERSE
Castalia bárbara. Buenos Aires, 1899
Castalia bárbara. Ed. 2, published with *País de sueño* and *País de sombra,* La Paz, Bolivia, 1918
Los mas bellos poemas. Introduction by Leopoldo Lugones. Mexico, 1920
    PROSE
Leyes de la versificación castellana. La Paz, 1912; ed. 2, La Paz, 1919

ology of ancient Greece nor among the artificialities of eighteenth-century Versailles. Influenced to some degree by Leconte de Lisle (*Poèmes barbares*) and by Wagner, he gratifies his taste for the exotic among the legends of the gods and heroes of Valhalla and of the great Wagnerian cycle. In this respect he offers a curious parallel to Thomas Gray, whose *Norse Odes* (1761) were his first response to the Romantic movement then just beginning in England. Moreover, the parallel does not end there. The two poets are very much alike in their devotion to scholarship, in their mild melancholy, in their revolt against prevailing standards and aims in literature, in the comparative meagerness of their poetic production, in the delicacy of their workmanship, and in the coldness and gloom that pervade their work. Jaimes Freyre's figures move in deep and pathless forests in an atmosphere of darkness and mystery, pierced now and then by flashes of fiery red. This at least is the impression produced by his first work, *Castalia bárbara,* and most notably by the poem, *Aeternum vale,* which is regarded by so competent a critic as Leopoldo Lugones as one of the finest poetic works in all Spanish-American literature. In this poem the poet symbolizes the rout of the older Teutonic gods before the advance of Christianity. Under an aged ash tree among the sacred woods a strange, new deity has been seen. The daughter of Thor (Thrud, the dense thundercloud) on her black steed carries the news to the assembled gods. There are strange noises among the branches, and the wild beasts flee before the approaching danger. Savage incantations are raised, and Thor, brandishing his mace, goes forth to do battle with the intruder. The gods look on while the whirling mace darkens the heavens. . . . When the sky has cleared, the sacred song has ceased; even the amorous voice of Freya is silent. The gods are in their last agony: "The silent God who holds his arms outstretched" has conquered.

In this poem, Jaimes Freyre uses very effectively the device of repeating the characteristic phrase,

el Dios silencioso que tiene los brazos abiertos,

evidently adapting to literary use the idea of the *leitmotif* that Wagner had already made popular in music (though even in music it was employed before Wagner's time). As used by Wagner, the musical phrase heard in one dramatic setting is brought in later, sometimes unchanged, but more often varied, developed, and transformed, to recall to the minds of the audience persons, events, and emotions associated with its earlier appearance. In music the effect is wonderful; in poetry it is less so. For words, though they come to the poet, trailing clouds of glorious association with them, are much more definite and restricted in their power of suggestion than music is. Hence, particularly in shorter poems, such as *Canción de la primavera* and *El canto del graal,* such repeated phrases, even though ingeniously worked in, are disappointing and not a little tedious. The scale of the work is too small. This, in fact, is the general impression left by the poems dealing with such subjects. They are inadequate to the somewhat grandiose conceptions of the poet. They are only faintly reminiscent or suggestive of their themes, like a Wagnerian score "written down" for a solo on the harpsichord.

For Jaimes Freyre, as for Hamlet, the world is weary, stale, flat, and unprofitable; and the result is a pervading melancholy. Even in the sonnet in which "the poet celebrates the joy of life," while he reminds his friend that

> La misteriosa sombra no cubre el horizonte
> sin que la luz fecunda prodigue sus raudales . . .

(or, in other words, that every cloud has a silver lining) he passes on his way

> por entre el bosque humano,
> soñador y nostálgico, y triste hasta la muerte.

Life as we know it being so dull and monotonous, surely, he thinks, it would be better to live amid the romance of feudal times. Hence, in *Pórtico,* he calls up four typical figures of that age—the churl, the knight, the troubadour, and the priest. He seizes upon one bright aspect in the life of his type (though in the churl's lot he has a difficulty in finding one), and firmly closes his eyes to all the cruelty, oppression, and corruption of which as a student of history he is perfectly well aware. He eternizes the one beautiful moment of his characters, assumes for the whole a beauty he has found in a part, and consequently finds beautiful the whole age that produced them. This romantic tendency is perceptible throughout his work. Only in one poem does he seem to come face to face with the facts of human suffering and human wickedness. In this poem, *Las noches,* we find him writing:

> Flotan extraños rumores
> en el seno de la noche callada;
> ecos de vagos gemidos
> de angustias lejanas;
> de tristezas pálidas;
> ecos de risas,
> dolorosas como la desesperanza. . . .

Here, he is aware of the pain, the bitterness, the despair, that night brings to many; but, in spite of all, for the poet

> juega bajo la luz de la luna
> una alegría en cada rayo de plata.

It is in purely descriptive writing that Jaimes Freyre is at his best. In *El alba* he shows a richness of imagination in the scenes he evokes and in the associations he brings with them that is wholly admirable. His picture of the dawn breaking over the sleeping town, for example, is worthy to be set alongside of Wordsworth's picture of London seen from Westminster Bridge.

> Las auroras pálidas
> * * * *
> bañan las torres erguidas,
> que saludan su aparición silenciosa,
> con la voz de sus campanas
> soñoliente y ronca;
> ríen en las calles
> dormidas de la ciudad populosa,
> y se esparcen en los campos
> donde el invierno respeta las amarillentas hojas.

The dawn, coming from the East, brings with it the exotic scents and sounds of the Orient, and memories of Arabian deserts, of the Isles of Greece and of Venus rising from the waves, of the sword lying rusty and forgotten under the oak (a favorite symbol of this poet for the triumph of reason over brute force); and over all he throws a shimmering, opalescent light, like that suggested by the music of Debussy.

Of an entirely different kind, but equally convincing, is the scene presented in *Las voces tristes*. Here, with a few rapid strokes in the impressionistic manner, Jaimes Freyre paints a picture in which every detail—the snow, the howling of the wolves, the solitary pine tree—serves to intensify the feeling of bleak desolation which even the coming of daylight cannot dispel.

LEOPOLDO LUGONES[31]

LEOPOLDO LUGONES is a man of great energy, an original and indefatigable worker, and a versatile and prolific writer. From the first he has been inspired with a passion for innovation, and each successive volume of verse has broken new ground and displayed a new aspect of his many-sided personality.

His first work, *Montañas de oro* (1897), though hailed with acclamation by Darío and Freyre and a few of the more discerning critics of the younger school, was sneered at or studiously ignored by the majority. As it was both in form and in content a defiance of the recognized canons of poetical composition, this cool reception is hardly surprising. Following the example set by Darío in *El país del sol* (in *Prosas profanas*), Lugones had cast his thoughts into unrhymed free verse, the lines being printed as ordinary prose and separated only by dashes. (The verse itself was in no way remarkable, and shows none of the extraordinary skill of his later volumes.) In the last section of the book he does not even write verse—unless Whitman's *Leaves of Grass* can be called verse—but produces a kind of apocalyptic prose.

In the early part, Lugones seems, like many other Spanish-American poets of this period, to be writing under the influence of Edgar Allan Poe. The following example will make this clear:

Posada sobre el pliego,—en el negro dintel de mis delirios,—está una inmóvil mariposa negra.—Es media noche; por sus largos hilos—descienden las arañas ponzoñosas; sobre el mundo dormido—cae el reflejo de una inmensa luna,—como el pálido lienzo que los vivos—echan sobre la faz de los difuntos;—canta

---

[31] Born at Córdoba, Argentina, 1874.
Poet, historian, journalist, Director of the National Council of Education.
WORKS*—

VERSE	PROSE (in part)
Las montañas de oro. 1897	*El imperio jesuítico.* 1905
Los crepúsculos del jardín. 1905	*La guerra gaucha.* 1905
Lunario sentimental. 1909	*Piedras liminares.* 1910
Odas seculares. 1910	*Prometeo.* 1910
El libro fiel. 1912	*Historia de Sarmiento.* 1911
El libro de los paisajes. 1917	*La torre de Casandra.* 1919
Las horas doradas. 1922	*Estudios helénicos.* 1924
Romancero. 1924	*Cuentos fatales.* 1924
Poemas solariegos. 1928	*Nuevos estudios helénicos.* 1928

*All the works were published in Buenos Aires. Of *El libro fiel* a second edition was published in Paris in 1912.

sus coplas de lujuria el Vicio,—quemando los fragantes alcoholes—que revuelven la hez de los fastidios.—Están dormidas las exhaustas núbiles;—los ensueños lascivos,—con sus brillantes alfileres punzan—carnes que tienen floración de lirio.—Hai ásperas pimientas difundidas—en la opaca redoma de los filtros;—un vasto desconsuelo en las estrellas;—una gran pena de mortales fríos;—un murmullo de álamos simbólicos—que se alzan a la orilla del camino,—como un cortejo de delgadas viudas—veladas por el luto de los siglos.

—*Rosas de Calvario.*

The well-known critic, Mas y Pi,[32] detects in this book the influence of the Brazilian Negro poet, Cruz e Souza (on whom Jaimes Freyre had lectured in Buenos Aires in the preceding year, 1896), and points particularly to the frequent repetitions in the passage describing the triumph of the iron horse, the locomotive:

And my spirit (ideal swallow) from its tower continues gazing; and it sees... how the sounding cars run along the parallel of iron, behind the steed of iron, whose soul is a thunder of iron, in whose throat coughs the hurricane, and whose heart is tempest-tossed with live coals; great horse, a great black horse devouring flame, great horse darting forward with a quiver of enormous muscles, with a cloud in its nostrils, panting as it gallops over thousands of leagues; a great horse, a great black horse that is never seen to sweat!

It seems to me, however, that there is more of Whitman than of Cruz here; still more in some of the later passages, as, for example, the following, where the resemblance to the catalogues that make up a large part of Whitman's work is very marked:

And my spirit (ideal swallow) from its tower continues gazing, and sees that the dawn is coming, and that a buxom girl is laughing and that her laughter scatters itself like a handful of silver rings. And it sees the ships departing for either continent—for red lands, for black lands where the sun goes down among palm trees; where there are serpents that seem like poisonous gems, and flowers more gaily painted than the tigers; and bisons, and elephants, and giraffes, and birds of Paradise, and fireflies, and resins, and essences, and balsams, and corals, and pearls (these in rose-colored shells, like the Host untouched between the lips of communicants), and sweet nuts, and gold-dust, and drums and gourds and great earthen jars that make the music of the gods; and naked princesses who love the kisses of their white lovers. And Christopher Columbus goes there, with a cross and a loyal sword; and Marco Polo, with a cosmographic treatise of the world in his hand; and Vasco da Gama on the mast with an astrolabe; and Hernando de Magellan with an axe at his belt; and Dumont d'Urville with a planisphere and an anchor; and Tasman with a compass; and the "Mayflower"

---

[32] Juan Mas y Pi, *Leopoldo Lugones y su obra* (Buenos Aires, 1911), Chap. III.

with the charter of King John; and Stanley with the pencil of the *New York Herald* and his cork helmet; and Livingstone, with his Bible and his wife—David Livingstone, the father of the Nile.

The *Montañas de oro* was, as has been said, a challenge to the established order. With its atmosphere of mystery and pain and passion, it revealed a vivid, though at times chaotic and incoherent poetic imagination; but it was little regarded, and has had no imitators. Its interest today is purely historic.

Eight years elapsed between the appearance of the *Montañas* and the publication of the poet's next volume of verse, *Los crepúsculos del jardín* (1905). In this work a remarkable change of tone is noticeable. The stormy passion of the *Montañas* has disappeared, or rather, it is subdued, or hidden behind a veil of irony. In the Prologue, the poet hints that he is not to be taken quite seriously. These poems, he says, are

> Pasatiempo singular
> tal vez, o harto inocente,
> como escupir desde un puente
> o hacerse crucificar;
>
> epopeya baladí
> que, por lógico resorte
> quizá sirva a tu consorte
> para su five o'clok tea.... *(sic)*

In some of the poems, for example, *Canto del amor y de la noche, Las loas de nuestra servidumbre,* and *Los doce gozos* (a series of sonnets), the sensual quality of the amorous sentiment becomes almost tropical; but the sensuality is carried off by the sheer brilliance of the language and the cleverness of the versification. Of the finer and more spiritual aspects of love these poems show no trace. In them Lugones employs all the devices of the Parnassians: lilies, coral, marble, lakes and swans, the perfumed twilight, and, of course, the moon—"conviene siempre mencionar la luna"; but, as he remarks in one poem, "el club del Parnaso cierra su biblioteca," being unable to do justice to the lady's charms.

The outstanding poem in this volume is *El solterón,* in which we find illustrated all the characteristics of the work of Lugones at this period.

The story is skillfully told, being gradually pieced together from the fragmentary recollections of the old man. The sound of distant music starts the train of thought; he recalls his sweetheart's figure, his love, the duel, his triumph and pride.... Then something went wrong. Now, provoked by the innocent diversions of the young people, his neighbors, the thought "both of lost happiness and lasting pain" torments him. Is happiness beyond recall? he asks; Is continued suffering inevitable? There must have been some mistake; he will write to her; they shall be happy yet; and, with his pen in hand, he sits dreaming for them a future of settled contentment together. But night descends, the dream vanishes, the futility of the attempt to bring back the past is too apparent; even the pen is past writing.

The whole tone of the poem is reminiscent of Poe, and not reminiscent only; for as the raven

> Perched upon a bust of Pallas just above my chamber door,

so in the chamber of this confirmed bachelor the bust of Balzac is the dominating presence (in virtue of his *Psychologie du mariage,* which painted in somber colors the inconveniences of matrimony). Reminiscent also of Poe is the manner in which every detail of the setting is made to contribute to the general atmosphere of gloom and squalid solitude. The realism of the description, particularly in the first part of the poem, with its almost photographic precision of detail, is a new thing in Spanish-American poetry. This realism becomes more striking in the later work of Lugones.[33]

One of the main contributions of Lugones to the literature of his time has been his insistence on the necessity for freshness of imagery, and the avoidance of the hackneyed and outworn. *El solterón* offers several admirable illustrations of his love for novelty; for example, the wheeling swallows,

> las golondrinas, en pos
> de invisibles mariposas,
> trazan letras misteriosas
> como escribiendo un adiós;

the cobwebs at the window,

> las telarañas
> que son inmensas pestañas
> del desusado cancel;

the racking headache,

> bajo su frente hueca
> la verdinegra jaqueca
> maniobra un largo ajedrez;

the weariness of solitude,

> Como en las cuevas sombrías
> en el fondo de sus días
> bosteza la soledad;

---

[33] See *Odas seculares.*

happiness in love,
> Epitalamios de flores
> la dicha escribió a sus pies;

the old man's dream of his elderly bride, with its touch of gentle irony,

> en su leve
> candor de virgen senil....

Worth noting is the onomatopoetic effect gained in

> Cuchicheará a ras del suelo
> su enagua un vago frú-frú;

Some of the force and suggestiveness of the "frú-frú" may be gathered from Amado Nervo's use of it in *Les Oiseaux s'envolent:*

> Se oyen dondequiera fru-frus de hojas difuntas,
> que fingen las pisadas de una mujer que llega.

Not all the figures of Lugones, however, are equally pleasing or effective. He speaks of

> los grandes años
> con sus cargas de algodón;

but even if we admit that age brings to one's hair a whitening to the color of cotton, it brings also a thinning out which hardly justifies the "cargas." In lines 106–110, also, apart from the word "punzo" (a Gallicism, Fr. *ponceau,* a deep poppy-red), the meaning is somewhat difficult to grasp. The idea seems to be that the splendor has gone out of the evening sky, and figuratively also from the old man's life, just as, in the decadent Roman Empire, to the emperor sated with luxury not even the richest beauty that nature could show could offer any pleasure.

In versification, Lugones is equally determined to avoid the commonplace. The octosyllable is apt to become monotonous; but it is not so in this poem. An analysis of twenty eight-syllable lines shows that in these there are no fewer than thirteen variations in the rhythm; and in the same number of seven-syllable lines, which naturally offer fewer opportunities for variety, there are eight distinct rhythms. Consequently, no two stanzas are alike in cadence, and the result of this on the whole poem is noteworthy.

In *Lunario sentimental* (1909) we find Lugones at his most extravagant and fantastic in his striving for novelty. In the preface he describes the work as

> especie de venganza con que sueño casi desde la niñez, siempre que me veo
> acometido por la vida.

But vengeance, as Bacon says, is a "wild kind of justice," injuring the avenger as often as it hurts his enemy; and it is difficult to believe that this book will add much to the poetical reputation of its author. As a "lunólogo," he says much that other poets have said before him, giving the reader a series of variations on the theme, "How sweet the moonlight sleeps upon this bank!" but adding a great deal that no one else could ever have dreamed of. Thus,

> A ella [the moon] va, fugaz sardina
> mi copla en su devaneo,
> frita en el chisporroteo
> de agridulce mandolina...

and again:

> como una dama de senos yertos
> clavada de sien a sien por la neuralgia
> cruza sobre los desiertos
> llena de más allá y de nostalgia
> aquella luna de los muertos.

The treatment is in general ironic, and in some poems the irony takes on an unpleasant tinge, as in *Los fuegos artificiales,* where the writer adopts the attitude of the "superior person" (which is somewhat surprising in a reputed Socialist); in some poems it is sentimental, and in one, *Luna de las tristezas,* it is marked by fine feeling and subtle characterization.

In *Lunario sentimental* more than in any other of this author's works, we note one of his favorite ways of achieving novelty at all costs, by the use of scientific terms drawn from chemistry, paleontology, physics, medicine, etc. Thus we have

> un jarabe hidroclórico...
>
> su faz sietemesina de bebé en alcohol...
>
> La nodriza, una flaca escocesa,
> va, enteramente isósceles, junto a la suegra obesa...

and many others. Such terms may serve as evidence of the author's wide reading and varied culture, but, occurring as they do, they seem to spoil the poetic effect. The whole essence of poetic language lies in its power of suggestion, of bringing to the mind of the reader echoes of the great heritage of fancy, of history, and of romance to which he has fallen heir. In the vocabulary of science, however, the denotation of each term is strictly defined, and its power of connotation hardly exists; in fact, is not intended to exist. One might go farther and say that in proportion as a scientific term gathers extraneous associations from use in ordinary writing, its value for the purposes of science is impaired. It seems to me that Lugones by his use of such terms deliberately cuts himself off from one of the most important sources of poetic effect.

Of course, Lugones is ready to defend his practice:

Language [he says in his preface] is a combination of images, each word conveying a metaphor [Archbishop Trench once described language as "fossil metaphor"]; so that to find new and beautiful images to express one's ideas with clearness and conciseness is to enrich the language, renewing it at the same time. Those entrusted with this work, as honorable at least as improving the breed of cattle, or administering the public revenues, seeing it is a social function, are the poets.... The commonplace is bad, having lost all expressive significance by excessive use, and originality remedies this by thinking out new ideas which demand new forms of expression.

On the same ground he would probably justify his occasional use of English words—a use that to English ears sounds at times very quaint:

> Milagrosamente blanca
> satina morbideces de *coldcream* y de histeria...
>
> Y bien que la nieve lunar fuera mucha,
> lucían, brillantes de *lawntennis* y ducha,
> como magnolias duras y claras.

An earlier example of this tendency is found in Herrera y Reissig, in *El canto de los meses:*

> Octubre, el Rey dandy canta de las blandas
> que en el aire dejan dulce de fragancia....

Here, however, there is more appropriateness in "dandy" than in most of the English words used by Lugones, for October, corresponding to our northern April, has something of the jauntiness of the beau or exquisite.

The celebration of the centenary of the independence of Argentina (1910) gave occasion for the display of a new aspect of the genius of Lugones. In *Odas seculares* of that year we have a series of poems to the glory of the Argentine Republic; and as "fire drives out fire," so the fire of patriotism has here for the time being quelled the more artificial glitter of mere literary cleverness. Stirred by patriotic emotion, the poet writes with greater simplicity and sincerity. The work contains odes to La Plata, to the Andes, to Buenos Aires, to Montevideo, and to Tucumán; but these are only the prologue to the hymn to his native country entitled *A los ganados y a las mieses,* in which he describes with enthusiasm and sympathy the life of this great country, and gives many charming and realistic sketches of rustic life and manners. One of these is given in translation. In this poem, as is evident even in this short selection, the poet allows himself considerable redundancy of expression, a feature conspicuously absent from the *Crepúsculos.* In *Lunario sentimental,* admitting his endless fund of weird comparisons, he speaks jestingly of "el gárrulo caudal de mis rimas," and in that work perhaps it was excusable. But this weakness is growing on him. In his latest work, *Poemas solariegos* (1928), though his realism is refreshing, his garrulity has become a serious blemish.

The two remaining poems translated from Lugones, *Lied de la boca florida* and *Desdén,* are from the volume, *Romancero* (1924), in which the poet goes back to his earlier manner and writes with a precision and polish that none of his contemporaries can rival.

◇ ◇ ◇

GUILLERMO VALENCIA[34]

THE PURELY PARNASSIAN PHASE of the Modernist movement reached its finest expression in the poem, *Leyendo a Silva,* written by Guillermo Valencia on the death of his friend and fellow-countryman, José Asunción Silva (1896). Like Silva, Darío, Lugones, Jaimes Freyre, and others of the same school, Valencia was a devoted student of Italian and French poetry, particularly of D'Annunzio, Verlaine, and Mallarmé, from whose works he made many translations. In him, as in the others named, we find a delicate sensitiveness to impressions of sensuous beauty, and a power of recording such impressions in language of a remarkably musical quality.

Throughout *Leyendo a Silva* Valencia makes references to different poems by his friend, though there are one or two (e.g., "la dama gótica..." lines 21–22) that the extant poems of Silva do not explain. It is possible that they refer to some of the works lost in the wreck of the "America." Further light is thrown on certain passages by Silva's prose work, *De sobremesa.* For example, it is in this book that we find the key to the passage beginning,

---

[34] Born in Colombia, 1872.
   WORKS—
      Poesías. Bogotá, 1898
      Ritos. London, 1914
      Catay, poemas orientales. Bogotá, 1929

"La rusa de ojos cálidos..." (lines 35-44). This lady was María Constantinova Bashkirtsev (1860-1884), an artist, whom Silva warmly defends from the brutal stigmatization of Max Nordau, and whose autobiography (*Journal de Marie Bashkirtseff*, Paris, 1890) and letters to Guy de Maupassant reveal a very remarkable personality. It is evident that in this lady the poet found an object of profound sympathy, admiring as he did her yearning to feel and know all that was to be felt and known, and to realize in a life already doomed to early extinction the dreams of magnificence in sculpture, painting, and social intercourse with which her mind was filled. Something of the same kind Silva puts into words of his own:

> You believe that the greater part of those who die have lived? Do not believe it; for most men, those struggling every minute to satisfy their daily needs, those shut up in a profession, in a special field, in a belief, as in a prison that has but a single window opening always on the same horizon—most men die without having lived, without getting from life more than a vague feeling of fatigue.... Ah! to live my life... that is what I desire, to feel all that there is to feel, to know all that can be known, to be able to do all that there is to do....[35]

These are the ideas that Valencia is working upon and has embodied with great skill and beauty in the remarkable passage (lines 91-114) beginning:

> Ambicionar las túnicas que modelaba Grecia...

and ending with actual quotation from María Bashkirtsev:

> Querer sentirlo, verlo y adivinarlo todo.

In this passage breathes the spirit of the whole Parnassian movement, with its restless seeking after novelty in sensuous experience and its pursuit of an exotic and unattainable beauty.

The passage (lines 47-62) beginning:

> La luna, como un nimbo de Dios...

takes the reader back to Silva's great elegy, *Nocturno III*, written on the occasion of his sister's death. It will be recalled that in the *Nocturno III* the poet, thinking of an earlier walk by moonlight, reflects that now

> mi sombra
> por los rayos de la luna proyectada
> iba sola,
> iba sola,
> iba sola por la estepa solitaria....

---

[35] *De sobremesa*, p. 16.

By utilizing this idea in the lines:

> La luna...
> dibuja sobre el llano la forma evanescente
> de un lánguido mancebo...

Valencia recaptures all the beauty and melancholy of the earlier poem as a background for his own: the death of Elvira, the mourning, the lament of the "bardo israelita," Jorge Isaacs, lead back to the brother's quest for his lost sister—"imitating the careful search that Isis made for the mangled body of Osiris."

Toward the end of the poem there is a certain incongruity not easy to explain. The appeal to Christ for pardon and saving grace seems natural enough; but why in such circumstances the poet should exclaim:

> Tallad un verso en ella, pagano y decadente...

is not clear. The call for a pagan and decadent epitaph seems more in keeping with the spirit of the poem; and, that being so,

> ¡Oh Señor Jesucristo! por tu herida del pecho,
> ¡perdónalo!...

may be regarded as a conventional utterance of distress.

Considering the whole spirit of this poem, and the delicacy and precision with which it is worked out, one feels that it would have been a fitting subject for the "pincel lapidario" of Aubrey Beardsley.

Los camellos is more Symbolist than Parnassian. In this poem, as in the older allegory, "more is meant than meets the ear." The Symbolist poet in his use of words, phrases, and ideas, attaches to them senses and associations that might not occur to the casual reader. One difficulty in dealing with poetry of this kind is that the mind of the reader is seldom so attuned to that of the poet that he can immediately grasp all the implications; and it may happen that, through lack of sympathy on the part of the reader, or through obscurity on the part of the writer, the key to the mystery is undiscoverable. Thus both may lose: the reader, the poet's meaning; and the poet, the appreciation his ideas might have gained if they could have been understood. In this sense, the Symbolist is a "poet's poet," demanding on the part of his reader something of the poet's insight; for, as Silva says, "Es que no quiero *decir* sino sugerir."

In *Los camellos* the camels represent the poet himself and a sympathetic friend, in all probability José Asunción Silva. Both are men of deep culture, with an intense love of beauty, and some scorn for the vulgar who care for none of these things. They have therefore abandoned their fellows and are sojourning in the desert. This, Solar Correa interprets as follows:

El desierto simboliza para él la *turba multa* de los hombres, la democracia igualataria, feroz y plana como la inmensa sábana de arenas. El camello—el alma de la soledad—es el poeta, el artista.[36]

But this, it seems to me, is a misreading of the poem. The camel certainly is the poet; but the desert represents rather the path of the man who deliberately chooses

> To scorn delights and live laborious days.

Moreover, the stanza beginning,

> Los átomos de oro que el torbellino esparce...

does not appear to support Solar's interpretation; for the dust of the desert, to the ordinary eye mere dust, seems to represent the gifts of the spirit, the fruits of the discipline of the way. In this desert path, the Pyramids, the Sphinx, the waving palms of the occasional oasis, all contribute their share to the poet's spiritual consolation. He feels himself an oddity among ordinary men—metaphorically speaking, he is humped; but the Pyramids whisper to him that the hump is merely the symbol of wisdom, of which they themselves are another expression. Yet the way is hard and painful. Caravans have attempted the course, and their bones lie bleaching in the sand. For them the true poetic life has been too exacting.

The appeal to the "flautistas de Bizancio" is evidently directed to Darío, then at the zenith of his fame. For him, the poet hints, an experience in the desert would be of service, bringing him back to a recognition of the higher aims for which the poet lives; for only the poet imbued with high purpose can serve humanity:

> sólo su arteria rota la Humanidad redime.

Toward the end of the poem only one camel is mentioned. This may be because in the interim Asunción Silva has died, and the poet, lonely and unappreciated by an unsympathetic world, can find comfort only in the contemplation of love and beauty in the eyes of his beloved.

---

[36] Eduardo Solar Correa, *Poetas de Hispano-América* (Santiago de Chile, 1926), p. 274.

JULIO HERRERA Y REISSIG[37]

A CURIOUS PHENOMENON in the literary life of Spanish America is the fact that many of those who have distinguished themselves in the field of poetry have been rewarded with important government positions, or have had other interests that have made them independent of poetry as a means of subsistence. Rubén Darío, for example, was minister for Nicaragua in Paris and Madrid, and wrote regularly for *La Nación* of Buenos Aires; Amado Nervo represented Mexico in Paris, and later at the Spanish court; Ricardo Jaimes Freyre and Enrique González Martínez both held professorial chairs; Gabriela Mistral, though a Chilean, was called by the Mexican government to coöperate with José Vasconcelos in the reform of Mexican education; while Leopoldo Lugones is Director of National Education in Argentina.

Julio Herrera y Reissig is exceptional in that he chose deliberately to be a poet, and that only. Though he belonged to a family that had been powerful in Uruguayan politics for three generations, he turned in disdain from the sordidness of political life and the material rewards it might have brought him. Only once did he seek a political office, that of consul at La Plata; but the letter he wrote to the minister who might have helped him to obtain it was of a kind to ensure his disappointment. The closing sentence is characteristic.

Mi ilustre amigo, el señor Bachini, en caso de serle grato, podría valientemente hacer valer mi nombre y mis palabras al señor Williman [the President] y tal vez algún día se me hiciera justicia y el país fuera digno de Julio Herrera y Reissig.[38]

As little did he feel he could sacrifice his ideals to descend to ordinary journalism. Hence he lived and died poor.

Being of delicate health, he was allowed to choose his own path. He read widely and with enthusiasm, and found special attraction in the writings of

---

[37] Born at Montevideo, Uruguay, 1875.
POETICAL WORKS (all published at Montevideo)—
Pascuas del tiempo. 1900
Los maitines de la noche. 1902
Los éxtasis de la montaña. 1904
Poemas violetas. 1906
Sonetos vascos. 1906
Los parques abandonados. 1908
Los éxtasis de la montaña (ser. 2). 1910
Los pianos crepusculares. 1910
Clepsidras. 1910

Obras completas. Published posthumously at the expense of the Uruguayan government, Montevideo, 1913. Five volumes

[38] This letter is given by Juan Mas y Pi in his Introduction to *Páginas escogidas de Julio Herrera y Reissig* (Barcelona, 1914), p. 19.

Baudelaire, Poe, Schopenhauer, and Nietzsche; so it was not unnatural that when Rubén Darío came to Buenos Aires, Herrera came under his influence. He established himself in the Calle Ituzaingó in an attic he somewhat magniloquently called *La torre de los panoramas,* not because it commanded a magnificent view of the harbor, but because a series of engravings by Gustave Doré adorned its walls. This *torre* became a center of revolt frequented by the youthful enthusiasts of the New Idealism. The novelty and extravagance of the poems that issued from the *torre* exasperated the critics and led to furious controversy, which Herrera brought to an end with the following:

DECRETO[39]

Abomino la promiscuidad de catálogo. ¡Solo y conmigo mismo! Proclamo la inmunidad literaria de mi persona.

Ego sum imperator. Me incomoda que ciertos peluqueros de la crítica me hagan la barba. . . .

¡Dejad en paz a los Dioses!

Yo, Julio.

Torre de los panoramas.

In somewhat the same vein as Darío had said a few years earlier (in *Palabras liminares* to his *Prosas profanas*), "Mi literatura es mía en mí," Herrera here declares he will not be one of the crowd. He claims for the poet perfect freedom to express himself as he pleases: no critic-barber shall trim his beard. It will be observed that here Herrera stops at the Quip Modest:

If I sent him word again "it was not well cut" he would send me word he cut it to please himself: this is called the Quip Modest.

But in a later prose passage he reaches the next stage in Touchstone's anabasis:

If again "it was not well cut," he disabled my judgment: this is called the Reply Churlish.

In Herrera's Spanish this reads as follows:

Yo siento a mi manera lo que cada uno siente a la suya. Hay quien tiene doble vista. Para el ciego siempre es noche. ¡Piafe el imbécil en su impotencia![40]

The violent aggressiveness of all this is apparent and shows itself in Herrera's poetry in various ways. For instance, he has a horror of the hackneyed or commonplace in the conception and expression of his ideas

---

[39] Mas y Pi, *op. cit.,* p. 18.   [40] Mas y Pi, *ibid.,* p. 23.

(though he does not recoil from the commonplace as subject-matter); hence the striving for novelty in the words he uses, in the connections in which they are used, and in his extravagant and sometimes confused metaphor. In method, he is often impressionistic, attempting to give a vivid picture by a series of apparently unrelated strokes. In his use of recondite references and in his power of condensation he resembles Browning, and like him is in consequence sometimes obscure. It is not to be wondered at, therefore, that in his lifetime he was little understood. Still, his influence on the poets of his own country was very great, and even in Spain he has been acknowledged as a precursor of the Creationist tendencies that were more fully developed later by González Martínez and Vicente Huidobro.

It has already been observed that in the choice of subjects Herrera had no objection to the common and ordinary; in fact, much of his best work consists of brilliant sketches of scenes and manners from his immediate surroundings. This is the more remarkable as, during the period of Herrera's main production, that is, from 1900 to 1910, Rubén Darío was at the summit of his achievement, and the highly artificial world that Darío had created for himself with its palaces and princesses, its lakes and swans, was much frequented by those who acknowledged him as leader. The independence of Herrera in this matter is admirable and refreshing.

Alba triste is from the volume, *Los maitines de la noche* (1902), and is so obscure that it may seem to have been written especially "pour épater les bourgeois." The general idea seems to be that the morning dreams of the poet have been broken in upon by foreboding signs—the heron over the bay, and the sibylline rattling at the window panes—suggesting dark thoughts to his mind. The poet realizes his misfortune when his sweetheart waves him good-bye and leaves him a prey to jealousy. For him the world seems coming to an end. The harsh note of the crow, like a Wagnerian theme for the bass trombone, is the echo to his thoughts, and the woods around seem to feel the approach of doom.

To English readers the lines:

>una garza pueril su absurda plana
>paloteaba en las ondas intranquilas ...

may seem puzzling. In Spanish-American countries, the "plana" is the sheet of paper on which the children learn to write, following the guide-lines (*palotes*) in making their earliest strokes. The comparison between the long, awkward legs of the heron and the *palotes* seems rather far-fetched; it is certainly novel.

In *Sombra dolorosa* (from *Parques abandonados,* 1908) Herrera is giving permanent expression to a fleeting sensation. Imagine a rural setting. It is evening, and the field workers are plodding home from their day's labor. There is a feeling of solemnity in the air, and the rays of the setting sun recall to the poet the fires of ancient holocausts and fill his mind with sadness. The lines:

> Bajo el misterio de los velos finos,
> evocabas los símbolos perplejos,
> hierática, perdiéndote a lo lejos
> con tus húmedos ojos mortecinos ...

are markedly in the Symbolist manner, and the poet's intention must be sought more in the general effect than in the individual words and phrases. The meaning may perhaps be rendered thus: The poet's sweetheart is beside him; under the fine lawn that covers her bosom, her breasts—symbols of love and motherhood—are indistinctly perceived, their appearance changing as the breeze moves the delicate fabric. She holds herself erect in the attitude of a priestess, her eyes suffused with emotion and fixed on the dim horizon. The unwelcome brother joins them, and, though his presence has snatched them from their dream of love, their hands, each in the other's grasp, still speak their message. Suddenly arises the doleful shadow—the momentary sight of a passing train—which raises in the minds of both the idea of separation, of absence, perhaps of death.

La cena (from *Los éxtasis de la montaña,* 1910) may be taken as an example of Herrera at his best. As a picture of an Uruguayan cottar's Saturday Night, it is as true to life as its Scottish counterpart. Its marked realism has led critics like Alfred Coester to suggest that the genesis of Argentine realism, attributed generally to Leopoldo Lugones, is really to be found in Herrera. This poem appeared in the volume of 1910, but Juan Mas y Pi, who knew Herrera personally, states that most of the poems in this volume were written in 1904. Realism in Lugones becomes important only in the *Odas seculares,* which appeared in 1910. Yet the realistic touch is unmistakable in *El solterón,* published in *Los crepúsculos del jardín* (1905). The truth probably is that Darío's artificial paradise was losing its attraction as a place of permanent habitation for the more advanced spirits of this decade; that reaction was in the air, and seized on the minds of those poets who were most open to new influences and ideas.

In *La cena* we may notice some of the chief characteristics of Herrera's art. The onomatopoetic effect in "Un repique de lata la merienda circula..." is striking. The curious use of the verb, "aploma," suggestive of a bricklayer setting bricks in their places, is no less remarkable. The simile describing the self-satisfaction of the peasant as he, because he is the breadwinner, appropriates to himself the largest share of the victuals, seems far-fetched, but is still effective. That peasant has the independence and complacency of an ecclesiastic with a papal dispensation in Lent to eat delicacies forbidden to others! And quite characteristic of Herrera is the line:

> arrullan, golosinas domésticas de invierno...

The poet calls the fairy tales the "dainties of the winter," and "arrullan" with "golosinas" suggests "golondrinas de verano." Thus the hidden sense comes to be that as the swallows are the harbingers of summer, so in due season the tales come up to cheer and brighten the winter. Further, it is worth noting that though the poet sees the grossness of the peasant and depicts it decisively, he does so with an irony that is quite free from either contempt or bitterness.

In *La gota amarga* (from *Los parques abandonados,* 1908) the phrase, "la Escocia de tus ojos verdes," will sound quaint to English, and still more, perhaps, to Scottish readers. The meaning, however, will be clear if we compare with this another sonnet in the same volume, *El juramento,* of which the opening lines are as follows:

> A plena inmensidad, todas las cosas
> nos efluviaron de un secreto mago.
> Walter Scott erraba sobre el lago,
> y Lamartine soñaba entre las rosas;

or another, *Los ojos negros de Julieta,* in which he speaks of the lady's eyes as

> Ojos de enigma sombrío,
> ojos de rapto severo;
> ojos que dicen:—¡Te Juro!—
> ojos que dicen:—¡Me muero!—
> ojos románticos, límpidos
> como dos lagos de Escocia....

Scotland, therefore, for this Uruguayan poet is still the Scotland of Sir Walter Scott and the *Lady of the Lake,* a land of enchantment, mystery, and romance.

It is not unusual with Herrera to make play with double meanings, not for purposes of equivocation, but to obtain a double suggestiveness. Thus, the line,

> que hablaban de romeros y de hinojos...

calls up not only the picture of kneeling pilgrims, but also the scent of fennel and rosemary, an effect impossible to reproduce in translation.

JOSÉ SANTOS CHOCANO[41]

IN FORM AT LEAST, Chocano belongs to the Modernist school. He pays the compliment of imitation to Leopoldo Lugones in *El verso futuro* (in *La selva virgen*), in which he welcomes free verse for the new liberty it gives the artist, but seems to fear it for the license of thought to which it may be allied. This poem was probably intended for satire; but satire is not Chocano's strong point. He experiments freely with the decasyllabic and dodecasyllabic forms of verse, and in a poem dedicated to Amado Nervo offers a new variant of the latter rhythm as a challenge to *El metro de doce*. Nervo's form is a line of four amphibrachs:

> El metro de doce son cuatro donceles ... ;

that of Chocano, three feet of the form introduced by Silva in his famous *Nocturno:*
> Musa prende nuevos ritmos en las liras ... ;

but what was appropriate and pleasing in Silva's nocturne seems flat and uninteresting in Chocano's poem. Much of his work in the later part of *Alma América* is in the form of free verse; for example, *El salto de Tequendama* and *La elegía del órgano,* the latter in the same measure as the *Nocturno* just mentioned. In both, and in other poems, he employs the device of repetition after the manner of Ricardo Jaimes Freyre, and in some very effectively, for example, in the *Elegía del órgano* with its refrain:

> Suena el órgano en el fondo de la noche;
> y hay un chorro de sonidos melodiosos en sus flautas.

Yet his point of view is distinctly new. Paris, the "spiritual home" and fountain of inspiration for Darío, Lugones, Herrera, Silva, and others, is for Chocano anathema. In *Flor de Hispania (La selva virgen)* he laments the fascination of Paris for the young American poet.

---

[41] Born in Peru, 1875.
WORKS—
En la aldea. Lima, 1893
Iras santas. Lima, 1895
Azahares. Lima, 1896
La epopeya del morro. Lima, 1899

Alma América. Madrid, 1906
Fiat lux. Paris, 1908
La selva virgen. Paris, 1909. Poems written, for the most part, before 1906

> Halla en Paris inspiración un día
> arrastrando tal vez el triunfal carro
> del Vicio, entre la falsa pedrería...
> * * * *
> Paris arde
> como un rubí de fúlgido brasero,
> cuando lo sopla el viento de la tarde;
> y corriendo en la hora vespertina
> por sus alegres calles, va la musa,
> como sombra que apenas se adivina,
> y que semeja, al resbalar confusa,
> alada aparición de Mesalina....
> ¡Oh musa! rompe los traidores lazos
> de esa sirena, que cantando mata;
> y busca amor en los robustos brazos
> del hispano león....

This passage gives the key to the work of Chocano, pointing as it does to the beginning of a revolt against French influence. In addition it voices the aspiration toward a cultural reunion with Spain, one of the happier results of the disastrous war which stripped the mother country of the last of her colonial possessions. This feeling finds eloquent expression in his *Ofrenda a España:*

> ¡Oh madre España! Acógeme en tus brazos,
> y, al compás de mi cántico sonoro,
> renueva el nudo de los viejos lazos;
> que un anillo de oro hecho pedazos
> ya no es anillo... ¡pero siempre es oro!

Chocano liked to think of himself as of noble Spanish blood, as having "come over" with the Conquistadores. In a later incarnation, he believes, he was one of the viceroys; but he insists that he is equally of noble Inca descent; for example, in *Blasón*. Above all, he is convinced that he is a poet, "the poet of America," with a sacred mission to sing the glories of the New World. His self-complacency in this matter is extraordinary:

> Ahora soy Poeta; soy divino, soy sagrado...
> —*Avatar*

and again:

> en mi canción, por eso, de múltiple cadencia,
> están todas las gracias, y todos los vigores.
> —*El alma fuerte.*

There is no denying the vigor of most of his poems; as for the graces, there is room for difference of opinion. He excels in description; for example, *Las punas, El salto de Tequendama,* and *Los Andes,* though to express the majesty of the Andes within the compass of a sonnet, as in the last named, may seem a bold undertaking. There is a certain sameness in his method of treatment; he feels that he must illustrate every detail by a simile, and the figure is so introduced as to give the reader the impression that the poet habitually first stated his idea and then went in search of his poetic illustration. Often the figure is interesting; sometimes it is absurd, as when in *Bajando la cuesta* he compares the barking of a dog to a long silk ribbon:

> Oigo el ladrido de un perro a veces,
> que se desdobla como una larga cinta de seda . . . ;

and occasionally the figure runs away with the poet, with ridiculous results, as in the last stanza of *La epopeya del pacífico.* And if the swan of Darío eventually wearied his readers, what shall we say of Chocano's condor, or, still more, of his snakes?—for in one way or another the serpent insinuates itself into at least two-thirds of all the poems in *Alma América.*

When Chocano leaves purely objective description and takes up narrative, he is less successful. He ventures into prophecy, and foretells that the Panama Canal will never be built, that the climate and disease will effectively prevent its completion; yet he looks forward to the benefits Peru will derive from the labors of the "brutal Saxon." For a moment, like Darío, he sees something in the strenuous life, for, as he pithily remarks:

> el trabajo no es culpa de un Edén perdido,
> sino el único medio de llegarlo a gozar.

He is more at home in romantic tales of the Incas and of the Spanish conquerors. In these, all his heroes are super-heroic:

> Hernán Cortés dió un paso; la acobardada tierra tembló toda . . . ;

and the Conquest, which at the best was a sordid and brutal business, assumes in his verse the aspect of a crusade of the noblest altruism. His greatly admired sonnet, *Seno de reina,* puts the matter shortly. A queen of Spain, driving through the streets, heard a child weeping at a corner. She stopped her coach, descended, and offered her breast to the cold and hungry child.

> Y es gloria de la estirpe, porque ese amor fecundo
> con que la reina al niño le dió de su seno un día
> ¡fué el mismo con que España le dió su seno a un mundo!

which seems a grotesquely sentimental misreading of history.

It is curious and significant that the only English poet with whose work Chocano shows any familiarity is Rudyard Kipling, whose praises he sings in a poem in *Fiat lux*. In this poem, Kipling figures as Shakespeare-plus-Orpheus, a tremendous hero, with strong muscles, hairy chest, and a proud and lofty forehead. Moreover, he is a mighty hunter who goes about always with ten knives at his belt! The Kipling of Chocano's imagination is in fact a kindred spirit, whose drum and cymbals would supply a fitting accompaniment to his own "épico clarín."

Of late years there has been a tendency to disparage the work of Chocano. Thus Alberto Hidalgo, another Peruvian, writes in his *Oda simplista a Arequipa:*

> Pasan las recuas de borricos
> con su rítmico trote
> aprendido en los versos de Chocano;[42]

and an Argentine critic, E. Suarez Calimano, is as little complimentary:

Santos Chocano hizo sonar el cuerno hueco de su palabrería insustancial tan estruendosamente que aturdió el Perú y aturdió ¡ay! Hispanoamérica desde ya hace más de veinte años. Olvidémoslo.[43]

This, however, is not entirely fair to Chocano. Since the publication of *Alma América* and *Fiat lux,* a change has come over the poet. His contacts with the ruling class in Peru, and his political adventures (he narrowly escaped being shot as a rebel in 1920), seem to have lessened his faith in the virtues of the Conquistadores and their descendants; and in consequence he has turned his attention to the descendants of the conquered. In his *Tres notas de nuestra alma indígena*,[44] it is a changed Chocano who is speaking: his old arrogance and egotism have disappeared, his style is less strident, and his studies of native manners are marked by a sympathetic insight as pleasing as it is unexpected.

---

[42] *Indice de la nueva poesía americana* (Buenos Aires, 1926).
[43] *Nosotros* (Buenos Aires, 1927).
[44] *Repertorio americano* (Costa Rica, 1922).

ENRIQUE GONZÁLEZ MARTÍNEZ[45]

THE EARLIEST PUBLISHED WORK of González Martínez was written, as critics have pointed out, under the influence of Gutiérrez Nájera and Manuel José Othón. Later, he came under the spell of the French writers, Baudelaire, J. M. de Heredia, and Verlaine. Of their works he made an intensive study, the results of which appeared in a volume of translations entitled *Jardines de Francia* and in the highly finished technique of his own early poems.

These works, however, were merely preparatory. His real power and originality first became apparent in the volume of 1909, *Silenter*. It is in this volume that he sets forth the aim and purpose of his writing—so to refine his sensibility and purify his spirit from all that is merely human that he may be able to penetrate into the mystery that surrounds our lives. Thus he lays down the rule (and the *ex cathedra* manner is characteristic) for the poetic life as follows:

> Que esquives lo que ofusca y lo que asombra
> al humano redil que abajo queda,
> y que afines tu alma hasta que pueda
> escuchar el silencio y ver la sombra.
>
> Que te ames en ti mismo, de tal modo
> compendiando tu ser, cielo y abismo,
> que sin desviar los ojos de ti mismo
> puedan tus ojos contemplarlo todo.
> —*Irás sobre la vida de las cosas.*

The philosophical idea behind the poetry of González Martínez and other recent writers, notably Vicente Huidobro, is thus explained by René Doumic:

> Idealism is the basis of the new poetry. Poetry is "such stuff as dreams are made on"; but we must give to the word *dream* its widest sense, and include even the theory of knowledge as it is understood by the philosophers: only we can know ourselves; in us are those beings whose hands we have clasped, and in us are the

---

[45] Born at Guadalajara, Mexico, 1871. Appointed Minister to Argentina, 1921.
WORKS—

Preludios. Mazatlan, 1903
Lirismos. Mocorito, 1907
Silenter. Mocorito, 1909
Los senderos ocultos. Mocorito, 1911

La muerte del cisne. Mexico, 1915
La hora inútil. Mexico, 1916
El libro de la fuerza, de la bondad y del sueño. Mexico, 1917

things we have touched; in us is the perfume of the flowers and the thorns that scratch us; and the obscure and distant paths in which our destiny has wandered lead only to our spirit; ... in the sense of the legend of Narcissus.[46]

But the only answer Narcissus could get from Echo was a fragmentary repetition of his own words. Thus the "imitation of nature" which critics have described as the function of the poet is at best a reproduction of the vision he has conceived, but fragmentary, and refracted and colored by his own experience and personality. For

> What hand and brain went ever paired?
> What heart alike conceived and dared?
> What act proved all its thought had been?
> What will but felt the fleshly screen?

The poet of *Los senderos ocultos* is a devotee of the contemplative life, one who has suffered, yet remains an optimist:

> Tristezas, ... sí, las tengo; mas cuando el alma llora
> un inefable goce con mi dolor se aduna....
> —*Yo voy alegremente.*

It must be said, however, that his joy finds little expression in his poetry. This is in general sad, and the tone of melancholy becomes monotonous and at times a little tiresome.

In contrast with the earlier poets of this period, González Martínez is not content with an ideal of Beauty as the end and aim of his searching. He regards himself as a serious-minded teacher; hence the dogmatic and didactic tone of much of his work. Even a passive piety, like that of Amado Nervo, is not enough: there must be a definite striving to shed light on the dark places of human destiny.

> Ha que labrar tu campo, hay que vivir tu vida,
> tener con mano firme la lámpara encendida
> sobre la eterna sombra, sobre el eterno abismo....
> —*Intus.*

There must be a higher and nobler conception of life as a whole, and of the function of the poet, than we find in Darío or in the earlier writers of the Symbolist school. Thus, though in these poems we find a spontaneity and perfection of form equal to Darío's, it is obvious that Beauty is not their sole end and aim: Art does not exist solely for Art's sake, but as a method of approach to Truth and Goodness.

---

[46] Quoted by Manuel Toussaint in his introductory study of González Martínez, in *Poesías escogidas de E. González Martínez* (Barcelona, 1917), pp. 16–17.

This new departure is signalized in the famous sonnet, *Tuércele el cuello al cisne*. Here González Martínez turns his back on the whole artificial world of pagan delights which Darío had created for himself. The latter loved the swan for its beauty, and that was sufficient; but for the former the swan as a symbol is inadequate. "El pasea su gracia no más"; it has merely its beauty to recommend it. The true poet must seek something more profound, and be able to hear the voice of nature and understand her spirit. If any symbol is to be taken, it must be the owl, the symbol of human wisdom. All this is not too kind to Darío, but the unkindest cut of all is that for the stick to beat him González Martínez has taken a line from Darío's poetical *vade mecum,* the *Art poétique* of his favorite, Verlaine:

> Prends l'Éloquence et tords lui son cou!

The conflict between carnal impulses and spiritual aspirations which occupied the minds of Darío and Nervo and found such poignant expression in their works, has little place in the mature poetry of González Martínez. Yet he had his own battle to fight, and the poem, *Y pienso que la vida,* exhibits at least one of its phases. As a poet and a dreamer—also as a Parnassian—he feels out of sympathy with the garishness of ordinary life. Instead of the "torre de marfil" or the "selva sagrada," however, he has as his safe retreat his "divina gruta" or his "hortus conclusus." There, though the voices of the world may be calling at the gate,

> El alma silenciosa y taciturna,
> ha encendido su lámpara nocturna,
> ha cerrado su puerta,... y no responde.
> —*Hortus conclusus.*

There he can pursue his meditations and receive the illumination of the spirit (the "interior llama infinita" of Darío), yielding himself to the attractions of books. But life, which passes "smiling by his side," is continually calling him. When he surrenders himself to study, he fears he is losing the joys the world has to offer:

> A vivir, a vivir... Y que sangre la herida;
> avizor vaya el ojo y el oído anhelante...
> Hay que asirse a la veste del efímero instante;
> ¡A vivir, a vivir, que se escapa la vida!
> —*Iba por el camino.*

and when engaged in mundane occupations and delights, he suffers as he thinks he is wasting hours that, dedicated to study, might enrich his eager spirit.

At times another question arises: Has his work as a poet any permanent value? For fashions come and go in poetry as in other things.

> Mañana los poetas seguirán su camino
> absortos en ignota y extraña floración,
> y al oír nuestro canto, con desdén repentino
> echarán a los vientos nuestra vieja ilusión.

In the sonnet, *Mañana los poetas,* González Martínez gives his answer. Poetry will and must go on; for so long as the great enigmas of life and love, of death and human destiny, remain unsolved, so long will ardent spirits feel the challenge and attempt their solution. As to the success they may attain he is not very sanguine; indeed, he seems to reach the same conclusion as Solomon some thousands of years before him:

> The thing that hath been, it is that which shall be; and that which is done is that which shall be done; and there is no new thing under the sun.

It will be noticed that this poet seems to live a strangely self-centered existence. In spite of his early declaration of the necessity for holding up the lighted torch for the guidance of humanity, the world of men seems remote and shadowy and makes little impact on the poet. He is, as it were, in a sound-proof chamber, broadcasting to an unseen audience.

The two remaining poems of González Martínez here translated, *La piedad que pasa* and *Esta tarde he salido* ..., illustrate one of the most genuine and constant traits in his poetry, a tender, almost sentimental love for the little, and little-regarded, things in nature.

◇ ◇ ◇

PEDRO PRADO[47]

BETWEEN THE WORK of González Martínez and that of Pedro Prado there is very little resemblance. They have in common only their seriousness of purpose. González Martínez, thanks to his early devotion to the study of

---

[47] Born, 1886. Was President of the Federación de Estudiantes and Director of the Museo de Bellas Artes, Santiago de Chile. Founded the *Revista moderna* and was one of the directors of *Los diez*.

WORKS—
Flores de cardo. Santiago, 1908
La casa abandonada. Buenos Aires, 1912
El llamado del mundo. Santiago, 1913
La reina de Rapa Nui. Santiago, 1914
Los pájaros errantes. Santiago, 1915
Los diez. Santiago, 1915
Ensayos. Santiago, 1916
Alsino. Santiago, 1921

French and Italian models, was a master of all the arts and artifices of the Parnassian school. The very limpidity of his style is evidently the fruit of much patient labor. With Prado it is different. His writing seems more spontaneous, and it would almost seem as if he deliberately eschewed any form of ornament, and depended for his emotional effect on his subject-matter alone. Yet his comparative plainness of statement may arise from lack of imagination—an inference to some extent borne out by the general vagueness of impression produced by his *Lázaro*. In the same way he seeks freedom from the restrictions of the conventional verse-forms by discarding rhyme and writing in free verse, or (as in *Pájaros errantes*) in a kind of elevated prose in which he has caught successfully the cadence of the Hebrew Psalms.

Though discarding rhyme, Prado makes free use of assonance, as in *Las manos;* and, as assonance is little favored in the practice of English poets, the translator is faced with an awkward choice: he must either use rhyme, and lose some of the fluidity of the original; or have recourse to blank verse, and lose some of the musical effect that Prado intended to produce. In this poem I have used rhyme, though I feel that the rhymes are rather too obtrusive.

Lázaro is generally regarded as Prado's best poem. It describes Lazarus rising or just risen from the tomb, and relating to the bystanders his experience of death and the transformation through which he was passing when recalled to life by the command, "Lazarus, come forth!" This poem, read alongside of Browning's *Epistle, Containing the Strange Medical Experience of Karshish, the Arab Physician,* supplies a measure by which we may compare a highly reputed Spanish-American poet with an acknowledged master in English poetry. Such a comparison reveals striking differences, not only in the outlook of the two poets on life and death, and on the life beyond death, but also in their powers of presentation, description, and characterization. For Prado, body and soul are one, and death is a change of state in which the elements of the body and the soul alike are transformed, and return to life in the sparkle of the rivers and the perfume of the flowers. There seems to be some inconsistency in the poem; for, though Lazarus declares that an impenetrable wall separates the states of life and death, and that death blots out the memory of life, as life the memory of death (that is, of our existence before birth), yet he is able to give a vivid account of his sensations while lying dead in the grave. In contrast with this materialistic view, Browning lays emphasis not on the purely physical changes, which indeed he hardly mentions, but on the deeper sense of moral and spiritual values attained by one who has passed within the veil.

Equally striking is the difference in descriptive power. There is nothing in Prado to compare with Browning's

> A black lynx snarled and pricked a tufted ear,
> Lust of my blood inflamed his yellow balls;
> I cried, and threw my staff, and he was gone;

nor with his description of the rocky pass from which the physician looked down on Bethany:

> I crossed a ridge of short, sharp, broken hills,
> Like an old lion's cheek tooth....

Compared with these, Prado's references to the "ardiente paisaje de Judea," or to the "suaves colinas de Bethania" over which Lazarus rambled as a boy, are pale and ineffective. So also, the writer of the epistle in Browning's poem is a vivid personality, with a keen eye for everything that might interest his correspondent. In *Lázaro,* the speaker is a vague figure, apparently one of the spectators. He tells us, "*Quedamos* con la luminosa y húmeda mirada de los vivos"; but toward the end of the poem we read:

> Entre las yerbas, Marta y María yacían agotadas;
> estremecidos los Apóstoles veían llorar a los judíos....

Evidently, therefore, the speaker was not one of these. Who then was the speaker? This may seem rather niggling criticism, but it points to an important difference between the work of a conscientious artisan and that of a poetical genius, in whose imagination the whole poetic conception rises complete and finished at the touch of a single suggestion from the outside.

We find the same difference between Browning's Lazarus, who is a very human figure, going about his daily work though haunted by the vision of splendor he has seen, and Prado's Lazarus, who is little more than a phantom, a mouthpiece for the materialistic monism of the poet.

CARLOS PEZOA VÉLIZ[48]

PEZOA VÉLIZ (1879-1908) is introduced here as a Realist poet writing before Realism had become the fashion in Spanish-American poetry, and writing thus, not because of any feeling of revolt from the prevailing mode, but because the grim environment in which he lived forced realism upon him. He was of humble origin, and his life, a hard struggle against adverse fate, reads like a picaresque novel. He had a keen eye for the beauty of outward nature, and an equally penetrating insight into the sordid reality of the lives of those with whom he had to do. His sympathies were unmistakably with the "under dog," and one almost feels, under the irony of his fragment, *Nada*, the poet's fear that at his own death he may be treated with the same callous indifference as the poor creature of whom he writes. He died in poverty. The lines, *Tarde in el hospital*, were written in his last illness, a few days before his death.

◇ ◇ ◇

VÍCTOR DOMINGO SILVA[49]

THE REALISM of Pezoa Véliz was the outgrowth of the bitterness of his own experience. In his contemporary, Víctor Domingo Silva, realism derives from deep human sympathy aroused by the sight of the misery of others in a plane socially beneath his own.

> El poeta egoista que ante la infamia calla,
> y calla ante el humano dolor, es un canalla.

In these lines we have the key to the most important work of Domingo Silva. He is above all a reformer. He has seen the sufferings of the laboring class in the niter fields of the north and in the coal mines of the south, and the cruelty of their lot has touched his heart. Hence his longer poems, for example, *La nueva marsellesa,* from which the above lines are quoted, and

---

[48] Since the death of Pezoa Véliz his works have been twice collected and republished, as *Alma chilena* (Santiago, 1912), and *Campanas de oro* (Paris, 1921).

[49] Born, 1882.
WORKS (all published in Santiago)—
Hacia allá. 1906
El derrotero. 1908
La selva florida. 1911
El romancero naval. 1912
Nuestras víctimas. 1912
Golondrina de invierno (ed. 5). 1923
Palomilla brava. 1923
Sus mejores poemas. 1923

Bajo el sol de la pampa, are powerful indictments of the system under which the laborers work, and touching appeals to the humanitarian instincts of men. The *Balada del violín* in short compass exhibits the same feeling. It is simple and direct in statement, and, though touched with irony, is not lacking in sympathy. In its freedom from sentimentality it offers a significant contrast to the treatment of a somewhat similar subject by Amado Nervo in *Perlas negras* (1898). In this volume is a series of short poems under the general title of *Album de Josefina Tornel*. In one of these Nervo tells how the lap dog of a countess one wintry night dozes in the midst of luxury. Meanwhile a poor musician comes along and plays his violin at the window, but is noticed by no one. Exhausted by cold and hunger, he drops down and dies. But

> Cuando despierta la luz primera,
> desciende un rayo sobre la acera,
> al niño muerto besa en la frente,
> presta matices a sus cabellos
> y luego forma por cima de ellos
> una corona resplandeciente.

Another ray enters the luxurious mansion and

> baña los rizos de blanca seda
> del falderillo de la condesa....

Silva saw no resplendent crown over the head of his dead fiddler; nor was the luxury of a pampered lap dog necessary to set off his tragedy. The stark reality was enough to stir men's pity. In this respect Silva points forward to the realistic writing of Gabriela Mistral and Pablo Neruda.

◇ ◇ ◇

ENRIQUE BANCHS[50]

THE SAME TENDENCY to discard the "precious" and rhetorical that has been noted in Pedro Prado is equally noticeable in the Argentine poet, Enrique Banchs. Banchs is only two years younger than Prado, and one might expect to find the same influences affecting both, and it is evident that they do.

---

[50] An Argentine poet, born in Buenos Aires, 1888.
WORKS (all published in Buenos Aires)—
Las barcas. 1907   *El cascabel del halcón.* 1909
El libro de los elogios. 1908   *La urna.* 1911
   The few poems and articles in prose that Banchs has published since 1911 have appeared in *Atlántida*.

In Banchs, however, the actual process of transition is more apparent than in Prado, in whom it seems already complete. In poems like *Elogio de una lluvia* and the *Balada del puñada de sol* his work is reminiscent of the poems of fancy we find in *Prosas profanas*. Like the rest of the Modernists, too, he has a grievance against life. Thus he describes a tiger:

> Espía mientras bate con nerviosa
> cola el haz de las férulas vecinas
> en reprimido acecho... así es mi odio.
> —*Tornasolando el flanco,* from *La urna.*

This attitude, however, seems to be a mere concession to the prevailing mode. The real personality of the poet is revealed in the poems of humble life in which he describes

> la plácida y quieta
> paz de los humildes, el callado
> vivir de los buenos.
> —*Elogio del reposo.*

The real or fictitious Bohemianism of Darío or Lugones finds no place in his work, and in his attitude toward women there is more of chivalry than of mere gallantry. In *Balbuceo* the sentiment is true and natural, and in the *Romance de la preñadita* the pathos is genuine and made more affecting by the restraint the poet exercises. His style, in keeping with his subjects, is simple and direct, and his versification is not distinguished by any notable or novel metrical effects. He has, nevertheless, a habit of repetition of words and phrases, such as we find in many Scottish and English ballads. The intention apparently is to give the illusion of entirely unpremeditated speech. In *Balbuceo,* where faltering utterance is the essence of the poem, this is appropriate and effective, but in most of the other poems in which it occurs it is a rather irritating mannerism:

> Y entonces vino una lluvia,
> vino una lluvia del cielo,
> lluvia que se parte en ruido
> de copla de romancero.
> —*Elogio de una lluvia.*

The group of sonnets entitled *La estatua* develops an idea of Darío's:

> Dichoso el árbol que es apenas sensitivo,
> y más la piedra dura, porque ésa no siente,
> porque no hay dolor más grande que el dolor de ser vivo.
> —*Lo fatal.*

It might be questioned whether there is actual matter here for four sonnets; the treatment is a little diffuse, and a greater poet would probably have condensed his statement considerably. Of the four the best is undoubtedly the last, though the poet's device of making one line do duty in both the first and the fourth sonnet might be regarded as a sign of poverty of invention. Withal, Banchs remains a notable poet, and it seems unfortunate that for twenty years now he has produced practically nothing.

◇ ◇ ◇

JUAN GUZMÁN CRUCHAGA[51]

GUZMÁN CRUCHAGA, born in the year of Darío's triumph with *Prosas profanas*, has grown to maturity in an environment in which Darío's influence has been gradually waning, and in which newer methods and different ideals have taken the place of those of the great Nicaraguan. In style he approaches Huidobro, though his poetry does not make such heavy demands on the imagination and patience of its readers as does Huidobro's. Guzmán Cruchaga, however, is not of the Creationist school; he is more properly described as an Impressionist. The Impressionist, be he painter or poet, seeks to give the fleeting impression of the moment only. For him reality is a continually changing series of impressions, each true by itself and for him; and truth, so far as it can be known or conveyed to another, is but the sum of these impressions. Hence, in painting, the impressionistic picture is made up of a number of apparently unconnected strokes or masses of color, and, in poetry, the narrative is broken up into a series of more or less unconnected details (the Germans call them *momentbilder*—snapshots); and the true artist reveals himself in the skill with which he presents these details so as to produce the feeling of unity by their combination.

This is the method followed by Guzmán Cruchaga in *Lejana* (1921). The theme of the poem is nostalgia or the poet's pain in the absence of one he loves. In the first part, however (to the end of Stanza V), the lovers are still

---

[51] Born in Santiago, 1896.
WORKS (all published in Santiago)—
Junto al brasero. 1914
La sombra [a drama]. 1918
La mirada inmóvil. 1919
Chopin. 1919
La princesa que no tenía corazón. 1920
Lejana. 1921
El maleficio de la luna. 1922
La fiesta del corazón. 1922

together, and one can gather something of the progress of their love. It is a strange wooing, for the lady, though she loves, seems distant:

> She never told her love,
> But let concealment, like a worm i' the bud,
> Feed on her damask cheek;

and the lover seems equally unable to reveal his passion. His words, "como la vertiente obscura," are more a veil to hide, than a lamp to throw light upon his true state of mind. Thus they part, their mutual love unacknowledged. The remaining stanzas (VI–XI) are a series of vivid pictures of the scenes through which the lover passes, haunted at all times by the memory of his love and the fragrance of the jasmines with which she lived surrounded.

The tone of melancholy and foreboding that is present even in the first part of the poem becomes deeper toward the close. Thoughts of death pursue the poet. The crow that settles on the mast is an evil omen. He dreams of livid opals on his fingers—portents of disaster. Even the innocent maid, who would have consoled him, only increases his sadness. The rain and the winter seem to say to him that his lady is dead; but still he hears a voice in the distance, and, dreaming of the impossible, he feels himself once more amidst the fragrance of her jasmines.

It can hardly be denied that in this poem the Impressionistic method has justified itself. The final impression is definite and complete, and the absence of mere verbiage makes the effect of the individual strokes all the more telling.

◇   ◇   ◇

GABRIELA MISTRAL

Lucila Godoy Alcayaga, who writes under the pen name Gabriela Mistral, is a native of Chile and was born at Vicuña in 1889. Her life has been a whole-hearted consecration of herself to the cause of the children and mothers of the poorer classes. Beginning her career as a teacher in a rural school, she attained so great distinction in her chosen profession that she was invited by the government of Mexico to assist in reorganizing the system of education there, and since then has held a post in the Institute of Intellectual Coöperation under the League of Nations.

Her published work consists of only one volume, *Desolación* (New York, 1922, and Santiago, 1923, the latter edition considerably augmented); but the individuality and power of these comparatively few poems have so deeply impressed competent critics, that Gabriela Mistral is now recognized as the preëminent poetess of Latin America.

In her early poems particularly, the religious tone is very manifest. She has her moments of spiritual exaltation; but mystic contemplation for her is not an end. Like Santa Teresa de Jesús, with whom she has much in common, she finds in her religion an incentive to a life of labor for the careless and the neglected. The people around her are spiritually dead:

> Estas pobres gentes del siglo están muertos
> de una laxitud, de un miedo, de un frío....
> —*Al oído del Cristo.*

If pity will not awaken them, then let the flames of adversity descend upon them! Even more than the apathy of the elders, the plight of the children of the poor touches her heart.

> Son también tus ovejas de vellón delicado.
> ¿Las vas a abandonar?

She will not abandon them. Rather, she will become as one of them, and in their innocent pleasures find the highest joy of her life. In *Rondas de niños* and in *El corro luminoso* we find her in this happy frame of mind. Even those whom physical infirmity has debarred from active participation feel the infection of her gaiety:

> Una niña que es inválida
> dijo:—¿Cómo danzo yo?—
> Le dijimos que pusiera
> a danzar su corazón....

This, however, is a passing mood; for the sufferings and neglected condition of the children evoke even more ardent sympathy. Thus her little poem, *Piececitos,* beginning,

> Piececitos de niño,
> azulosos de frío,
> ¡cómo os ven y no os cubren,
> Dios mío!

wakens the same sort of emotion as was aroused in England by George Smith of Coalville's *Cry of the Children* (1871), and cannot fail to have an equally beneficial effect.

Inspired by the same sympathy, and perhaps more important, is the poem, *La maestra rural.* In this poem Gabriela Mistral paints a vivid and fascinating picture of the rural teacher, pure-minded, poor, but happy in her work; yet pained by the thoughtlessness and ingratitude of the parents whose ignorance and stupidity blind them to the greatness of the teacher's sacrifice for the children. Her life has been saintly, and when she dies the fragrance of sanctity hovers over her grave.

The thought of the last stanza finds a curious parallel in the *Rubáiyát* of Omar Khayyám:

> And in the winding-sheet of Vine-leaf wrapt,
> So bury me by some sweet garden-side,
>
> That even my buried ashes such a snare
> Of perfume shall fling up into the air
>   As not a true believer passing by
>   But shall be overtaken unaware!

The most memorable part of Gabriela Mistral's poetry, however, is not to be found in the section under the heading *Escuela,* important though it is, but in the poems grouped under the heading *Dolor,* and dealing with the great passion and tragedy of her life. The story may be very briefly told. While still young, she had been filled with a passion of love as pure as it was fervent.... There followed a momentary infidelity of her lover: "El pasó con otra; yo le ví pasar...." The lover returns and pleads with her, but pleads in vain ... and the drama ends with his suicide, and an eternity of desolation and regret for her, haunted as she is by his spirit:

> Me toca en el relente;
> se sangra en los ocasos;
> me busca con el rayo
> de luna por los antros ...
>   —*La obsesión.*

Some idea of the intensity as well as of the individual quality of this passion may be gathered from the poem, *Intimo.* It is as far removed from the somewhat cynical gallantry of Leopoldo Lugones on the one side as from the crude, carnal passion of Pablo Neruda on the other. Here, apart from the gruesome details of physical disintegration, which we might have been spared, we have a serious attempt to figure forth a conception of love that is deeply personal and so spiritual as to be almost beyond the power of words to express. Withal, there is something naïve and almost primitive in it. The woman is a prey to jealousy, and the bitterness of this experience is made more poignant by the complete indifference of nature, and even, apparently, of God, to the anguish she suffers. This is the theme of the poem, *Balada,* which as a refutation of the so-called "pathetic fallacy" takes rank with Tennyson's *Break, break, break.*

In *El ruego*,[52] love appears in another aspect, that in which the woman is the active, dominating, exigent power, for whom the man is no more than "el panal de mi boca...el ceñidor de mi veste." In other words, the possessive instinct, which Galsworthy has portrayed in the *Forsyte Saga* as the fixed idea and moving force in the love of the man, is here revealed as the predominant passion in the woman. She is jealous of her love, of her lover; and not only in his lifetime, but even when the grave has closed over him:

> Me alejaré cantando mis venganzas hermosas,
> ¡porque a este hondor recóndito la mano de ninguno
> bajará a disputarme tu puñada de huesos!
> —*Sonetos de la muerte.*

It is not surprising to find in a poetess so sensitive and so original in outlook as Gabriela Mistral that the contemplation of outward nature has inspired some of her finest work. The fourth section of her volume is entitled *Naturaleza,* and contains only nature-poems; but included in the first section, under *Vida,* and in the second, under *Escuela,* are a number of fine poems of this kind. Separating *Vida* and *Escuela* from *Naturaleza* is the section entitled *Dolor,* the record of the tragedy that cast its shadow over her life; and the difference in tone between the first two sections and the last finds its explanation in the tragedy there unfolded.

The distinctive point of view of this writer is worth observing. For her, nature is no mere spectacle, to be painted objectively, nor is it, as with Wordsworth, the outward and visible manifestation of the creative spirit of God. In the first two sections, she regards the trees, the brooks, the stars, the fleecy clouds, as fellow-mortals, as frail as we are, but friendly, beneficent, and wiser, and therefore able to influence our lives for the better. This one might illustrate from various poems; for example:

> Arbol que donde quiera aliente
> tu cuerpo lleno de vigor,
> asumes invariablemente
> el mismo gesto amparador:
>
> haz que a través de todo estado
> —niñez, vejez, placer, dolor—
> asuma mi alma un invariado
> y universal gesto de amor!
> —*Himno al árbol.*

---

[52] In the translation of *El ruego* I have taken the liberty of departing from the stanza form of the original, and have given a rendering in blank verse. The quatrain of Gray's *Elegy,* which is the nearest equivalent in English, does not lend itself to the expression of emotion so passionate and dramatic as this poem contains.

> Grávidos van nuestros ojos de llanto
> y un arroyuelo nos hace sonreír;
> por una alondra que erige su canto
> nos olvidamos que es duro morir.
> —*Palabras serenas.*

Thus she finds tongues in trees, books in the running brooks, messages even in the falling snow, and in all nature a consolation for the sorrows of life. Moreover, the tree is for her a brother, "árbol hermano," and in *Plegaria por el nido* it is for the nest, "un hermano, indefenso y hermoso," that she prays. Gabriela Mistral is a poetess of the order of St. Francis.

The poems of the fourth section are more somber in tone. They are, as it were, the reflection of her prevailing mood thrown over the objects surrounding her. The whole atmosphere of these poems is charged with melancholy. The objects depicted seem to have been chosen for their gloomy suggestiveness. In *Desolación* the Patagonian landscape

> tiene su noche larga
> que cual madre me esconde....

(Here, there seems to be a certain amount of poetic exaggeration, for the night at Punta Arenas, where the poetess was teaching, is no longer than that of London.) Autumn for Keats was the "season of mists and mellow fruitfulness"; but in *Otoño* we have only the bitter reflection:

> el amor al que tendí
> para salvarme, los brazos,
> se está muriendo en mi alma
> cual un arrebol desflocado.

The thorn bush is

> el espíritu del yermo
> retorcido de angustia y sol.
> —*El espino.*

The sunsets are laden with tragic associations:

> Que la tarde quebró un vaso de sangre
> sobre el ocaso...
> —*La montaña de noche.*

Even the gentle rain from heaven is "esta agua medrosa y triste"; and the writer asks:

> ¿Dormiréis, mientras afuera
> cae, sufriendo, esta agua inerte,
> esta agua letal, hermana
> de la Muerte?
> —*La lluvia lenta.*

The originality of this point of view is undeniable, and that it should have shocked some of the critics is hardly surprising. Like other Modernist poets, however, Gabriela Mistral does not write to please the critics. The thoughts that arise in her mind torture her till they find utterance, and, if the ordinary language of men is weak and insufficient for her needs, other language must be found. For her burning ideas

> las palabras caducas de los hombres
> no han el calor
> de sus lenguas de fuego, de su viva
> tremolación...
>   *   *   *   *
> ¡Terrible don! ¡Socarradura larga
> que hace aullar!

Hence, her disregard of mere beauty (though beautiful phrases appear at unexpected moments); her broken rhythms; her imperfect rhymes (for example, *era, praderas; mundo, profundos; mieses, padece*—all arising from phonetic peculiarities of Chilean Spanish); her tendency to exaggerated imagery:

> De las greñas le nacen flores.
> (Así el verso le nació a Job.)
> Y como el salmo del leproso,
> es de agudo su intenso olor.
>   —*El espino.*

> Y sube de la herida [in the tree trunk] un purpurino
> musgo, como una estrofa ensangrentada.
>   —*Arbol muerto.*

and her fondness for gruesome details, to which reference has already been made. Still, when all this has been allowed for, there remain the deep sincerity, the rich imagination, and the emotional power that single out Gabriela Mistral as the greatest living poetess in the Spanish language.

ARTURO TORRES-RÍOSECO[53]

A CERTAIN NUMBER of the poems of Gabriela Mistral appeared in magazines and reviews before their publication in book form as *Desolación* (1922). They aroused widespread interest and stimulated younger writers, among whom Torres-Ríoseco was outstanding. He has since gained a considerable reputation as a lyric poet as well as a critic. As a disciple of Mistral, he shows in his work the same personal touch, the same directness of vision and expression, and the same impulsion of passion. His passion, however, is not, like hers, blended with religious idealism, but is in conflict with his religious aspirations. He has less depth and intensity of feeling, but in compensation he contrives to get more music into his verse. This musical quality is exemplified in *Campanita nocturna*.

Besides his lyric gift, Torres has leanings toward satire. Of the righteous indignation from which satire springs we have the expression in *Versos de profecía,* a poem in dodecasyllables rhyming in triplets—a novel experiment, and here a successful one. It is obviously an early effort, for youth is as prone to prophecy as age is to the conviction of its fatuous futility. The germ of the poem is to be found in a group of three sonnets by Gabriela Mistral, entitled *Al oído del Cristo* and dedicated to Torres-Ríoseco. The first sonnet begins thus:

> Cristo, el de las carnes en gajos abiertas;
> Cristo, el de las venas vaciadas en ríos;
> estas pobres gentes del siglo están muertas
> de una laxitud, de un miedo, de un frío! ...

and the third sonnet ends with the sestet:

> ¡Llanto, llanto de calientes raudales
> renueve los ojos de turbios cristales
> y les vuelva el viejo fuego del mirar!

---

[53] Born in Chile, 1897; a student of the University of Chile, Santiago; in the University Club there, a member of a group of young writers among whom was Vicente Huidobro; has taught in the Universities of Minnesota, Texas, and California; has written both poetry and criticism, much of which has appeared in the *Repertorio americano* (Costa Rica), *Nosotros* (Buenos Aires), and *Cuba contemporánea* (Havana).

WORKS—
En el encantamiento. San José de Costa Rica, 1921
Walt Whitman. San José de Costa Rica, 1922
Precursores del modernismo. Madrid, 1925
Rubén Darío. Harvard, 1931
Ausencia. Santiago, 1932

¡Retoñalos desde las entrañas, Cristo!
Si ya es imposible, si Tú bien lo has visto,
si son paja de eras... ¡desciende a aventar!

The winnowing wind would be a severe trial for the chaff, but at least it would leave the wheat behind. Torres is more ruthless. He prays to the Christ "de las suavidades" to overwhelm the whole world, wise and foolish, wicked and righteous alike (though even Sodom and Gomorrah were to be spared if only ten just men could be found in them). Apart from the Mistral sonnets, *Versos de profecía* seems to have been influenced by recollections of Dante's *Inferno,* mingled with reminiscences of the "Schrecklichkeit" of the Great War, and of the "Yellow Peril," a favorite European bogy some twenty-five years ago. Still, due allowance being made for the exuberance of youth, it is evident from this poem, and from *Broadway,* published at the same time, that the critics were justified in believing that a new poetic luminary had arisen on the Chilean horizon.

Though Torres-Ríoseco first appeared as a disciple of Gabriela Mistral, his latest work shows that his period of discipleship is long past. He has developed a style of his own. He discards Dame Mistral's somewhat strained vocabulary and her complicated metaphors, and seeks to convey his meaning in the simplest words available, in this respect exemplifying the tendency already noticed in Enrique Banchs and Pedro Prado; while his imagery, though not complicated in the same way as hers, seems to be condensed or blended after the manner of the Futurist or Creationist school. There is, however, in his later poems a depth and complexity of thought to which this style serves to give force and vividness.

These characteristics are fully exhibited in *Ausencia.* In this poem the poet contemplates his long exile from the land of his birth and the prospect of return. For fourteen years he has been haunted by memories of the scenes of his youth. Like other young Americans, he has felt the lure of Paris, and has exerted his poetic powers to bring others under its spell. Now he looks with distaste on those wasted years. The old memories come back; but can his country be the same to him now? His patriotism and his liberal opinions, which were the cause of his banishment, are as strong as ever; but he is a man now, with years of varied experience and disillusionment behind him. Even his exile has not been without compensations, for it has brought him a renown he might not have gained at home. He has also heard of incidents that have reflected little honor on his country and on the political junta responsible for her international reputation. Even his own words have given her pain. But his country is suffering, a prey to despotism and selfish interests. Knowing, therefore, that he has in his hands the balm for her wounds, in the ideals he cherished for her in his youth, he will return and bring her peace, and in her smile find peace for his own soul.

It is evident that the writer of this poem has traveled far, both technically and spiritually, since he wrote *Versos de profecía* and *Cuando me muera*, and that finer work still may be expected from his pen.

It is a sign of the change that was going on that satire was beginning to reassert itself in Spanish-American poetry. Under the Parnassian and Symbolist domination, poets had deliberately shut their eyes to human weakness and depravity, and had found in their own fancy the satisfaction of their aesthetic instincts and the theme of their songs; but, as has been observed in considering the work of Pezoa Véliz and Domingo Silva, the idea of human brotherhood had emerged as a new source of inspiration. Of this idea satire is only another aspect.

◇ ◇ ◇

ALFONSINA STORNI[54]

IN A SHORT POEM, entitled *Moderna*, Alfonsina Storni describes herself as a "pagana de un siglo empobrecido," and it would be difficult to find a phrase that more aptly or succinctly sums up her attitude to life. In her work there is none of the religious mysticism that is so marked in that of Gabriela Mistral. Instead we find an ardent longing for the enjoyment of every passionate and sensuous experience. The theme of love is predominant in her poetry. She yearns for the virile hero,

> el tremendo varón que se despierta
> y es un torrente que se ensancha en río,

who will carry her off, as in some modern Rape of the Sabines. But the hero does not appear, and her passionate dreams end in frustration:

> Que está la tarde ya sobre mi vida [aged 28],
> y esta pasión ardiente y desmentida
> la he perdido, Señor, haciendo versos!
> —*El ruego,* from *Languidez.*

---

[54] Born in the province of San Juan, Argentina, 1892; by profession a teacher; contributes frequently to *La Nación* under the pseudonym Tao-Lao.
WORKS (all published in Buenos Aires)—
La inquietud del rosal. 1916
El dulce daño. 1918
Irremediablemente. 1919
Languidez. 1920
Ocre. 1925

It is an impoverished age, a poor world! Yet this world, disappointing as it is, she regards with keenly observant eyes and depicts with vivid strokes. She could be caustically sarcastic, but only occasionally does she permit the note of irony to obtrude in her writing, as in the lines, *Cuadrados y ángulos:*

> Casas enfiladas, casas enfiladas,
> casas enfiladas.
> Cuadrados, cuadrados, cuadrados,
> casas enfiladas.
> Las gentes ya tienen el alma cuadrada,
> ideas en fila
> y ángulo en la espalda.
> Yo mismo he vertido ayer una lágrima,
> Dios mío, ¡cuadrada!

Here it is evident the monotony of the city streets and squares, and the dull, commonplace uniformity in the lives of the citizens, afflict her with a sense of weariness. On another occasion it is the sense of futility that finds expression in her verse:

> Preparé un himno, y se murió gorgeo,
> Me eché a ser río, y terminé canal.
> —*La inútil primavera,* from *Irremediablemente.*

In *Carta lírica* it is the feeling that life has passed her by; she is one who goes "vagando por afuera de la vida," and is able to look on happiness only through the eyes of others. This poem is a powerful piece of psychological analysis, exposing to us the passionate working of the woman's mind, with the force, and something of the manner, of Browning's dramatic monologues.

It may be argued that in this apparent lack of sympathy with her environment the attitude of the poetess more nearly approaches that of Modernism than of the new Americanism; yet her rendering of the American scene as she sees it, even if her glasses are tinted, is genuine, native poetry. She is emphatically, as Darío would say, "de su tierra."

PABLO NERUDA

PABLO NERUDA represents one of the later phases of the reaction from the Parnassian and Symbolist schools of Spanish-American verse. He was born in Chile in 1904, and has published two collections of poems, *La canción de la fiesta* (1921) and *Crepusculario* (1923), the latter of which was received with unreserved acclamation. He is given a place almost as exalted as that assigned to Gabriela Mistral, and is regarded as one of the most interesting lyrical personalities in Chile today.

The attitude of Neruda and other poets of his school toward their immediate predecessors is prophetically described by Shakespeare:

> They surfeited with honey, and began
> To loathe the taste of sweetness whereof a little
> More than a little is by much too much.

That is to say, the perfection of rhythm and cadence, the preciosity of language, the sensitiveness to the finer shades of feeling, the tendency to artificiality and idealization, even the quest for beauty as an end, or as a means to something greater, which marked the poetry of Darío, Nervo, Lugones, and González Martínez, were found too cloying for their taste. Hence, in Neruda, the intention of the poet is obviously to be sternly and starkly realistic. In *Maestranzas de noche,* for example, there can be no mistaking the grim power of his description, and the intensity of his emotional reaction to the weird shapes and sounds that haunt the foundry at night.

Metrically, there is nothing remarkable about this or the other poem here translated. Beauty or novelty of versification is no part of the poet's aim. The lines vary in length, and to this extent his verse is "free"; but in their internal structure they are, with a few exceptions, normal.

Poemas de amor illustrates both Neruda's realism and his freedom from the ordinary restraints that governed the older practitioners of verse. As a motto for these poems he quotes a passage in translation from Walt Whitman, taken from his early poem, *Starting from Paumanok:*

> And I will make the poems of my body and of mortality,
> For I think I shall then supply myself with the poems of
> my soul and of immortality.

Neruda, however, puts into the mouth of Whitman a statement of fact, whereas Whitman merely offers an opinion; though "Así tendré los poemas de mi Alma y lo Inmortal," Neruda's translation, may be held justified by a later passage in the same poem:

> Behold, the body includes and is the meaning, the main
> concern, and includes and is the soul.

Neruda has evidently studied Whitman to some purpose: his heaping up of images to describe the relentless advance of the sea, and thereby the storm of his own passions, is quite in the Whitman manner. He believes he is following directly the line laid down by the master. Whitman sang of the body in all its phases, seeing in them the revelation of the soul of man and the perfection of the work of nature. His songs of praise to the body are in reality paeans to the God of Nature. With Neruda it is far otherwise. In this poem we have a glorification of the animal instinct, not as a manifestation of the miracle of nature, but as an end in itself. This tendency in Neruda is even more marked in other poems, for example, *Morena, la besadora,* which becomes little more than an orgy of rampant eroticism.

Had his reading of Whitman led him to the *Democratic Vistas,* he would have found an instructive passage:

> "The true question to ask," says the librarian of Congress in a paper read before the Social Science Convention at New York, October, 1869, "The true question to ask respecting a book, is, *has it helped any human soul?*" This is the hint, statement, not only of the great literatus, his book, but of every great artist. It may be that all works of art are to be first tried by their art qualities, their image-forming talent, and their dramatic, pictorial, plot-constructing, euphonious and other talents. Then, whenever claiming to be first-class works, they are to be strictly and sternly tried by their foundation in, and radiation, in the highest sense and always indirectly, of, the ethic principles, and eligibility to free, arouse, dilate.[55]

This is not an ideally perspicuous piece of English prose, but the general idea is clear enough, and it supplies us with one test which we may apply to the work of Neruda. Has this poem, we may ask, helped any human soul? And to this question the answer is almost certainly, No. The one possible exception would be the writer himself, who probably felt relieved when he had cleansed his stuffed bosom of the perilous stuff that weighed upon his heart.

It might be useful to apply the criteria of another and more recent critic. Theodore Watts-Dunton, discussing the nature of poetry, says:

---

[55] Walt Whitman, *Leaves of Grass* and *Democratic Vistas,* Everyman edition (London, 1916), p. 353.

The questions to be asked concerning any work of art are these: Is that which is here embodied really permanent, universal, and elemental? and, Is the concrete form embodying it really beautiful—acknowledged as beautiful by the soul of man in its highest moods? Any other question is an impertinence.[56]

Now, while the poem before us abundantly satisfies the first criterion, it does not (to my mind) satisfy the second; therefore as a work of art it is imperfect.

A Chilean critic, Armando Donoso, says of Neruda:

Here we have a poet whose coming we must greet as we would the springtime. He has power and grace, for he can be the most human and the least bookish of all, and his verse knows the harmonious secret of every string.[57]

There is, indeed, no denying the power of these verses, but the power is so ill regulated that they frequently become merely incoherent. They show occasional flashes of beauty, for example,

> Ella, tallada en el corazón de la noche
> por la inquietud de mis ojos alucinados;

and gropings after the expression of the inexpressible, for example,

> Algo de inmensa huida,
> que no se va, que araña dentro,
> algo que en palabras cava tremendos pozos ...

which may be compared with a similar effort on the part of Wordsworth to grasp and hold the impalpable:

> But for those obstinate questionings
> Of sense and outward things
> *Fallings from us, vanishings,*
> Blank misgivings of a creature
> Moving about in worlds not realized;

but Donoso's claim for Neruda that "su verso no ignora el secreto harmonioso de cada cuerda" seems to me strangely exaggerated. Neruda seems to have become obsessed by sex and sensual instinct; to be, in fact, a promising case for the psychopathologist. Still, he is young, and, where there is so much power in reserve, we may be justified in looking forward for something richer and more mellow as the years bring more matured judgment.

English taste will probably be shocked by the brutal crudeness of the sentiments expressed in these poems, as if human affection were nothing finer

---

[56] Theodore Watts-Dunton, "Poetry," *Encyc. Brit.* (Cambridge, 1911), XXI:877.
[57] Armando Donoso, *Nuestras poetas* (Santiago, 1924), Introduction, p. xxx.

than the instinct of the gray beasts of the field. To judge by what Neruda has written, not only has the age of chivalry departed, but we have got back to the morals of the cave-dwellers or of some beings still more primitive. Still more shocking will be the morbid suggestion of the lines:

> Y tú, en tu carne encierras
> las pupilas sedientas con que miraré cuando
> estos ojos que tengo se me llenen de tierra.

The same idea, rather more fully developed, occurs in another poem by this author, the piece entitled *Farewell* (using the English word):

> Desde el fondo de ti y arrodillado
> un niño, triste como yo, nos mira.
> Por esa vida que arderá en sus venas
> tendrían que amarrarse nuestras vidas.
>
> Por esas manos, hijas de tus manos,
> tendrían que matar las manos mías.
> Por sus ojos abiertos en la tierra,
> veré en los tuyos lágrimas un día. . . .

Here the poet, addressing his mistress, speaks of the child, as yet unborn, the fruit of their illicit amour. He declares it will be a bond between them—a bond he would now lightly break for ever, and prophesies that it will inherit the same wild instincts as now dominate the father: through the child's hands the father's hands will kill; through the child's eyes, alive and open upon the earth, the eyes of the father will look forth upon the tears of the mother. But our present knowledge of the working of heredity is too scanty to enable anyone to make forecasts of this kind with security. Had Ramón Pérez de Ayala's *Prometeo* (Madrid, 1924) been available when Neruda was writing, he might have been less sure in his prognostication. In this grim study, Pérez de Ayala shows how little reliance can be placed on the theories of the eugenists. The poet's offspring might just as readily have become a great philanthropist, or a mere nonentity.

VICENTE HUIDOBRO[58]

REPRESENTATIVE OF PERHAPS the most advanced ideas in Spanish-American poetry is Vicente Huidobro, a Chilean, born in 1893. He has lived for many years in Paris. Much of his work is in French and is in line with the most modern writing of men like Paul Valéry, Tzara, Reverdy, Dermée, and Cendras.

His poems illustrate the method of Creationism; for, as the ordered world arose out of chaos at the fiat of the Creator, so the poet summons into being his own world, as might a magician by the waving of his magic wand. In his inner consciousness the poet sees everything that he has made, and behold, it is very good; to the uninitiated, however, the result seems chaotic, and at times barely intelligible.

In a short poem, *Arte poética,* Huidobro sets forth some of his principles.

> Que el verso sea como una llave
> que abra mil puertas....

That is, poetry should be a stimulus to the imagination of the reader. The practice of the older poets has been so to stimulate the reader that his mind will picture approximately the same images as filled the mind of the poet, together with such pleasing associations as his own reading and experience may suggest. With the best intentions, the reader of Huidobro finds it difficult to imagine what the poet had in mind. The key may open a thousand doors, but he may search long before he comes upon the right one. Huidobro continues:

> Una hoja cae; algo pasa volando;
> cuanto miren los ojos creado sea
> y el alma del oyente quede temblando;

in other words, for the poet the act of perception is the act of creation; and when he has translated into words what he has perceived, the hearer must tremble with emotion at the wonder of it. This is obviously a continuation

---

[58] Born in Chile, 1893.
WORKS—
Canciones en la noche. Santiago, 1913
La gruta del silencio. Santiago, 1913
Pasando y pasando. Santiago, 1914
Las pagodas ocultas. Santiago, 1916
Adán. Santiago, 1916
La Tour Eiffel. Paris, 1920

Horizon carré. Paris, 1920
Poemas árticos. Paris, 1920
Hallali. Paris, 1920

Mío Cid Campeador, hazaña (prose). Madrid, 1928

and development of the theory preached and practiced by Herrera y Reissig, and by González Martínez, as in the poem, *Irás sobre la vida:*

> Que te ames en ti mismo, de tal modo
> compendiando tu ser, cielo y abismo,
> que sin desviar los ojos de ti mismo
> puedan tus ojos contemplarlo todo.

A little later, Huidobro adds:

> Inventa mundos nuevos y cuida tu palabra;
> el adjetivo, cuando no da vida, mata...

which is perfectly sound: the otiose adjective has seldom been more effectively disposed of; but there is nothing original in the idea. Again,

> ¿Por qué cantáis la rosa, oh Poetas?
> Hacedla florecer en el poema...

is good advice, for the best poets are remarkable mainly for their avoidance of mere generalities. His closing lines sum up the whole:

> Solo para vosotros
> viven todas las cosas bajo el Sol.
>
> El Poeta es un pequeño Dios.

For Huidobro, this is a clear statement. It has even the advantage of punctuation, a convention which in his later work he throws overboard. But as a definition of the aims and function of the poet it gets us no farther than Shakespeare's incidental reference to the subject:

> The poet's eye, in a fine frenzy rolling,
> Doth glance from heaven to earth, from earth to heaven;
> And as imagination bodies forth
> The forms of things unseen, the poet's pen
> Turns them to shapes, and gives to airy nothing
> A local habitation and a name.

The poetic idea in the mind of the poet exists in the form of more or less definite images, which for him are perfectly satisfying. To him the words in which these find expression are still satisfying, for the links by which they are held together—and these may be merely emotional—are still present to his mind. But the reader, having no access to these links, may easily go astray in his attempt at interpretation. This, of course, is not peculiar to Vicente Huidobro, or to Spanish-American poetry. Thus, in *Tendencies of*

Modern American Poetry, Amy Lowell quotes with approval the following, by John Gould Fletcher:

> THE WELL
>
> The well is not used now
> Its waters are tainted.
> I remember there was once a man went down
> To clean it.
> He found it very cold and deep,
> With a queer niche in one of its sides,
> From which he hauled forth buckets of bricks and dirt.

and adds:

The picture as given is quite clear and vivid, but the picture which we see is not the poem, the real poem lies behind, is only suggested.[59]

Were it not for the fact that American poets, and especially American poetesses, are portentously serious persons, one might suspect that Miss Lowell was here indulging in the gentle game of "pulling the leg" of her readers. Such a thing, however, is unthinkable; and we are thrown back on the declaration of Huidobro that "the Poet is a little God," whose ways are beyond the searching of ordinary humanity.

In the poems here translated, the peculiarities of Huidobro's style are fairly evident. Punctuation is erratic, perfunctory, or nonexistent. The use of capitals is arbitrary, and more confusing than helpful. His vocabulary is limited; even in the few examples here given we note the recurrent use of such words as "estrella," "palpitar," "agonizar." The violence of his metaphors and his apparent efforts to fuse two metaphors into one have a disturbing effect on the reader; for example,

> Llevo sobre el pecho
> Un collar de tus calles luminosas ...
>
> Una luz que agoniza entre los dedos....

Yet, some of his figures are very suggestive, such as

> Los balandros que pacen en las tardes ...

a pleasing image for the boats on the Seine, that disappear in the west like sheep to their pasture; and again,

> Pájaros de ala inversa que mueren
> entre las tejas ...

---

[59] Amy Lowell, *Tendencies of Modern American Poetry* (New York, 1917), p. 247.

describing how the birds are lost to sight among the tiles of the roofs, conveys a really beautiful picture.

Adiós gives a vivid impression of Paris at daybreak. The morning star, the sculptured angels on the towers of Notre-Dame, the white and glistening dome of the church of the Sacré-Coeur dominating the city from the heights of Montmartre,

> Baja el sol a tu hostia que se eleva ...

and the windmills in the same quarter, all contribute to the effect, and produce the desired atmosphere; while the luminous streets, the symbolic banners, the ships setting out down the river, and the Seine gliding under its bridges, all suggest the pain of departure in the poet's mind.

In *Horizonte* the poet seems to look back on the home of his youth and the love of his mother. Why the lady's beauty should close her lips, however, is not obvious. Still, the memory remains, and at unexpected moments the old scenes and the old affection revive and the poet feels a new inspiration.

Hijo offers many openings for conjecture. It may continue the thought of the preceding poem; and, remembering that the poet left his native Chile to live in Paris, we may interpret it thus: The son finds himself far from home and among squalid and dismal surroundings. He is in the midst of strangers; night comes on, and in his mind he can hear the nightingale that sang unheeded while he was a boy; the moon, shining through the snow, casts a vivid light over him and the memories that wring his heart.

Mañana primavera seems to be another recollection of the life of the home. The tranquillity of the family circle, the simple songs, the son in his pride eager to see the world, the brooks that suffer in his absence—these will all come back to him.

La senda era tan larga is even more cryptic than the poems just considered, though like them it probably refers to the poet's voluntary exile. The wind that bore the poet from his native land carried him as on its wings. Days passed with storm and tempest. The homing gulls left feathers in his hands, symbols of an instinct he defied. Days passed into months; the last trace of land was lost; he seemed entirely cut off from old associations; still there was one song in his heart, as yet unsung, "posthumous" inasmuch as it belonged to the land he had left—a land that still claimed him to such an extent that, though in body he was far from his country, his spirit was still there. For him a complete severance was impossible.

Campanario is an impressionistic sketch in which the reader feels that a more generous allowance of punctuation would be useful. As it stands, the fifth line, "Donde ha caído...," may belong either to what precedes or to what follows. The same applies to the next line, "Al fondo de la tarde." Moreover, the subject (or object), "las llamas vegetales," would be more intelligible with a predicate. All this being admitted, however, it is still possible to see that the poet has evoked a very striking picture. The dominating feature is the belfry of the village church, from which the birds come flying at the sound of the bells. Wheeling in their flight ("de ala inversa" is a poetic hyperbole for the movement known among aviators as "banking" for a turn), they are lost to view among the tiles of the roof-tops, where their morning songs have been heard. It is evening, and in the west the vegetation seems like tongues of fire, each leaf as if filled with emotion. As the poet passes along, the stars begin to appear. Something of the feeling of the surroundings passes into his heart and causes a tremor in his voice, while in the distance a clock tolls out the hour.

In spite of the irregularity and apparent eccentricity of these poems of Huidobro's, there is something fascinating about them. They certainly stimulate the imagination, and their very obscurity acts as an incentive to further reading. "L'appétit vient en mangeant." Presently progress becomes easier.

◇ ◇ ◇

JORGE LUIS BORGES[60]

BORGES, THOUGH HE WAS EDUCATED ABROAD and had associated with the most advanced poetic minds in Spain, returned to Argentina a more ardent admirer of his country than when he had left it. He had no sympathy with what he calls *Rubenismo:* its pessimism and its "nostalgia for Europe" irritated him. Even with Alfonsina Storni he has little in common, for her feeling of boredom with the rectangularity of the city and with the *bourgeois* life of the citizens seems to him only an effete phase of Rubenism. This that

---

[60] Born in Buenos Aires, 1900; studied in Geneva during the War; thereafter lived for three years in Spain, where he took part in the early activities of the Ultraists; returned to Argentina, 1921, a prophet of Ultraism.

POETICAL WORKS (all published in Buenos Aires)—
    Fervor de Buenos Aires. 1923   *Cuaderno San Martín.* 1929
    Luna de enfrente. 1925

Collaborated with Vicente Huidobro and Alberto Hidalgo in the *Indice de la nueva poesía americana.* Buenos Aires, 1926.

surrounds us, he declares, is reality, a complete and unified reality, an ample theme for any poet. Hence his own poetry is a vivid presentation of the life he finds around him, viewed with sympathy and understanding. It is, in perhaps greater measure than the work of any other living poet, the realization of the new Americanism of which Darío dreamed and to which Chocano aspired.

Of this new poetry the essential elements are free verse and the image or metaphor. The poet must have absolute freedom. He rejects rhyme as a convention that has become tiresome. He uses lines long or short as he pleases, and accepts the traditional rhythms or invents others as he sees fit. Some of the lines seem hardly distinguishable from prose, while others have a fine musical quality; but always the rhythm is subordinate to the emotion of the moment. For him the image is all-important; "La imagen es, hoy por hoy, nuestro universal santo y seña";[61] and the more daring the better. In its use Borges is masterly. How better could a poet convey the idea of the illimitable prairie than by such figures as the following:

> Ví una loma que arrinconan
> quietas distancias...
>
> Ví el único lugar de la tierra
> donde puede caminar Dios a sus anchas...?

The whole poem, *La guitarra,* from which these lines are taken, is a magnificent piece of evocation. The old crone strumming the guitar is unseen; but the whole spirit of the Pampa rises before us, and we appreciate its vastness, the struggles of its early settlers, and the fruitful labors of its present inhabitants.

Borges, however, is a town-dweller. In *Dulcia linquimus arva* he paints another striking picture of the Pampa where his ancestors had lived and labored; but of himself he confesses:

> Soy un pueblero y ya no sé de esas cosas,
> Soy un hombre de ciudad, de barrio, de calle;
> Los tranvías lejanos me ayudan la tristeza
> Con esa queja larga que sueltan en las tardes.

Yet, even in the town there is poetry, and his *Calle desconocida* is ample proof that he has the art to reveal it.

---

[61] *Indice de la nueva poesía americana,* Introduction, p. 17.

BIBLIOGRAPHY

Historical and Critical

Blanco Fombona, Rufino
 El modernismo y los poetas modernistas (Madrid, 1929).
Coester, Alfred
 Anthology of the Modernista Movement in Spanish America (Boston, 1924).
 Literary History of Spanish America (New York, 1919).
Daireaux, Max
 Littérature hispano-américaine (Paris, 1930).
Donoso G., Francisco
 Al margen de la poesía (Paris, 1927).
Fitzmaurice-Kelly, James
 The Oxford Book of Spanish Verse (Oxford, 1925).
Goldberg, Isaac
 Studies in Spanish-American Literature (New York, 1920).
González Blanco, Andrés
 Estudio preliminar [de Darío] (Madrid, 1910).
Hurtado, Juan, and González Palencia, Angel
 Historia de la literatura española (Madrid, 1921–1922).
Jowett, Benjamin
 The Dialogues of Plato (translated: Oxford, 1892).
Lauxar, pseud. (Osvaldo Crispo Acosta)
 Motivos de crítica hispanoamericanos (Montevideo, 1914).
Lowell, Amy
 Tendencies of Modern American Poetry (New York, 1917).
Mapes, Erwin K.
 L'Influence française dans l'oeuvre de Rubén Darío (Paris, 1925).
Marinetti, Filippo Tommaso
 Le Futurisme (Paris, 1910).
Mas y Pi, Juan
 Leopoldo Lugones y su obra (Buenos Aires, 1911).
Menéndez y Pelayo, Marcelino
 Historia de la poesía hispanoamericana (Madrid, 1893).
Navarro Tomás, Tomás
 "La cantidad silábica en unos versos de Rubén Darío," *La revista de filología española* (Madrid, 1922), vol. 9.

Rodo, José Enrique
  "Rubén Darío," in *Cinco ensayos* (Madrid, 1915).
Roxlo, Carlos
  Historia crítica de la literatura uruguaya (Montevideo, 1913–1916), 7 vols.
Silva Uzcátegui, R. D.
  Historia crítica del modernismo en la literatura castellana (Barcelona, 1925).
Torres-Ríoseco, Arturo
  En el encantamiento (San José de Costa Rica, 1922).
  Walt Whitman (San José de Costa Rica, 1922).
  Precursores del modernismo (Madrid, 1925).
  Rubén Darío, Casticismo y Americanismo (Harvard, 1931).
  Ausencia (Santiago, 1932).
Valera y Alcala Galiano, Juan
  Cartas americanas (Madrid, 1889).
Vargas Vila, José María
  Rubén Darío (Madrid, 1917).

Poetical

Banchs, Enrique
  Las barcas (Buenos Aires, 1907).
  El libro de los elogios (Buenos Aires, 1908).
  El cascabel del halcón (Buenos Aires, 1909).
  La urna (Buenos Aires, 1911).
Baudelaire, Charles
  Fleurs du mal (Paris, 1857).
Borges, Jorge Luis
  Fervor de Buenos Aires (Buenos Aires, 1923).
  Luna de enfrente (Buenos Aires, 1925).
  Cuaderno San Martín (Buenos Aires, 1929).
Casal, Julián del
  Hojas al viento (Habana, 1890).
  Nieve (Habana, 1892).
  Bustos y rimas (Habana, 1893).
  Sus mejores poesías (Madrid, 1916).
Carducci, Giosue
  Antologia Carducciana (Bologna, 1929).
Chocano, José Santos
  En la aldea (Lima, 1893).
  Iras santas (Lima, 1895).
  Azahares (Lima, 1896).
  La epopeya del morro (Lima, 1899).
  Alma América (Madrid, 1906).
  Fiat lux (Paris, 1908).
  La selva virgen (Paris, 1909).

Darío, Rubén
> VERSE
>
> *Primeras notas* (Managua, 1885).
> *Abrojos* (Valparaiso, 1887).
> *Azul* (Valparaiso, 1888).
> *Prosas profanas* (Buenos Aires, 1896).
> *Cantos de vida y esperanza* (Madrid, 1905).
> *Oda a Mitre* (Paris, 1906).
> *El canto errante* (Madrid, 1907).
> *Poema de otoño y otros poemas* (Madrid, 1910).
> *Canto a la Argentina* (Buenos Aires, 1910).
> *Sol de domingo* (posthumous) (Madrid, 1917).
>
> PROSE
>
> *A de Gilbert* (San Salvador, 1889).
> *Los raros* (Buenos Aires, 1893).
> *Castelar* (Madrid, 1899).
> *Peregrinaciones* (Paris, 1901).
> *España contemporanea* (Paris, 1901).
> *La caravana pasa* (Paris, 1903).
> *Tierras solares* (Madrid, 1904).
> *Opiniones* (Madrid, 1906).
> *Parisiana* (Madrid, 1907).
> *El viaje a Nicaragua* (Madrid, 1909).
> *Letras* (Paris, 1911).
> *Todo al vuelo* (Madrid, 1912).
> *Historia de mis libros* (Buenos Aires, 1912).
> *Autobiografía* (Barcelona, 1916). Appeared in *Caras y caretas* (Buenos Aires, 1912).
> *Cabezas* (Buenos Aires, 1916).
> *El oro de Mallorca* (posthumous) (Madrid, 1917).
>
> *Obras completas* (Mundo Latino, Madrid, 1917-1919).

For an exhaustive bibliography of works dealing with Darío see Torres-Ríoseco's *Rubén Darío, Casticismo y Americanismo* (Harvard, 1931).

Donoso, Armando
> *Nuestros poetas: antología chilena moderna* (Santiago, 1924).

Gautier, Théophile
> *Emaux et camées* (Paris, 1856).

Ghiraldo, Alberto
> *Antología americana* (Romantic period) (Madrid, 1922), 5 vols.

González Martínez, Enrique
> *Preludios* (Mazatlán, 1903).
> *Lirismos* (Mocorito, 1907).

González Martínez, Enrique *(concluded)*
  Silenter (Mocorito, 1909).
  Los senderos ocultos (Mocorito, 1911).
  La muerte del cisne (Mexico, 1915).
  La hora inútil (Mexico, 1916).
  El libro de la fuerza, de la bondad y del sueño (Mexico, 1917).

  Poesías escogidas, with an introductory study by Manuel Toussaint (Barcelona, 1917).

Gutiérrez Nájera, Manuel
  Poesías (posthumous collection) (Mexico, 1896).
  Cuentos frágiles (Mexico, 1883).
  Sus mejores poesías, with an introduction by Rufino Blanco Fombona (Madrid, 1916).

Guzmán Cruchaga, Juan
  Junto al brasero (Santiago, 1914).
  La sombre (a drama) (Santiago, 1918).
  La mirada inmóvil (Santiago, 1919).
  Chopin (Santiago, 1919).
  La princesa que no tenía corazón (Santiago, 1920).
  Lejana (Santiago, 1921).
  El maleficio de la luna (Santiago, 1922).
  La fiesta del corazón (Santiago, 1922).

Herrera y Reissig, Julio
  Pascuas del tiempo (Montevideo, 1900).
  Los maitines de la noche (Montevideo, 1902).
  Los éxtasis de la montaña (Montevideo, 1904).
  Poemas violetas (Montevideo, 1906).
  Sonetos vascos (Montevideo, 1906).
  Los parques abandonados (Montevideo, 1908).
  Los éxtasis de la montaña (ser. 2; Montevideo, 1910).
  Los pianos crepusculares (Montevideo, 1910).
  Clepsidras (Montevideo, 1910).

  Obras completas (Montevideo, 1913), 5 vols.
  Páginas escogidas, with an introduction by Juan Mas y Pi (Barcelona, 1914).

Hidalgo, Huidobro, and Borges
  Indice de la nueva poesía americana (Buenos Aires, 1926).

Huidobro, Vicente
  Canciones en la noche (Santiago, 1913).
  La gruta del silencio (Santiago, 1913).
  Pasando y pasando (Santiago, 1914).
  Las pagodas ocultas (Santiago, 1916).

HUIDOBRO, VICENTE *(concluded)*
    Adán (Santiago, 1916).
    La Tour Eiffel (Paris, 1920).
    Horizon carré (Paris, 1920).
    Poemas árticos (Paris, 1920).
    Hallali (Paris, 1920).
    Mío Cid Campeador, hazaña (prose) (Madrid, 1928).

JAIMES FREYRE, RICARDO
    Castalia bárbara (Buenos Aires, 1899).
    Castalia bárbara (ed. 2, published with *País de sueño* and *País de sombra;* La Paz, Bolivia, 1918).

    Leyes de la versificación castellana (La Paz, 1912; ed. 2, 1919).
    Los más bellos poemas de R. Jaimes Freyre, with an introduction by Leopoldo Lugones (Mexico, 1920).

JIMÉNEZ, JUAN RAMÓN
    Poesías escogidas (New York, 1917).

DE LISLE, LECONTE
    Poèmes barbares (Paris, 1862).

LUGONES, LEOPOLDO
    VERSE

    Las montañas de oro (Buenos Aires, 1897).
    Los crepúsculos del jardín (Buenos Aires, 1905).
    Lunario sentimental (Buenos Aires, 1909).
    Odas seculares (Buenos Aires, 1910).
    El libro fiel (ed. 2; Paris, 1912).
    El libro de los paisajes (Buenos Aires, 1917).
    Las horas doradas (Buenos Aires, 1922).
    Romancero (Buenos Aires, 1924).
    Poemas solariegos (Buenos Aires, 1928).

    PROSE

    El imperio jesuítico (Buenos Aires, 1905).
    La guerra gaucha (Buenos Aires, 1905).
    Piedras liminares (Buenos Aires, 1910).
    Prometeo (Buenos Aires, 1910).
    Historia de Sarmiento (Buenos Aires, 1911).
    La torre de Casandra (Buenos Aires, 1919).
    Estudios helénicos (Buenos Aires, 1924).
    Cuentas fatales (Buenos Aires, 1924).
    Nuevos estudios helénicos (Buenos Aires, 1928).

MISTRAL, GABRIELA, pseud. (LUCILA GODOY ALCAYAGA)
    Desolación (New York, 1922; Santiago, 1923).

Neruda, Pablo
   La canción de la fiesta (Santiago, 1921).
   Crepusculario (Santiago, 1923).
Nervo, Amado
   Verse
   Perlas negras (Mexico, 1898).
   Poemas (Paris, 1901).
   El éxodo (Mexico, 1902).
   Las flores del camino (Mexico, 1902).
   Perlas negras, Místicas, Las voces (Paris, 1904).
   Los jardines interiores (Mexico, 1905).
   En voz baja (Madrid, 1909).
   Serenidad (Madrid, 1914).
   Elevación (Madrid, 1916).
   El estanque de los lotos (Madrid, 1918).
   El arquero divino (posthumous) (Madrid, 1920).
   Los cien mejores poesías, with an introduction by E. González Martínez (Mexico, 1919).
   Prose
   El bachiller (Mexico, 1896).
   Otras vidas (Barcelona, n.d.).
   Almas que pasan (Madrid, 1906).
   Juana de Asbaje (Madrid, 1910).
   Ellos (Paris, 1912).
   Mis filosofías (Paris, 1912).
   El diablo desinteresado (Madrid, 1916).
   Plenitud (Madrid, 1918).
   Obras completas (Madrid, 1920–), 28 vols.
Noé, Julio
   Antología de la poesía argentina moderna, 1900–1925 (Buenos Aires, 1925).
Ortiz, Alberto
   Parnaso nicaragüense (Barcelona, n.d.).
Pezoa Véliz, Carlos
   Alma chilena (Santiago, 1912).
   Campanas de oro (Paris, 1921).
Prado, Pedro
   Flores de cardo (Santiago, 1908).
   La casa abandonada (Buenos Aires, 1912).
   El llamado del mundo (Santiago, 1913).
   La reina de Rapa Nui (Santiago, 1914).
   Los pájaros errantes (Santiago, 1915).
   Ensayos (prose) (Santiago, 1916).
   Alsino (Santiago, 1921).

SILVA, JOSÉ ASUNCIÓN
   Poesías, with an introduction by Miguel de Unamuno (Barcelona, 1908).
   Poesías (ed. defin., Paris, 1913).
   De sobremesa (prose) (Bogotá, 1926).
SILVA, VÍCTOR DOMINGO
   Hacia allá (Santiago, 1906).
   El derrotero (Santiago, 1908).
   Nuestras víctimas (Santiago, 1908).
   La selva florida (Santiago, 1911).
   El romancero naval (Santiago, 1912).
   Palomilla brava (Santiago, 1923).
   Golondrina de invierno (Santiago, 1923).
   Sus mejores poemas (Santiago, 1923).
SOLAR CORREA, EDUARDO
   Poetas de Hispano-América (Santiago, 1926).
STORNI, ALFONSINA
   La inquietud del rosal (Buenos Aires, 1916).
   El dulce daño (Buenos Aires, 1918).
   Irremediablemente (Buenos Aires, 1919).
   Languidez (Buenos Aires, 1920).
   Ocre (Buenos Aires, 1925).
TORRES-RÍOSECO, ARTURO
   Ausencia (Santiago, 1932).
VALENCIA, GUILLERMO
   Poesías (Bogotá, 1898).
   Ritos (London, 1914).
   Catay, poemas orientales (Bogotá, 1929).
VERLAINE, PAUL
   Oeuvres complètes (Paris, 1899), 3 vols.